Scene Reconstruction Pose Estimation and Tracking

Scene Reconstruction Pose Estimation and Tracking

Editor

Danel Jaso

scitus
academics

Scene Reconstruction Pose Estimation and Tracking
Edited by **Danel Jaso**

ISBN: 978-1-68117-584-3
Library of Congress Control Number: 2016946439

SCITUS Academics LLC,
616, Corporate Way, Suite 2, 4766,
Valley Cottage, NY 10989

www.scitusacademics.com

Printed in United States of America on Acid Free Paper

Preface

Scene Reconstruction Pose Estimation and Tracking envisages contemporary advances in the use of pattern recognition techniques for computer and robot vision. The disciplines of pattern recognition and computational vision have been intimately entangled since their early days, some four decades ago with the development of fast digital computing. It is generally easy for a person to differentiate the sound of a human voice, from that of a violin; a handwritten numeral "3," from an "8"; and the aroma of a rose, from that of an onion. Though, it is difficult for a programmable computer to solve these kinds of perceptual problems. These problems are difficult because each pattern usually contains a large amount of information, and the recognition problems typically have an inconspicuous, high-dimensional, structure. Pattern recognition is the science of making inferences from perceptual data, using tools from statistics, probability, computational geometry, machine learning, signal processing, and algorithm design. Thus, it is of central importance to artificial intelligence and computer vision, and has far-reaching applications in engineering, science, medicine, and business.

In particular, advances made during the last half century, now allow computers to interact more effectively with humans and the natural world (e.g., speech recognition software). However, the most important problems in pattern recognition are yet to be solved. Pattern recognition is generally categorized according to the type of learning procedure used to generate the output value. Supervised learning assumes that a set of training data (the training set) has been provided, consisting of a set of instances that have been properly labeled by hand with the correct output. All computer vision techniques could be regarded as a form of pattern recognition, in the broadest sense of the term.

Table of Contents

Chapter 1

Iterative Multiview Side Information for Enhanced Reconstruction in Distributed Video Coding

Mourad Ouaret, Frédéric Dufaux and Touradj Ebrahimi

Multimedia Signal Processing Group (MMSPG), Ecole Polytechnique Fédérale de Lausanne (EPFL)

ABSTRACT

Distributed video coding (DVC) is a new paradigm for video compression based on the information theoretical results of Slepian and Wolf (SW) and Wyner and Ziv (WZ). DVC entails low-complexity encoders as well as separate encoding of correlated video sources. This is particularly attractive for multiview camera systems in video surveillance and camera sensor network applications, where low complexity is required at the encoder. In addition, the separate encoding of the sources implies no communication between the cameras in a practical scenario. This is an advantage since communication is time and power consuming and requires complex networking. In this work, different intercamera estimation techniques for side information (SI) generation are explored and compared in terms of estimating quality, complexity, and rate distortion (RD) performance. Further, a technique called iterative multiview side information (IMSI) is introduced, where the final SI is used in an iterative reconstruction process. The simulation results show that IMSI significantly improves the RD performance for video with significant motion and activity. Furthermore, DVC outperforms AVC/H.264 Intra for video with average and low motion but it is still inferior to the Inter No Motion and Inter Motion modes.

1. INTRODUCTION

Multiview video is attractive for a wide range of applications such as free viewpoint television (FTV) [1] and video surveillance camera networks. The increased use of multiview video systems is mainly due to the improvements in video technology. In addition, the reduced cost of cameras encourages the deployment of multiview video systems.

FTV is one of the promising applications of multiview. FTV is a 3D multiview system that allows viewing the scene from a view point chosen by the viewer. Video surveillance is another area where multiview can be beneficial for monitoring purposes. In addition, the multiple views can be used to improve the performance of event detection and recognition algorithms. However, the amount of data generated by multiview systems increases rapidly with the number of cameras. This makes data compression a key issue in such systems.

In DVC [2], the source statistics are exploited at the decoder by computing the SI of the WZ frame using different techniques. In this paper, a review of different SI techniques for multiview DVC is first provided, including a thorough evaluation of their estimation quality, complexity, and RD performance. Moreover, all the SI techniques are combined in the ground truth (GT) fusion, which combines the different SIs using the original WZ frame at the decoder. Even though this is not feasible in practice, it gives the maximum achievable DVC performance. Further, a new technique called iterative multiview side information (IMSI) is proposed to improve the DVC RD performance especially for video with significant motion. IMSI uses an initial SI to decode the WZ frame and then constructs a final SI which is used in a second reconstruction iteration. Finally, the performance of multiview DVC is compared with respect to AVC/H.264 [3] Intra, Inter No Motion (i.e., zero motion vectors), and Inter Motion.

The paper is structured as follows. First, the paradigm of distributed video coding is presented in Section 2. Multiview DVC is described in Section 3, whereas, Section 4 reviews the different intercamera estimation techniques. The IMSI technique is proposed in Section 5. Then, the test material and simulation results are presented and discussed in Section 6. Finally, some concluding remarks are drawn in Section 7.

2. DISTRIBUTED VIDEO CODING (DVC)

2.1. Theoretical DVC

DVC is the result of the information-theoretic bounds established for distributed source coding (DSC) by Slepian and Wolf [4] for lossless coding, and by Wyner and Ziv [5] for lossy coding with SI at the decoder. Lossless DSC refers to two correlated random sources separately encoded and jointly decoded by exploiting the statistical dependencies.

If we consider two statistically dependent random sequences *X* and *Y*, rates R_X and R_Y can be achieved by entropy coding such that $R_X \geq H(X)$ and $R_Y \geq H(Y)$, where $H(X)$ and $H(Y)$ are the entropies of *X* and *Y*, respectively. The Slepian-Wolf theorem proves that a better rate can be achieved with joint decoding and gives tighter bounds for the total rate $R_X + R_Y$. The admissible rate region established by SW, which corresponds to the shaded area depicted in Figure 1, is defined by

$$R_X \geq H(X \mid Y), \qquad R_Y \geq H(Y \mid X),$$
$$R_X + R_Y \geq H(X, Y). \tag{1}$$

Decoding with SI is considered as a special case of DSC. In this case, the source *X* depends on some SI *Y*, which corresponds to the black dot on the region border in Figure 1. Later on, Wyner and Ziv established bounds for lossy compression with SI at the decoder as an extension to the Slepian and Wolf theorem. In this case, the source *X* is encoded without having access to the SI *Y*. On the other hand, the decoder has access to the SI to produce *X* with a certain distortion *D*.

2.2. Practical DVC

Figure 2 shows the DVC architecture used in this work [6].

At the encoder, the frames are separated into two sets. The first one is the key frames which are fed to a conventional AVC/H.264 Intra encoder. The second set is the WZ frames. The latter are transformed and then quantized prior to WZ encoding. The same 4×4 separable integer transform as in AVC/H.264 is used with properties similar to the discrete cosine transform (DCT) [7]. Then, the same bands are grouped together and the different bit planes are extracted and then fed to a turbo encoder [8]. The latter offers near-channel capacity error correcting capability. Furthermore, a cyclic redundancy check (CRC) [9] is computed for each quantized bit plane and transmitted to the decoder. The frequency of the key frames is defined by the group of pictures (GOPs).

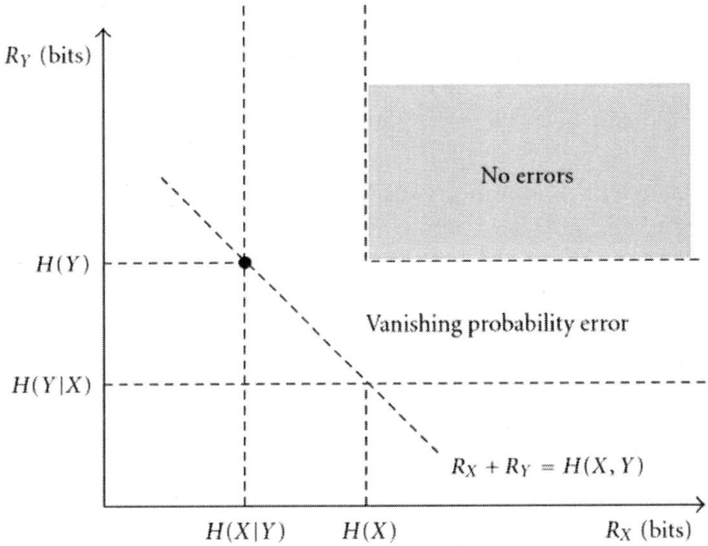

Figure 1. Achievable rate region defined by the Slepian-Wolf bounds.

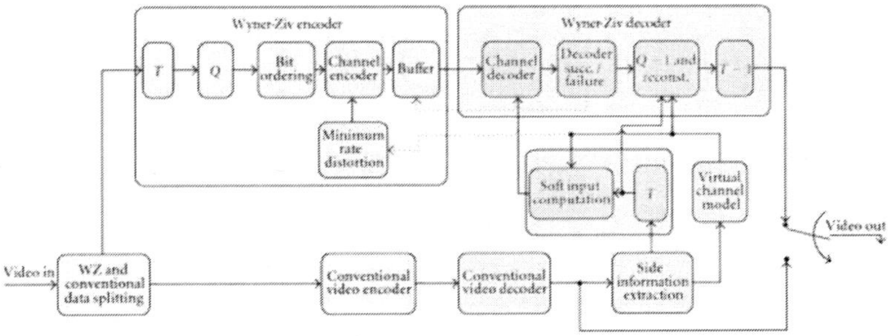

Figure 2. Conventional DVC architecture.

At the decoder, the key frames are conventionally decoded and then used to generate the SI for the WZ decoder. In the monoview case, motion compensation temporal interpolation (MCTI) [10] is used to generate the SI. For this purpose, MCTI uses the key frames to perform motion estimation. The resulting motion vectors are interpolated at midpoint as illustrated in Figure 3.

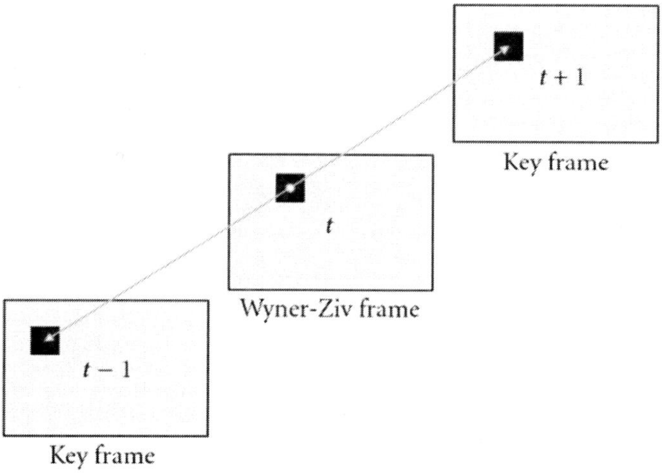

Figure 3. Motion compensation temporal interpolation (MCTI). MV is a motion vector in the forward direction.

A virtual channel is used to model the correlation between the DCT coefficients of the original and SI frames. It is shown that the residual of the DCT coefficients follows the Laplacian distribution [2]. The reconstruction process [11] uses the SI along with decoded bins to recover the original frame up to a certain quality. The decoder accepts the SI DCT value as a reconstructed one if it fits into the quantization interval corresponding to the decoded bin. Otherwise, it truncates the DCT value into the quantization interval. This DVC scheme is decoder driven as the request for parity bits from the encoder is performed via a feedback channel until successful decoding. The decoding is considered successful if the decoded bit plane error probability is lower than 10^{-3} and its CRC matches the one received from the encoder.

The multiview DVC scheme used in this research is exactly the same as the monoview DVC described above except for the SI extraction module as it is explained further in Section 3.

3. MULTIVIEW DVC (MDVC)

MDVC is a solution that allows independent encoding of the cameras and joint decoding of the different video streams as shown in Figure 4.

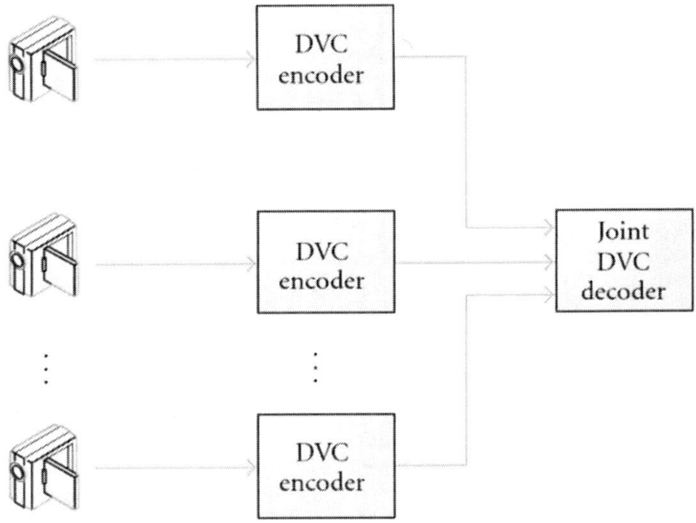

Figure 4. MDVC scheme. The different views are separately encoded and jointly decoded.

It differs from monoview DVC in the decoder. More precisely, the SI is constructed not only using the frames within the same camera but using frames from the other cameras as well.

A fusion technique between temporal and homography-based side information is introduced in [12]. The fusion considers the previous and the forward frames as predictors of the WZ frame. The logical operation OR is used to combine the different predictors for each pixel. In other words, MCTI is chosen if it is a better predictor than homography for at least one of the two frames. Otherwise, homography is chosen as predictor as illustrated in Figure 5. The results in [12] report that the fusion outperforms monoview DVC by around $0.2 \sim 0.5$ dB for video with significant motion for a spatial resolution of 256×192 at 15 fps for a three cameras setup. In the latter, only the central camera contains WZ frames while the side ones are conventionally coded in Intra mode. This is called*decoder-driven fusion*.

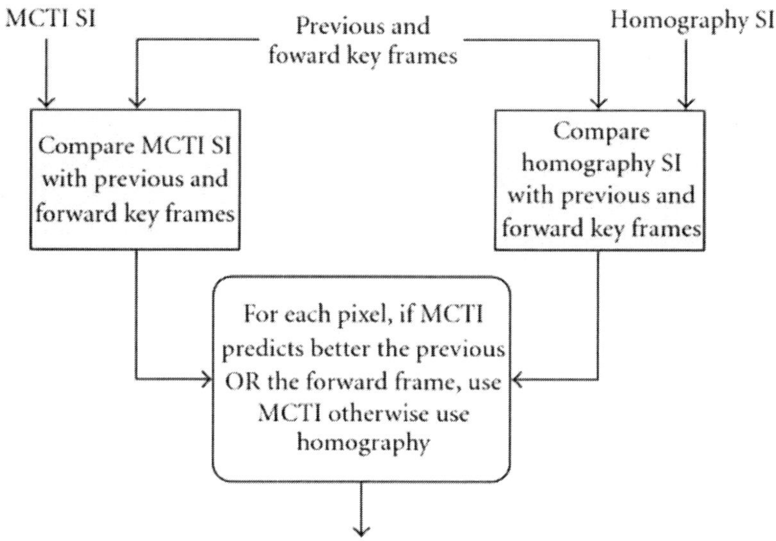

Figure 5. Decoder-driven fusion [12].

Artigas et al. [13] proposed two novel fusion techniques between temporal and intercamera side information. In the first technique, temporal motion interpolation is performed between the previous and the forward frames from the side cameras. The result is subtracted from the current frame and then thresholded to obtain a binary mask. The latter is projected to the central camera to perform the fusion as shown in Figure 6(a). The second algorithm uses the previous and the forward frames as predictors for the current frame on the side cameras to compute a reliability mask. The latter is projected to the central camera and used to perform the fusion as depicted in Figure 6(b). It is reported that the fusions improve the average PSNR of the SI using high resolution video (1024×768 at 15 fps). On the other hand, the RD performance of DVC is not investigated, and the simulations are run using the originals, which is in practice not feasible.

Moreover, depth maps are required to perform the intercamera estimation which is a hard problem for complex real-world scenes.

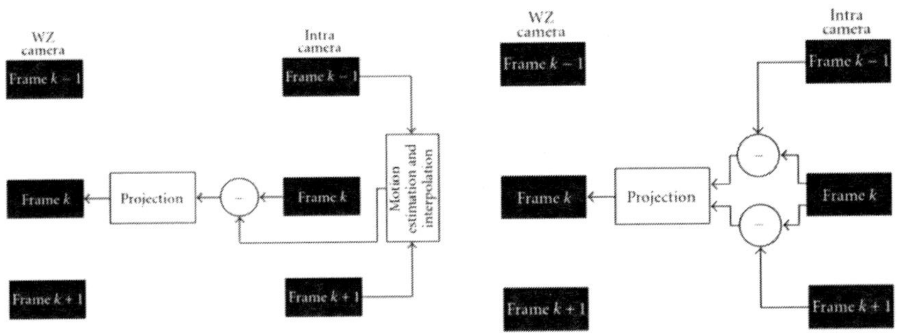

Figure 6. Fusion techniques proposed by Artigas et al. [13].Motion estimation is performed on the side camera to compute a fusion mask for the central cameraFrame difference w.r.t the previous and forward frames on the side camera is used to compute the fusion mask

In [14], the wavelet transform is combined with turbo codes to encode a multiview camera array in a distributed way. At the decoder, a fusion technique is introduced to combine temporal and homography-based side information. It thresholds the motion vectors and the difference between the corresponding backward and forward estimations to obtain a fusion mask. The mask assigns the regions with significant motion vector and estimation error to homography SI, and the rest is assigned to temporal SI (i.e., regions with low motion and relatively small prediction error). It is reported that the hybrid SI outperforms the temporal one by around 1.5 dB in PSNR. In addition, it outperforms H.263+ Intra by around $4.0 \sim 7.0$ dB. A video content with spatial resolution 320×240 is used in the evaluation.

Further, a flexible estimation technique that can jointly utilize temporal and view correlations to generate side information is proposed in [15]. More specifically, the current pixel in the WZ frame is mapped using homography to the left and right camera frames. Then, AVC/H.264 decision modes are applied to the pixel blocks in the left and right camera frames. If both resulting modes are intermodes, the SI value is taken from temporal SI. Otherwise, it is taken from homography SI. The simulation results show that this technique significantly outperforms conventional H.263+ Intra coding. Nevertheless, comparison with AVC/H.264 Intra would be beneficial as it represents state-of-the-art for conventional coding.

A fusion technique based on some prior knowledge of the original video is introduced in [16]. This is called *encoder-driven fusion*. Initially, a binary mask is calculated at the encoder as illustrated in Figure 7. It is compressed using a bilevel image compression [17] encoder and then transmitted to the decoder.

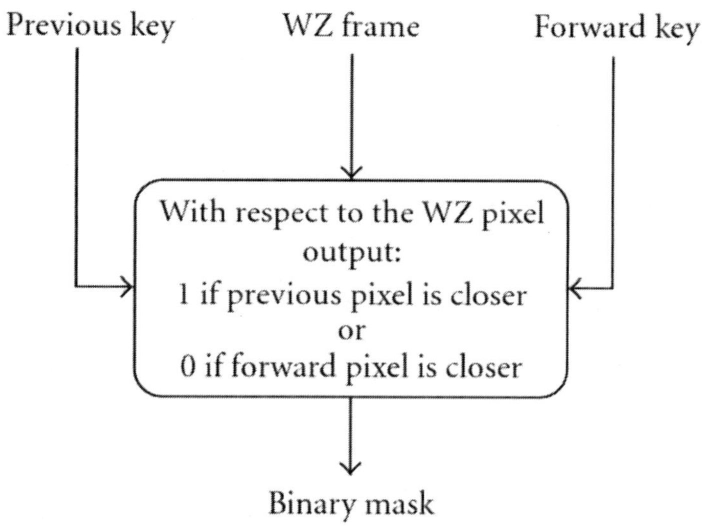

Figure 7. The *encoder-driven fusion* at the encoder side [16].

For each pixel, the mask informs the decoder whether the previous or the forward pixel is a better predictor of the same pixel in the original frame to perform fusion at the decoder (Figure 8). The results report a maximum gain up to 1.0 dB over monoview DVC in the same conditions as [12]. Furthermore, there is a slight increase in the encoder complexity as it has to perform the additional task of compressing the binary mask.

In [18], coding of multiview image sequences with video sensors connected to a central decoder is investigated. The *N* sensors are organized in an array to monitor the same scene from different views as shown in Figure 9. Only decoders 2 to *N* perform DVC using disparity compensated output of decoder 1. In addition, the video sensors are able to exploit temporal correlation using a motion compensated lifted wavelet transform [19] at the encoder. The proposed scheme reduces the bit rate by around 10% by performing joint decoding when compared to separate decoding for video content at 30 fps and 256×192 spatial resolution.

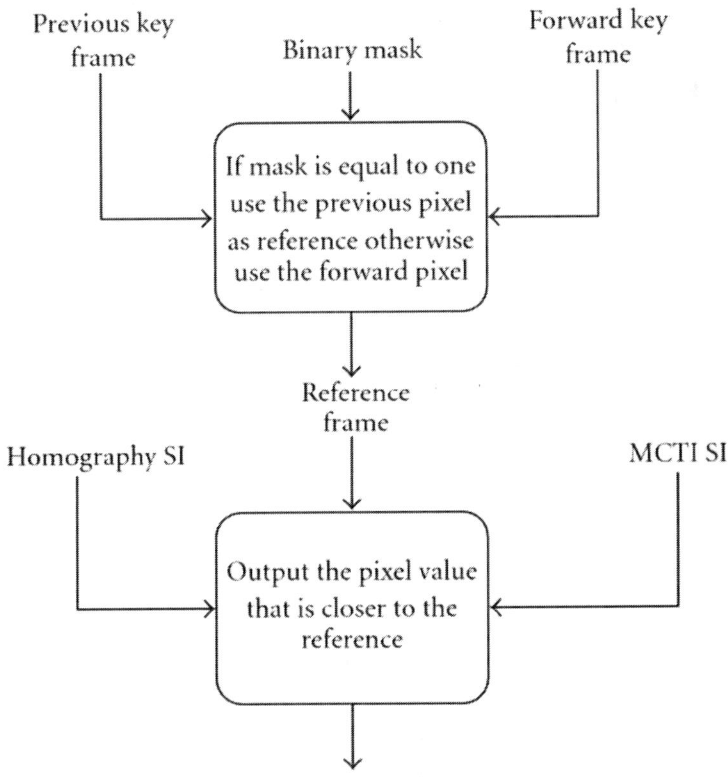

Figure 8. The *encoder-driven fusion* at the decoder side [16].

Finally, ways of improving the performance of multiview DVC are explored in [20]. Several modes to generate homography-based SI are introduced. The homography is estimated using a global motion estimation technique. The results show an improvement of SI quality by around 6.0 dB and a gain in RD performance by around $1.0 \sim 2.0$ dB for video content with a spatiotemporal resolution of 256×192 at 15 fps. However, the reported results assume an ideal fusion mask, which requires the knowledge of the original at the decoder. This is not feasible in a practical scenario.

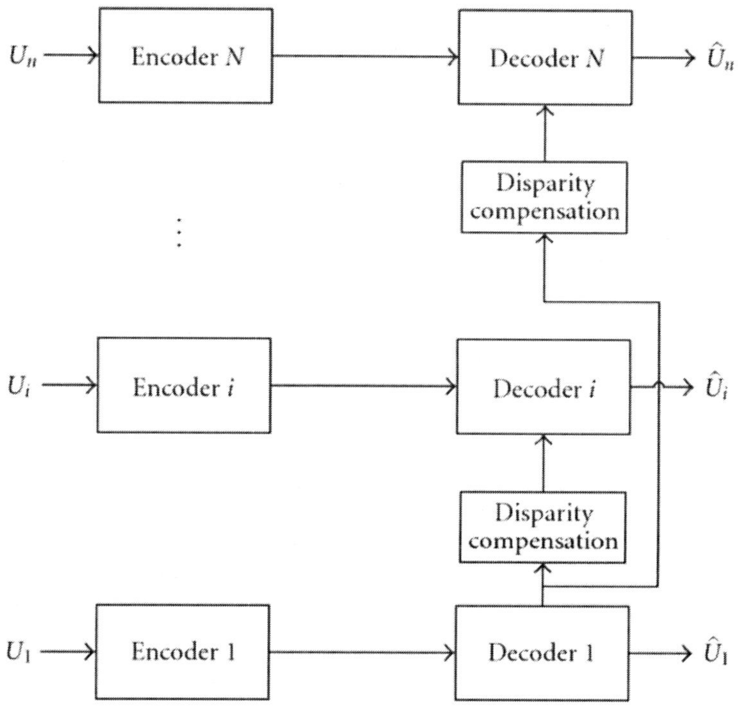

Figure 9. Distributed coding scheme with disparity compensation at the central decoder [18].

4. INTERCAMERA PREDICTION

In this section, different SI techniques for multiview DVC are reviewed. The different techniques are described for 3 cameras setup, where the central camera is predicted from both neighboring cameras, as depicted in Figure 10.

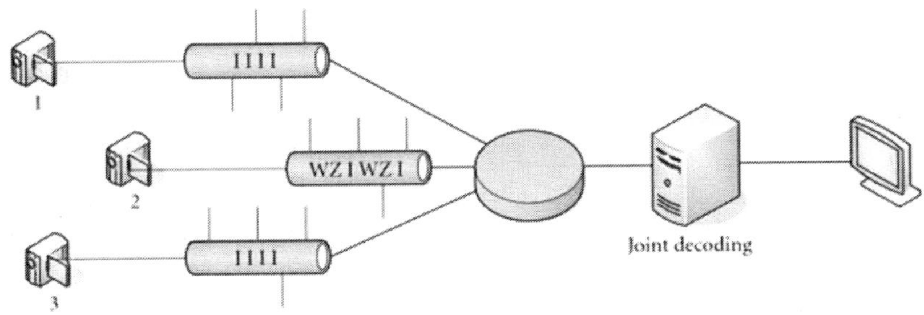

Figure 10. The multiview camera setup considered in this work. I stands for intraframe and WZ for Wyner-Ziv frame.

4.1. Disparity Compensation View Prediction (DCVP)

DCVP [16] is based on the same idea as MCTI, but the motion compensation is performed between the frames from the side cameras. A slight modification is applied to DCVP to improve the SI quality. Instead of interpolating the motion vectors at midpoint, an optimal weight is computed in [16]. For this purpose, the first frame of each camera is conventionally decoded. Then, motion compensation is performed between the side camera frames. The motion vectors are weighted with the weights $0.1, 0.2, \ldots, 0.9$. Further, the SI PSNR is computed for each weight. The weight with maximum PSNR is maintained and used for the rest of the sequence. Nevertheless, the SI generated by DCVP has usually a poorer quality than the one generated by MCTI. This is due to the larger disparity between the side camera frames when compared to the one between the previous and forward frames.

4.2. Homography

The homography, *H*, is a 3×3 matrix transforming one view camera plane to another one as shown in Figure 11.

It uses eight parameters *a, b, c, d, e, f, g,* and *h*. The homography maps a point (x_1, y_1) from one plane to a point (x_2, y_2) in the second plane up to a scale λ such that

$$\lambda\begin{pmatrix} x_2 \\ y_2 \\ 1 \end{pmatrix} = \begin{pmatrix} a & b & c \\ d & e & f \\ g & h & 1 \end{pmatrix}\begin{pmatrix} x_1 \\ y_1 \\ 1 \end{pmatrix}. \quad (2)$$

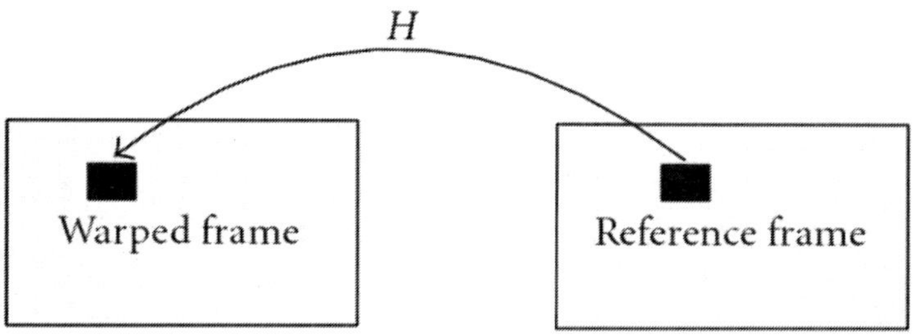

Figure 11. Homography matrix *H* relating one view to another.

This model is suitable when the scene can be approximated by a planar surface, or when the scene is static and the camera motion is a pure rotation around its optical center. The homography can be calculated using various techniques. In this work, we consider a global motion estimation technique introduced in [21] to compute the homography. The parameters are calculated such that the sum of squared differences E between the reference frame and the warped side frame is minimized:

$$E = \sum_{i=1}^{N} e_i^2 \quad \text{with } e_i = I_w(x_{w_i}, y_{w_i}) - I(x_i, y_i), \quad (3)$$

where $I_w(x_{w_i}, y_{w_i})$ and $I(x_i, y_i)$ are the pixels from the warped and reference frames, respectively. The problem is solved using the Levenberg-Marquardt gradient descent algorithm to iteratively estimate the parameters. To remove the influence of such outliers, a truncated quadratic is used. In other words, only pixels for which the absolute value of the error term is below a certain threshold are taken into account in the estimation process, other pixels are ignored. Therefore, the algorithm will count mainly for global motion

$$E = \sum_{i=1}^{N} \rho(e_i) \quad \text{with } \rho(e_i) = e_i^2 \text{ if } |e_i| \geq T \text{ else } 0, \tag{4}$$

where T is a threshold.

In multiview DVC, the warped frame is computed from the left (H_L) and right (H_R) camera frames as shown in Figure 12. Therefore, three side information are possible. The one entirely warped from each side camera and the average (H) of both side cameras. The latter is the only one considered in this work.

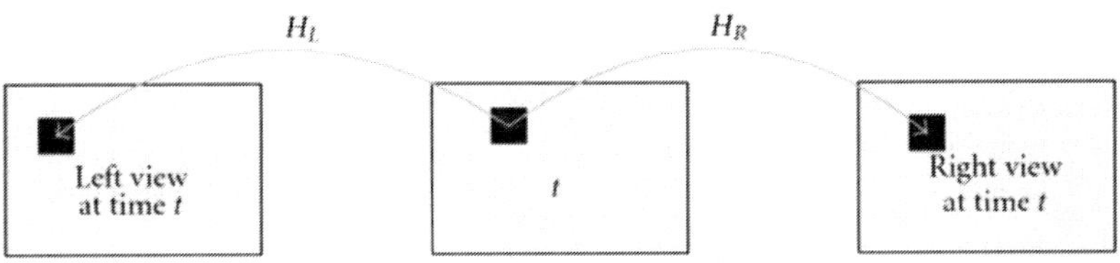

Figure 12. Homography-based SI.

The advantage of this technique is that once the homography relating the central camera with the side ones is estimated, computing the SI becomes very simple in terms of computational complexity when compared to techniques based on exhaustive block-based motion estimation. Moreover, this technique is suitable for scenarios, where the global motion is highly dominant with respect to local variations as it would generate a good estimation in this case. On the other hand, if the scene has multiple significant objects moving in different directions, the estimation would be of a poor quality as the technique would only account for global motion.

4.3. View Synthesis Prediction (VSP)

The previously mentioned techniques do not take advantage of some important features of multiview. That is, the speed at which an object is moving in a view depends on its depth information. In addition to this, rotations, zooms, and different intrinsic parameters are difficult to model using a motion vector, which is a simple translational model. Furthermore, the homography tries to estimate a global motion and ignores local motion using a truncated error function, which is not the case of VSP [22]. In the latter, the camera parameters, intrinsic and extrinsic, are used to predict one camera view from its neighbors.

For simplicity, the case of one neighboring camera is considered as shown in Figure 13. The view from camera c_2 can be synthesized from camera c_1. Each pixel $I(c_1, x, y)$ from camera c_1 is projected into the 3D world reference using its depth information:

$$\lambda\begin{pmatrix} x \\ y \\ 1 \end{pmatrix} = A\begin{pmatrix} R & T \\ 0 & 1 \end{pmatrix}\begin{pmatrix} X_{3D} \\ Y_{3D} \\ Z_{3D} \\ 1 \end{pmatrix}, \tag{5}$$

where *A* is the intrinsic parameters matrix, and *R* and *T* are the rotation and translation matrices with respect to the 3D world reference. Moreover, the depth information is equal to Z_{3D}, which corresponds to the *Z* coordinate of the point in the 3D world coordinates. It is substituted in (5), and the resulting system is solved for X_{3D} and Y_{3D}. Then, the 3D point is projected back to the 2D plane of camera c_2. This process is performed for each pixel of camera c_1.

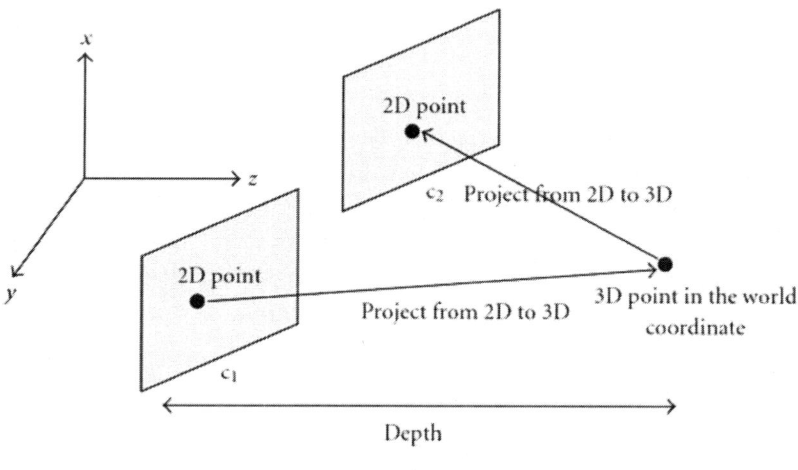

Figure 13. View synthesis prediction.

In the multiview camera setup used in this research, the pixel in the central camera is mapped to both side cameras. The pixel value is taken as average of both side camera pixels.

The drawback of this technique is the difficulty to estimate depth for real-world complex scenes. In addition, the quality of the SI depends on the precision of the camera calibration and depth estimation.

4.4. View Morphing (VM)

Image morphing can generate compelling 2D transitions between images. However, differences in object pose or viewpoint often cause unnatural distortions in image morphs. Using basic principles of projective geometry, one can perform a simple extension to image morphing that correctly handles 3D projective camera and scene transformations. The view morphing requires the computation of the fundamental matrix, which is the algebraic representation of epipolar geometry. Suppose that we have a point P in the 3D world coordinates. This point is visible in both cameras with optical centers C_0 and C_1 as P_0 and P_1, respectively. The three points P, C_0, and C_1 define a plane called the epipolar plane Π. The line intersection of the epipolar plane with each image plane is called an epipolar line as shown in Figure 14. The fundamental matrix is derived from the mapping between a point in one camera and its epipolar line in the other camera. Therefore, matching points should be calculated between the two images.

VM [23] is used to get an image from a virtual camera that could be placed between two real cameras as shown in Figure 15. The input of the view morphing algorithm is two images from real cameras and information about the correspondences between regions in the two images or projection matrices of the side cameras from 3D world coordinates to 2D coordinates in each camera plane. The output of the algorithm is a synthesized image (i.e., a view from the virtual camera).

The VM of a virtual camera with optical C_s is illustrated in Figure 16. Initially, both images I_0 and I_1 are warped across the scanlines to get $\tilde{I}_0$ and $\tilde{I}_1$, respectively, which are in the same plane. The latter are morphed across the position of the virtual camera C_s to get $\tilde{I}_s$. Finally, $\tilde{I}_s$ is unwarped to get I_s. As in the case of DCVP, an optimal weight s is computed for the virtual camera C_s such that the PSNR is maximized for the warped frame with respect to the central view frame.

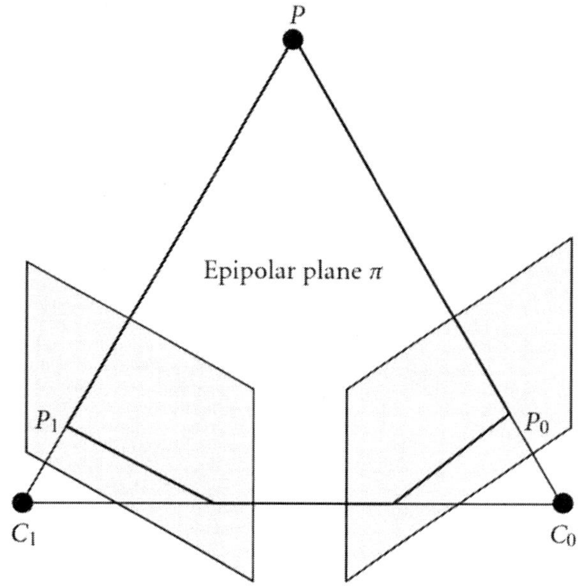

Figure 14. The epipolar line and plane.

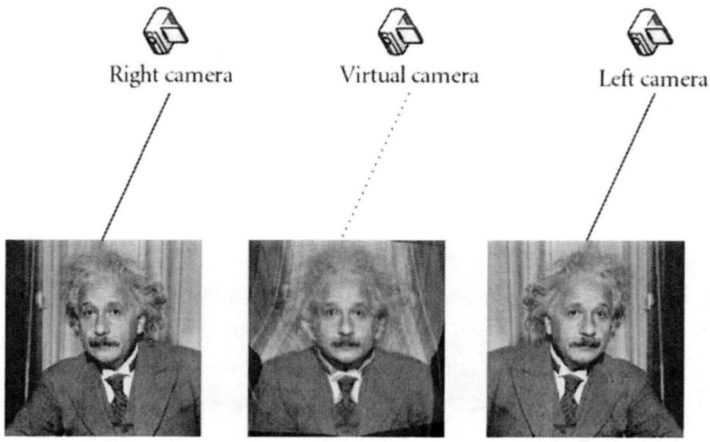

Figure 15. The virtual camera in view morphing.

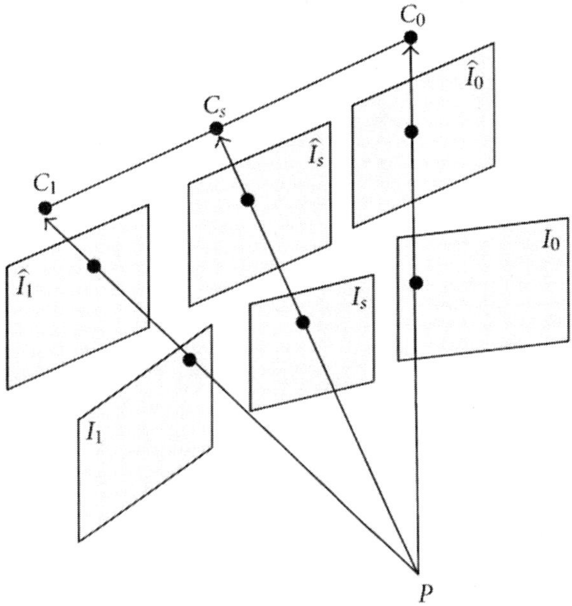

Figure 16. VM of a virtual camera with optical center C_s.

The problem with VM is that it works very well for simple scenes with a central object infront a uniform background. In this case, extracting matched feature points with a high degree of accuracy from the scene is simple as these points are used to compute the fundamental matrix. On the other hand, VM fails for real-world scenes as the matched feature points task becomes a more challenging task.

4.5. Multiview Motion Estimation (MVME)

MVME [24] finds the motion vectors in the side cameras and then applies them to the central camera to estimate the WZ frame as shown in Figure 17. The motion vectors computed in one view should be transformed before being used in another view. Nevertheless, they can be directly reused if all the cameras lie in the same plane and point in the same direction.

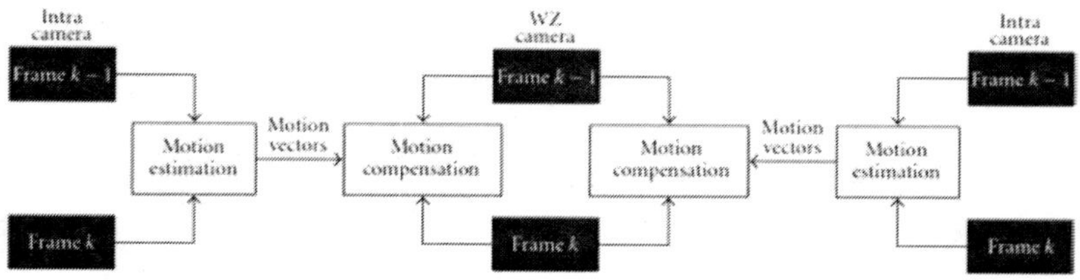

Figure 17. Conceptual scheme. Motion vectors are found in the intracamera and used in the WZ camera.

First, a *disparity vector* $\overrightarrow{dv}$ is obtained by block-based full search between the WZ and the intracameras for frame $k-1$. The vector $\overrightarrow{dv}$ estimates the location of each block from the WZ camera in the intracamera. Then, the *motion vector* $\overrightarrow{mv}$ is computed by searching in frame *k* in the intracamera for the best match for the block obtained in the previous step as illustrated in Figure 18(a). Finally, the *motion vector* $\overrightarrow{mv}$ is applied to the aligned block in frame *k* in the WZ camera as depicted in Figure 18(b).

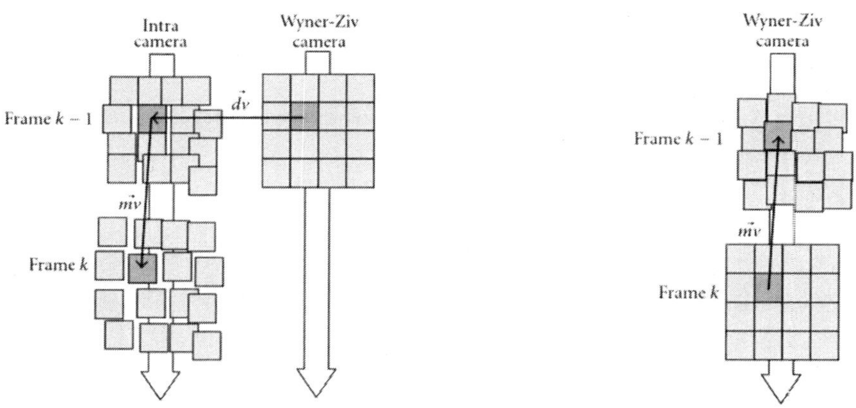

Figure 18. (a) Motion estimation scheme and (b) motion compensation scheme [24].

Figure 19 shows the possible motion paths to estimate the WZ frame, which are a total of 8 paths, 4 inner paths, and 4 outer paths, each generating one estimate. The inner paths are computed as described above by performing disparity estimation followed by motion estimation on the intracamera (Figure 19(a)). The outer paths are computed by doing the opposite of inner paths computation, starting with motion estimation on the intracamera followed by disparity estimation (Figure 19(b)). The simplest way to generate the final SI is by taking the average of these estimates. A better strategy is to compute a reliability measure for each path on a block or pixel basis and weight the estimates before taking the sum. For this purpose, mean square error (MSE) or mean absolute difference (MAD) computed between the original and the candidate blocks is used as a reliability measure.

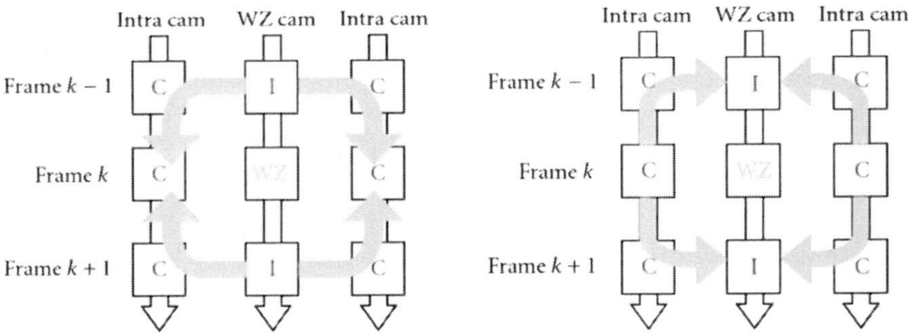

Figure 19. The 8 possible paths when using two intracameras and two reference frames in each camera [24]. Inner pathsOuter paths

5. ITERATIVE MULTIVIEW SIDE INFORMATION (IMSI)

We initially introduced iterative SI for the monoview scenario in [25], where the final SI depends not only on the key frames but also on the WZ bits as well. This final SI is used to refine the reconstruction of the decoded WZ frame. This is done by running the reconstruction process in a second iteration to enhance the quality of the decode frame. The process of IMSI is illustrated in Figure 20. IMSI differs from monoview iterative SI [25] in the fact that the initial SI depends on the input video in the multiview case. In the latter, the refinement process is applied to all the blocks, while a threshold is used to select the refined blocks based on the estimation error in [25].

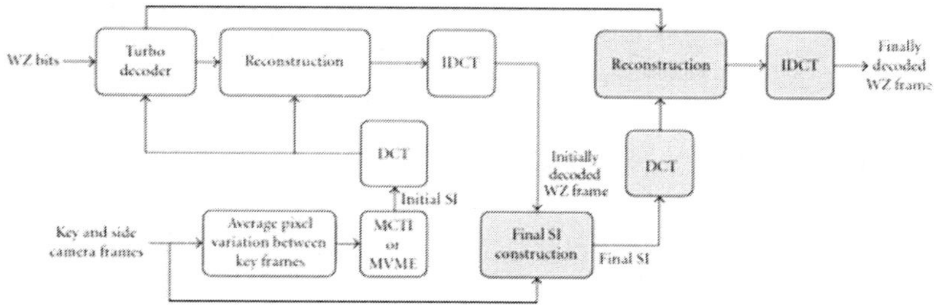

Figure 20. The IMSI generation process.

Initially, the reconstruction process of DVC is described in this section. Then, IMSI is introduced.

5.1. DVC Reconstruction

This stage in the decoding process is opposite to the quantization step at the encoder. After turbo decoding, the decoder knows perfectly the quantization bin of each decoded band. Relying on the assumption that the WZ frame is correlated with the SI, the reconstruction block uses the SI along with decoded bins to improve the reconstruction quality as described in [11]. The principal consists in either accepting an SI value as a reconstructed value if it fits into the quantization interval corresponding to the decoded bin or truncating the SI value into this quantization interval. The reconstruction is performed independently for every transform coefficient of every band.

Let Y be the SI value, d' the decoded quantized index, Δ the quantization step, and $\hat{X}$ the reconstructed value. In the case of the DC band, the reconstructed value $\hat{X}$ is computed as

$$\hat{X} = \begin{cases} Y & \text{if } d\Delta \leq Y \leq (d+1)\Delta, \\ d\Delta & \text{if } Y < d\Delta, \\ (d+1)\Delta & \text{if } Y > (d+1)\Delta. \end{cases} \tag{6}$$

For the AC bands, the reconstructed value $\hat{X}$ is computed in a similar way. The only difference is that a quantizer with a dead zone is used for the AC coefficients as they take positive and negative values. On the other hand, the DC coefficient takes only positive value.

5.2. IMSI for Enhanced Reconstruction

Hereafter, the proposed IMSI is described.

a. First, the initial SI to use in the WZ frame decoding is chosen depending on the nature of the video. This is done by computing the average luma variation per pixel between the key frames at the decoder, which is compared to a threshold. If it is below the threshold, the motion is considered not significant and MCTI is used as the initial SI. Otherwise, MVME is taken as initial SI. This is motivated by the results presented further in Section 6.2. Namely, MCTI shows better estimation quality for low-motion video content. On the other hand, MVME is shown to have a better performance for video with significant motion.

b. WZ decoding is performed using the initial SI, which implies turbo decoding followed by a first reconstruction stage.

c. The decoded WZ frame from the first stage is then predicted by block-based motion search and compensation as in conventional video coding using four references: the previous, forward, left camera, and right camera frames. More specifically, for each block in the decoded frame, the best matching block with minimum distortion is selected using the square absolute difference (SAD) as the distortion metric as shown in Figure 21. This generates a final SI.

d. Finally, the final SI is used in a second iteration in the reconstruction block.

It is important to stress the fact that this method does not use the original WZ but rather the decoded WZ frame using the initial SI. IMSI is expected to be efficient in situations where motion is significant as the difference in estimation quality between the initial and final SIs is more important. The reason is that the final SI is highly correlated with the WZ frame in the case of high activity video content. Therefore, most of the SI values map into the decoded bin in the reconstruction process (i.e., the SI value is taken as the reconstructed value). This produces a better reconstruction with lower distortion as less SI values are truncated into the quantization interval, when compared to the initial reconstruction phase, using the initial SI.

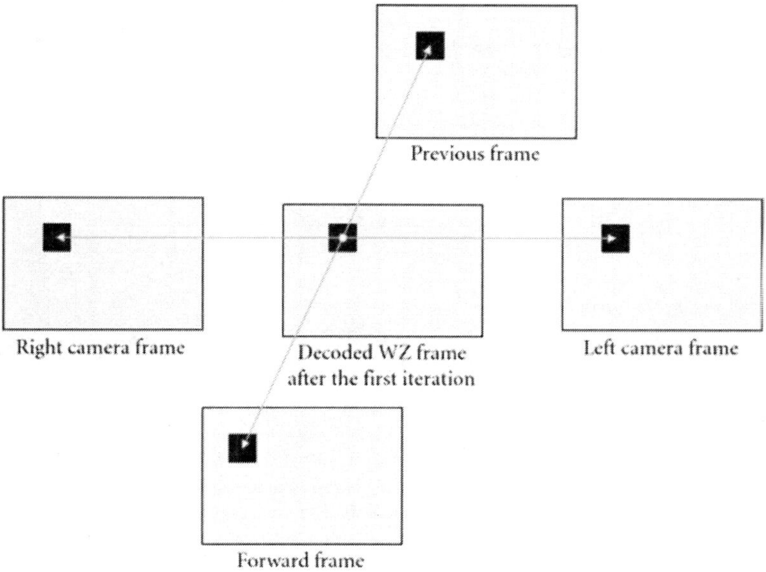

Figure 21. The final SI construction in IMSI.

The improvement for low-motion video is negligible as both side information, initial and final, are close in terms of estimation quality.

IMSI generates a better estimation of the WZ frame than the initial SI, since it uses the decoded WZ frame from the first iteration to compute the estimation. On the other hand, the price to pay for this good estimation is the initial WZ rate spent to initially decode the WZ frame. In addition, there is an increase in the decoder complexity due to the additional motion search task.

6. SIMULATION RESULTS

6.1. Test Material and Evaluation Methodology

The sequences *Breakdancers, Ballet,* and *Uli* shown in Figure 22 are used for evaluating the performance of the different SI techniques. *Breakdancers* and *Ballet* contain significant motion. This makes the motion estimation a difficult and challenging task. On the other hand, *Uli* is a conference-like video sequence, which contains more or less static video content. The spatial resolution is 256×192 for all the sequences. The temporal resolutions are 15 fps for *Breakdancers* and *Ballet*, and 25 fps for *Uli*.

Figure 22. Sequences *Breakdancers, Ballet,* and *Uli* .

In this paper, three camera views are used, and the performance is evaluated only for the central camera. For DVC simulations, the DISCOVER codec [6] is run with the following settings.

- Only luminance data is coded.
- The central camera is the only one containing WZ frames. The side cameras (i.e., left and right) are conventionally encoded in the intramode, while the central one contains WZ frames, as depicted in Figure10.
- Four RD points are computed per SI. They correspond to the following quantization matrices:

$$QI_1 = \begin{pmatrix} 32 & 8 & 0 & 0 \\ 8 & 0 & 0 & 0 \\ 0 & 0 & 0 & 0 \\ 0 & 0 & 0 & 0 \end{pmatrix}, \quad QI_2 = \begin{pmatrix} 32 & 16 & 8 & 4 \\ 16 & 8 & 4 & 0 \\ 8 & 4 & 0 & 0 \\ 4 & 0 & 0 & 0 \end{pmatrix},$$

$$QI_3 = \begin{pmatrix} 64 & 16 & 8 & 8 \\ 16 & 8 & 8 & 4 \\ 8 & 8 & 4 & 4 \\ 8 & 4 & 4 & 0 \end{pmatrix}, \quad QI_4 = \begin{pmatrix} 128 & 64 & 32 & 16 \\ 64 & 32 & 16 & 8 \\ 32 & 16 & 8 & 4 \\ 16 & 8 & 4 & 0 \end{pmatrix}. \tag{7}$$

Each element of the matrices corresponds to the number of quantization levels to the corresponding coefficient band. For example, the DC coefficient has 32, 32, 64, and 128 quantization levels, respectively, in the 1st, 2nd, 3rd, and 4th RD points, and so on.

- The same quantization parameter (QP) is used for the side cameras and the key frames of the central camera. A QP is defined per quantization matrix such that the decoded key and WZ frames have a similar quality.

- The GOP size is equal to 2.

For AVC/H.264 coding, the publicly available reference software (JM 11.0) [26] is used with the following settings:

a) Intra, Inter No Motion, and Inter Motion modes. For the Inter No Motion mode, each motion vector is equal to zero, which means that each block in a P frame is predicted from the colocated block in the previous I frame. For the Inter Motion mode, the motion search range is set to 32. In both modes, the GOP size is equal to 12;

b) high profile with CABAC;

c) the 8×8 transform enabled.

6.2. Side Information Estimation Quality

In this section, the SI PSNR is evaluated for the SI techniques at the different RD points. *Uli* is not provided with depth maps. In addition, the feature point matching performs poorly due to highly textured scene background in the sequence. For this reason, the VSP and VM techniques are not evaluated for *Uli*.

For IMSI, Figure 23 shows the luma pixel variation between the key frames for the three video sequences at the highest RD point. By picking a threshold equal to 1.7, *Breakdancers* and *Ballet* are classified as sequences with significant motion (i.e., MVME is used as the initial SI) and *Uli* is classified as a low-motion video content (i.e., MCTI is used as the initial SI) at all RD points.

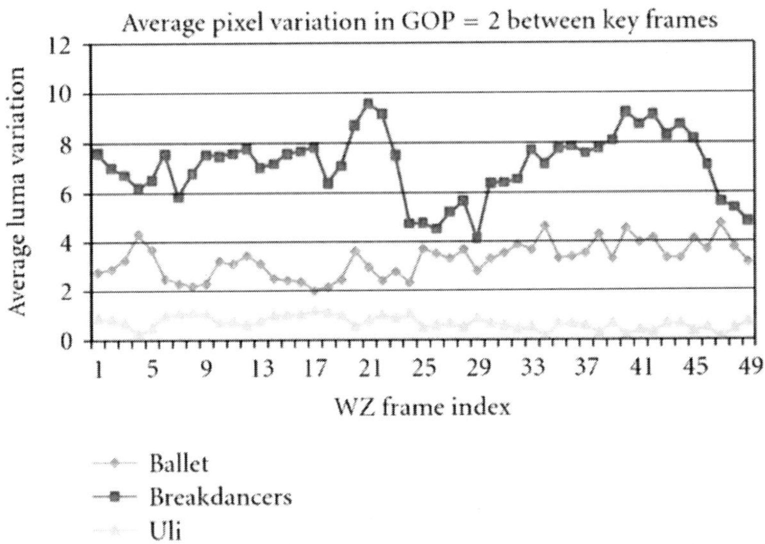

Figure 23. Average luma pixel variation for *Breakdancers, Ballet* , and *Uli* at the highest RD point.

Figures 24, 25, and 26 show the SI PSNR for *Breakdancers, Ballet*, and *Uli*, respectively. Obviously, the GT fusion and IMSI produce the best estimation for all sequences at all RD points as they use, respectively, the original frame and the decoded WZ frame to construct the estimation. Thus, the comparison will mainly focus on the other SI techniques. For *Breakdancers*, MVME produces the best SI quality followed by MCTI. On the other hand, the worst performance is for VSP. However, VSP requires two input parameters, camera calibration, and depth estimation. The quality of the SI depends on the precision of these parameters. We can observe that most of the techniques perform quite well in terms of SI quality for this sequence as homography and DCVP are quite close to MCTI in estimation quality.

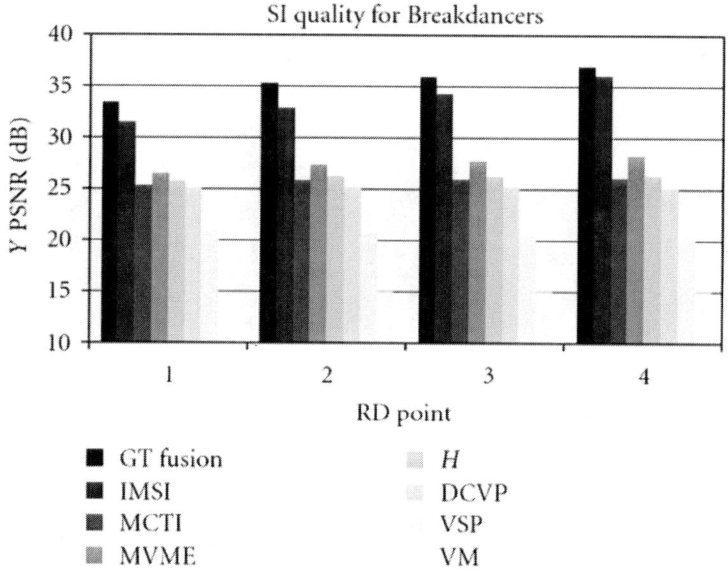

Figure 24. Side information quality for *Breakdancers* .

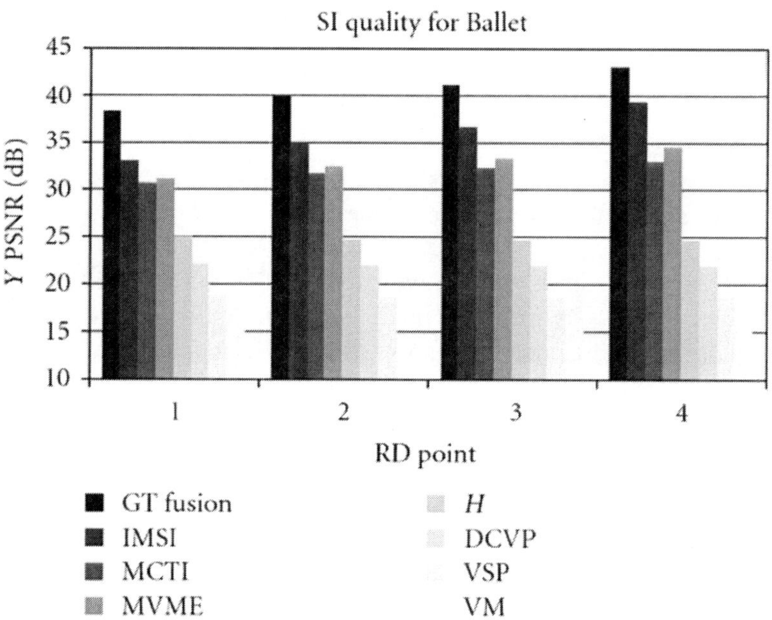

Figure 25. Side information quality for *Ballet* .

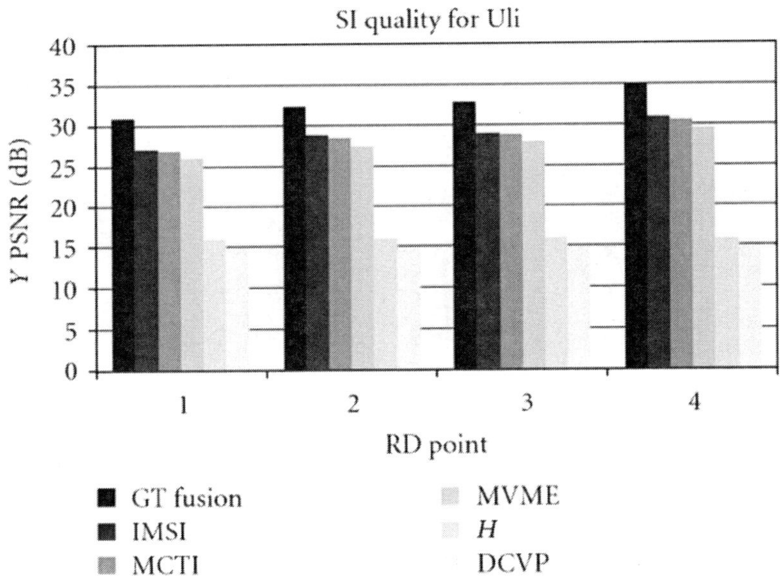

Figure 26. Side information quality for *Uli* .

For *Ballet*, MVME produces the best SI quality followed by MCTI. *Ballet* contains motion but it is less significant than in the *Breakdancers* case. This explains the increase in PSNR gap between MCTI and the other SI techniques. As for *Breakdancers*, we have homography followed by DCVP, then VM, and finally VSP in a decreasing order in terms of SI quality.

Since *Uli* contains little motion, we expect MCTI and MVME to work very well, since MCTI performs a pure temporal interpolation and MVME performs an intercamera disparity estimation followed by a temporal motion estimation.

In summary, we can see clearly that MVME and MCTI produce by far better estimations than other SI generation techniques for *Ballet* and *Uli*. On the other hand, MVME, MCTI, homography, and DCVP are not very far from each other in terms of SI quality for *Breakdancers*.

Figure 27 illustrates the contribution of the different side information to the GT fusion for *Breakdancers*. It is obvious that MCTI has the largest contribution around 43 % ~ 55 % out of the total number of frame pixels.

It is followed by homography-based SI. The homography is the one that brings most innovation to the GT fusion. MVME and DCVP are highly correlated with MCTI. This is explained by the fact that these methods are of the same block-based nature. Finally, VSP and VM have the worst contribution to the GT fusion.

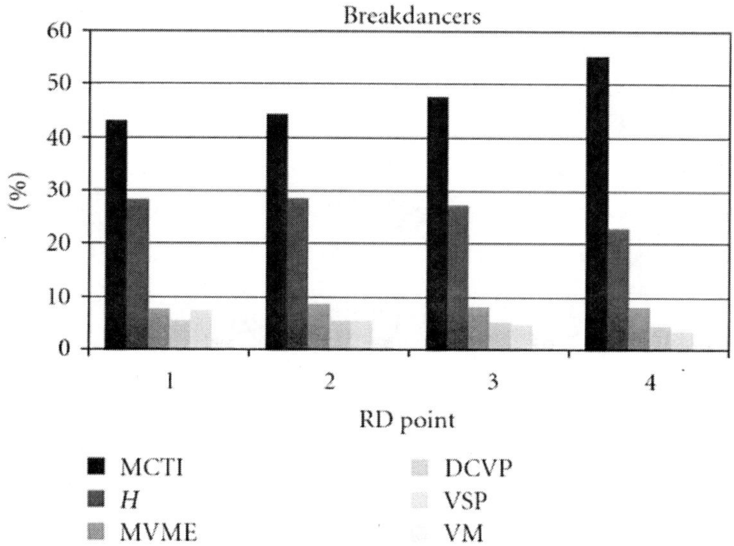

Figure 27. The percentage of contribution of the different side information in the GT fusion for *Breakdancers* .

The contribution of the different side information to the GT fusion for *Ballet* is illustrated in Figure 28. As for*Breakdancers,* MCTI has the largest contribution, around 45% ~ 64% . It is larger than in the *Breakdancers* case, since *Ballet* contains less motion than *Breakdancers.* It is followed by homography-based SI. Then, MVME comes in the third place followed by DCVP. Finally, VSP and VM are the worst in terms of contribution to the GT fusion.

Since *Uli* contains low-motion content, MCTI has the largest contribution to the GT fusion, around 54% ~ 73% , out of all pixels. It is followed by homography-based SI and then MVME. Furthermore, the rest of side information have a poor contribution to the GT fusion. This is illustrated in Figure 29.

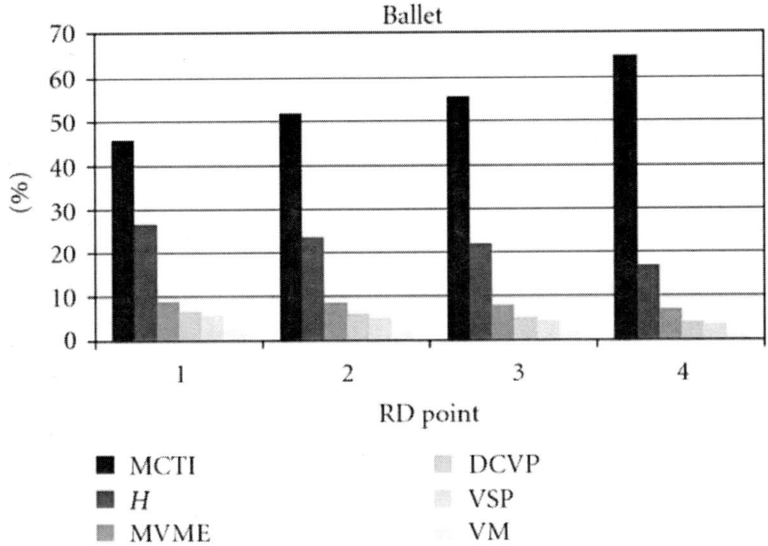

Figure 28. The percentage of contribution of the different side information in the GT fusion for *Ballet* .

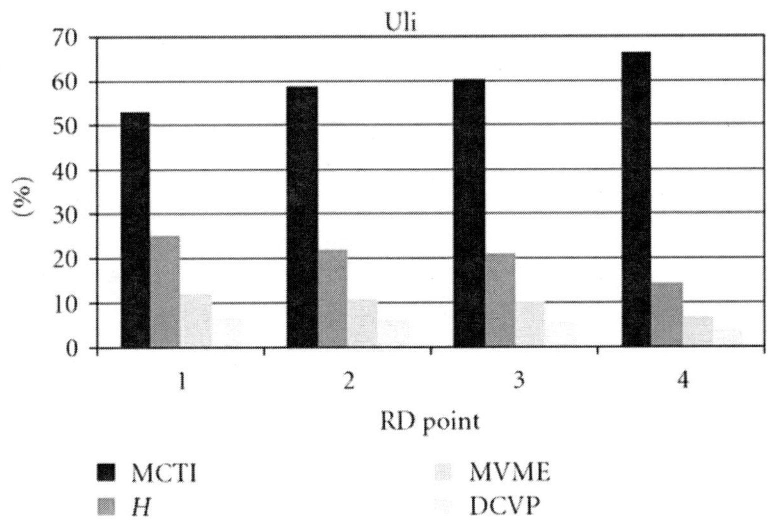

Figure 29. The percentage of contribution of the different side information in the GT fusion for *Uli* .

For the three sequences, homography-based SI is the one that brings most innovations to the GT fusion as it is the least correlated SI with MCTI. Therefore, we can conclude that possible fusion algorithms combining MCTI and homography-based SI represent a good tradeoff between performance improvement and complexity increase.

6.3. Side Information Complexity

The different techniques complexities are compared in terms of the total number of arithmetic operations (i.e., additions, subtractions, multiplications, and divisions) required to generate the side information. The image dimensions are the height, *H*, and the width, *W*. For the block-based methods, a search range r and block size w are considered.

6.3.1. MCTI and DCVP

Both MCTI and DCVP have the same complexity. The only difference between both techniques is the input frames. For each block match, w^2 subtractions are required. Then, the error is computed, which requires $w^2 - 1$ additions. This is performed for each position within the search range. Thus, $(2w^2 - 1)r^2$ operations are required to find a match for each block. Finally, all the blocks should be processed. Therefore, $(2w^2 - 1) * r^2 * (H * W / w^2) \approx 2 * H * W * r^2$ is the number of operations required to estimate the motion between the two frames.

6.3.2. MVME

There is a maximum of 8 paths. For each one, motion estimation is performed twice with the Intracamera and then across the side and the central cameras. Therefore, $2 * O(\mathrm{MCTI})$ operations are required for each path. Thus, a total of $16 * O(\mathrm{MCTI})$ operations is required for all the paths. In other words, MVME is approximately 16 times more complex than MCTI.

6.3.3. Homography

Initially, the homography matrices are computed offline. A total of 15 operations is required to compute the mapping for each pixel using the 3×3 homography matrix. Therefore, the complexity of the homography-based side information generation from both view is $2 * 15 * H * W = 30 * H * W$.

6.3.4. VM

In VM, both side frames are warped, which requires $2 * 15 * H * W$ operations. Then, the resulting warped frames are morphed across the virtual camera position. The latter needs $3 * H * W$ operations. Finally, the morphed frame is unwarped to obtain the side information. Therefore, the total complexity is $3 * H * W + 3 * 15 * H * W = 48 * H * W$ operations.

6.3.5. VSP

For each pixel, the projection from the image plane to the 3D world coordinates requires 38 operations. Moreover, the projection back to the central camera requires 23 operations. This is performed for each pixel, which results in a total complexity of $61 * H * W$. It important to mention that this estimation does not take into account the depth estimation. This complexity applies given that the depth map is already available.

6.3.6. IMSI

The complexity of IMSI depends on the initial SI used, which is either MVME or MCTI. Then, the final SI generations requires $O(\text{MCTI})$ operations. This implies a maximum complexity of $9 * O(\text{MCTI})$ when MVME is used as the initial SI.

6.4. RD Performance

In this section, the RD plots for the different sequences are presented for the different side information. It is important to mention that only SI with a significant RD performance is presented. Therefore, the performance of VM and VSP is not plotted for *Breakdancers* and *Ballet*. For *Uli*, only IMSI, MCTI, and MVME are plotted as they significantly outperform the other side information. On the other hand, the GT fusion combines all the side information even the ones that are not plotted.

For *Breakdancers*, IMSI has the best RD performance out of all SI techniques as it is superior to MVME by around 0.4 dB and 0.7 dB at low and high bit rates, respectively. The SI quality is better for MVME than MCTI. This explains the performance gap between MVME and MCTI in Figure 30. This gap is more or less constant and around 0.2 dB. Further, homography and DCVP are inferior to MCTI by a maximum gap of around 1.0 dB and 2.0 dB, respectively, at high bit rates. At average bit rates, this gap is around 0.5 dB and 1.2 dB, respectively. The homography has a similar performance to MCTI at low bit rates and DCVP is inferior by 1.0 dB.

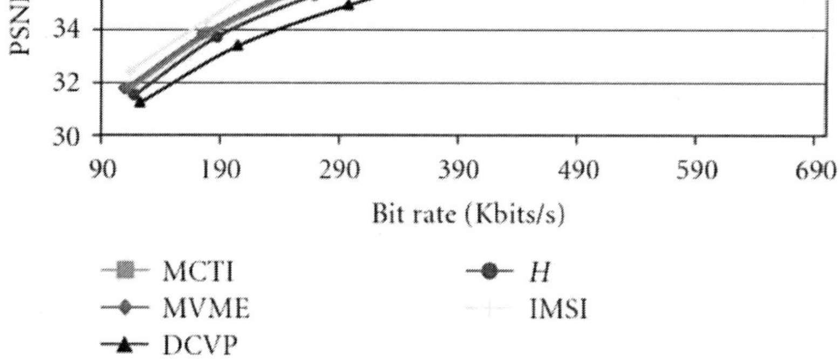

Figure 30. RD performance for *Breakdancers* .

For IMSI, Figure 31 shows the quality of the reconstructed WZ frames for *Breakdancers* in the first and second reconstruction iterations for the highest RD point. In the initial one, around 13% of the SI values are truncated while this percentage is around 5% in the second reconstruction iteration resulting in a less-distorted reconstruction.

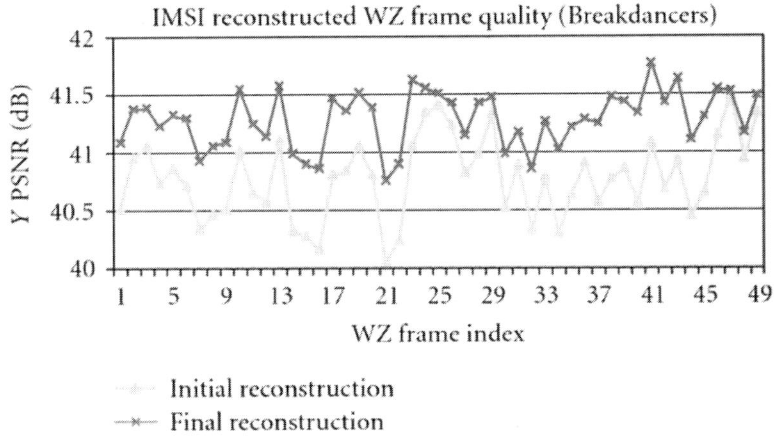

Figure 31. The reconstructed WZ frames quality for the initial and final reconstructions for *Breakdancers* for the highest RD point.

For *Ballet*, IMSI has the best RD performance slightly outperforming MVME by around 0.1 dB at high bit rates. Obviously, the performance improvement is less important than in the *Breakdancers* case as this sequence has less motion. Further, MVME and MCTI have a similar performance as shown in Figure 32. Even though MVME has a slightly better SI quality than MCTI for all RD points, it is not translated to a better RD performance. The reason is that the DVC scheme operates in the DCT domain not the pixel domain. Thus, a better SI PSNR, which is computed on the pixel values, does not automatically imply better performance for transform domain WZ decoding.

Finally, the reduction in the number of truncated SI values with IMSI is less significant (i.e., around 2%) for *Ballet*than in the case of *Breakdancers*. This leads to less improvement in the reconstruction as shown in Figure 33.

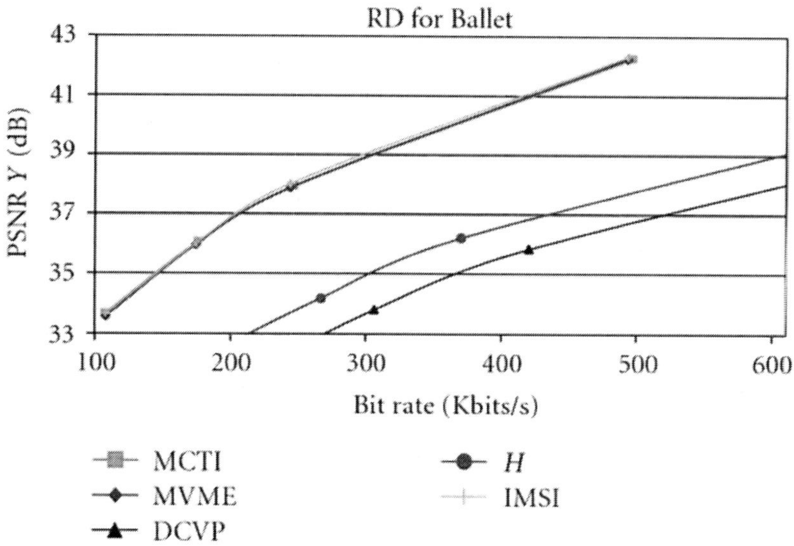

Figure 32. RD performance for *Ballet* .

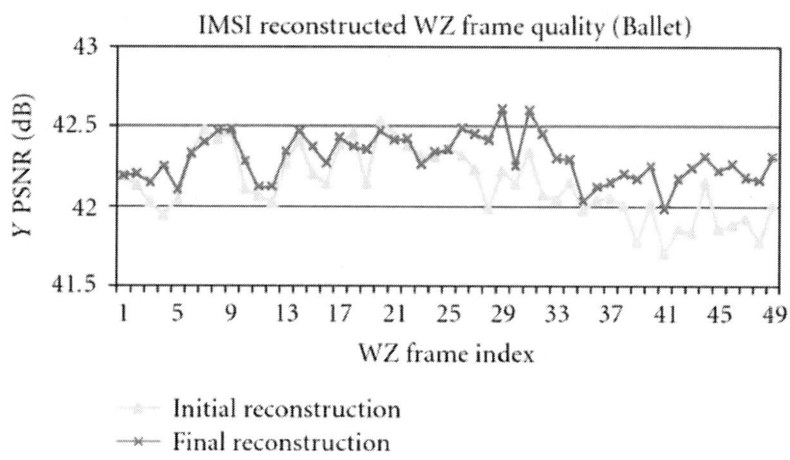

Figure 33. The reconstructed WZ frames quality for the initial and final reconstructions for *Ballet* for the highest RD point.

As mentioned previously, *Uli* contains very low-motion video content due to its nature. Therefore, both IMSI and MCTI have the best performance, but IMSI does not bring any improvement in this case. Both side information outperform MVME by around 0.5 dB as shown in Figure 34.

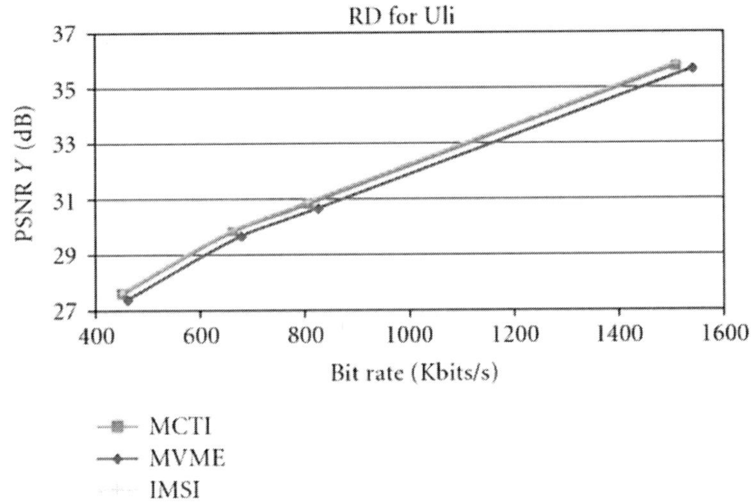

Figure 34. RD performance for *Uli* .

Next, the GT fusion, IMSI, and the fusion techniques introduced in [12, 16], combining MCTI and homography (i.e., the least correlated side information), are compared to AVC/H.264 Intra, Inter No Motion, and Inter Motion. The choice of the Intra and Inter No Motion modes is motivated by the fact they are very close to DVC in terms of encoding complexity. In addition, the DSC theorems state that the performance of a codec that performs joint encoding and decoding (i.e., Inter Motion Mode) should also be achievable (asymptotically) by a DVC codec.

For *Breakdancers*, even though the encoder driven fusion is slightly superior to IMSI at low bit rates but overall, IMSI produces the best performance out of the DVC techniques as it outperforms both fusion algorithms (Figure35). The performance gap is more significant at high video quality. Nevertheless, IMSI is still inferior to AVC/H.264 in its different modes. This sequence is very challenging in terms of motion estimation, which generates a low-correlated SI with the WZ frame. This results in a poorer coding performance when compared to conventional codecs.

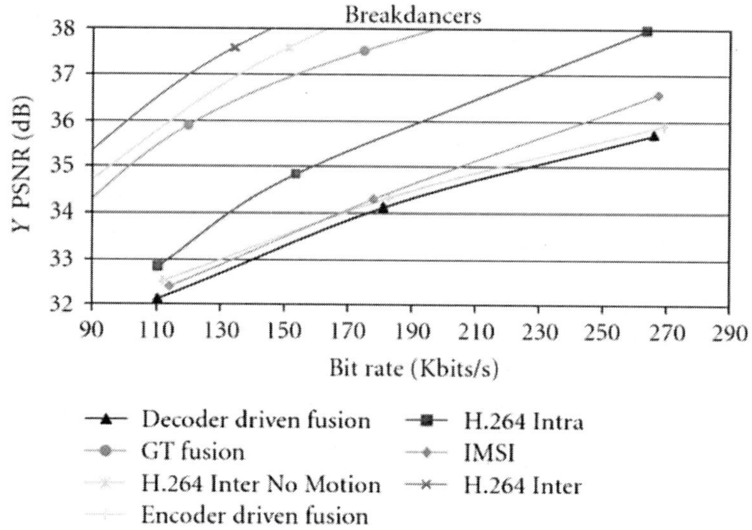

Figure 35. RD performance for *Breakdancers* .

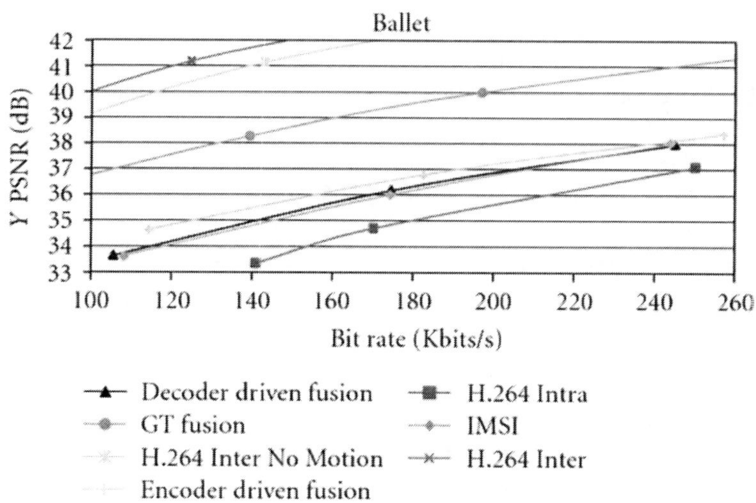

Figure 36. RD performance for *Ballet* .

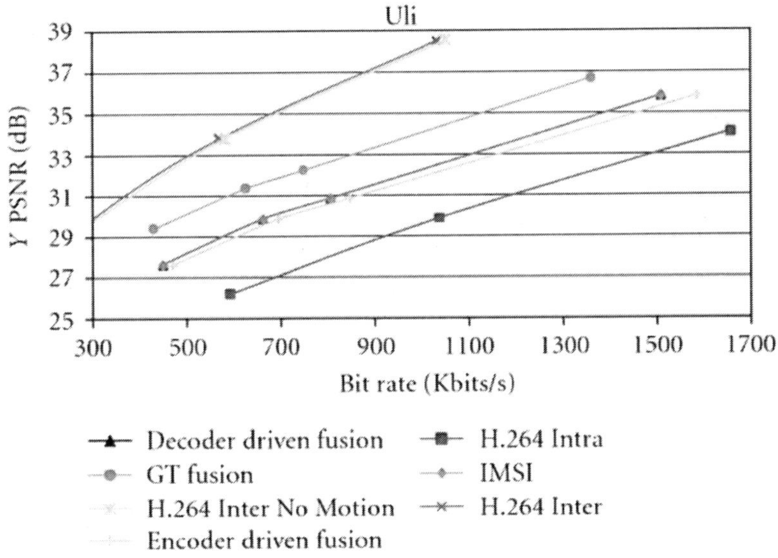

Figure 37. RD performance for *Uli* .

For *Ballet*, IMSI is superior to AVC/H.264 Intra by around 1.0 dB, and significantly outperformed by AVC/H.264 Inter No Motion and Inter Motion. Both fusions in this case improve the performance over IMSI. More specifically, the decoder-driven fusion improvement is around 0.25 dB. Moreover, the encoder-driven fusion improves the performance even further especially at low and average bit rates by a maximum gap of around 1.0 dB.

For *Uli*, IMSI, which is similar to MCTI in performance, improves the performance over AVC/H.264 Intra by around 3.0 dB. Moreover, it has a poorer performance than AVC/H.264 Inter No Motion and Inter Motion. The fusions do not result in any improvements as the decision is always made in favor of MCTI for the decoder-driven fusion. In other words, performing the fusion in this case is useless for *Uli*. For the encoder-driven fusion, the improvement in SI estimation quality is insignificant, and since additional rate is spent to send the binary mask, the overall performance drops below MCTI.

Overall, the performance of DVC is superior to AVC/H.264 Intra for two sequences out of three. On the other hand, it has a poorer performance than AVC/H.264 Inter Inter No Motion and Inter Motion for all the sequences, even with the GT fusion. Concerning DVC, IMSI is better for video content with very significant motion occupying a large part of the scene. MCTI is suitable for more or less static video content as it generates highly correlated SI with the WZ frame, resulting in superior compression efficiency than intraconventional coding, but inferior to conventional intercoding. For video with average motion, the encoder driven fusion produces the best performance for the DVC compression. Finally, the GT fusion shows that there still a large gap for improvement as it reduces the bit rate for DVC up to 50% for video with significant motion with respect to MCTI.

7. CONCLUSION

In this work, different SI generation techniques are studied for multiview DVC. For video with significant motion, the proposed IMSI significantly improves the performance over other SI techniques. It is followed by MVME and then MCTI. On the other hand, IMSI is more complex than MVME, which is much more complex than MCTI. For videos with average and low motion, MCTI and MVME improve the RD performance over AVC/H.264 Intra. Nevertheless, MCTI has the advantage of having a similar or better RD performance and being less complex than MVME in this case.

Further, we show that it is possible to reduce up to 50% the bit rate with respect to monoview DVC (i.e., MCTI) with the GT fusion. Nevertheless, the GT fusion requires the original video at the decoder, which is not feasible but it shows the maximum possible gain when the different SIs are ideally combined. It shows as well that MCTI, MVME, and DCVP generate highly correlated side information since they belong to the same block-based category techniques. On the other hand, MCTI and homography represent a good tradeoff between performance improvement and complexity increase. Moreover, fusion techniques combining these two side information show significant improvement for video with high motion.

Many improvements are possible over this work. Initially, a better fusion algorithm should be found to exploit the combination of the different side information without needing the original frame and close the gap on the GT fusion. Moreover, fusion between MCTI and homography should be considered as they produce the least-correlated side information, and represent a good tradeoff between performance improvement and complexity increase.

Further, the MVME technique is very complex. Therefore, the complexity of this technique can be reduced by using fast motion search techniques such as a multigrid [27] approach instead of a fixed block size in addition to an *N*-step [28] search instead of a full search.

Finally, the additional complexity in the IMSI technique can be significantly reduced by selecting the blocks for which the reestimation is performed as defined in [25]. More specifically, a block is reestimated in the final SI if the residual error between the initially decoded WZ frame and the initial SI is greater than a certain threshold for this block. Otherwise, the block from the initial SI is just copied into the final SI.

ACKNOWLEDGMENTS

This work was partially supported by the European project Discover (http://www.discoverdvc.org) (IST Contract 015314) and the European Network of Excellence VISNET II (http://www.visnet-noe.org) (IST Contract 1-038398), both funded under the European Commission IST 6th Framework Program. The authors also would like to acknowledge the use of the DISCOVER codec, a software which started from the IST WZ software developed at the Image Group from Instituto Superior Técnico (IST) of Lisbon by Catarina Brites, João Ascenso, and Fernando Pereira.

REFERENCES

1. **Free Viewpoint Television (FTV)** http://www.tanimoto.nuee.nagoya-u.ac.jp/study/FTV

2. Girod B, Aaron AM, Rane S, Rebollo-Monedero D: **Distributed video coding.** *Proceedings of the IEEE* 2005,**93**(1):71-83.

3. Wiegand T, Sullivan GJ, Bjøntegaard G, Luthra A: **Overview of the H.264/AVC video coding standard.** *IEEE Transactions on Circuits and Systems for Video Technology* 2003,**13**(7):560-576.

4. Slepian D, Wolf J: **Noiseless coding of correlated information sources.** *IEEE Transactions on Information Theory*1973,**19**(4):471-480.

5. Wyner A, Ziv J: **The rate-distortion function for source coding with side information at the decoder.** *IEEE Transactions on Information Theory* 1976,**22**(1):1-10.

6. Artigas X, Ascenso J, Dalai M, Klomp S, Kubasov D, Ouaret M: **The DISCOVER codec: architecture, techniques and evaluation.** *Proceedings of the Picture Coding Symposium (PCS '07), November 2007, Lisbon, Portugal*

7. Malvar HS, Hallapuro A, Karczewicz M, Kerofsky L: **Low-complexity transform and quantization in H.264/AVC.** *IEEE Transactions on Circuits and Systems for Video Technology* 2003,**13**(7):598-603.

8. Berrou C, Glavieux A, Thitimajshima P: **Near Shannon limit error-correcting coding and decoding: turbo-codes.1.***Proceedings of the IEEE International Conference on Communications (ICC '93), May 1993, Geneva, Switzerland* **2:** 1064-1070.

9. Peterson WW, Brown DT: **Cyclic codes for error detection.** *Proceedings of the IRE* 1961,**49**(1):228-235.

10. Ascenso J, Brites C, Pereira F: **Improving frame interpolation with spatial motion smoothing for pixel domain distributed video coding.** *Proceedings of the 5th EURASIP Conference on Speech and Image Processing, Multimedia Communications and Services, July 2005, Smolenice, Slovak*

11. Aaron A, Zhang R, Girod B: **Wyner-ziv coding for motion video.** *Proceedings of the 36th Asilomar Conference on Signals, Systems and Computers, November 2002, Pacific Grove, Calif, USA*

12. Ouaret M, Dufaux F, Ebrahimi T: **Fusion-based multiview distributed video coding.** *Proceedings of the 4th ACM International Workshop on Video Surveillance and Sensor Networks (VSSN '06), October 2006, Santa Barbara, Calif, USA*139-144.

13. Artigas X, Angeli E, Torres L: **Side information generation for multiview distributed video coding using a fusion approach.** *Proceedings of the 7th Nordic Signal Processing Symposium (NORSIG '06), June 2007, Reykjavik, Iceland* 250-253.

14. Guo X, Lu Y, Wu F, Gao W, Li S: **Distributed multi-view video coding.** *Visual Communications and Image Processing (VCIP), January 2006, San Jose, Calif, USA, Proceedings of SPIE* **6077:**

15. Guo X, Lu Y, Wu F, Zhao D, Gao W: **Wyner-ziv-based multiview video coding.** *IEEE Transactions on Circuits and Systems for Video Technology* 2008,**18**(6):713-724.

16. Ouaret M, Dufaux F, Ebrahimi T: **Multiview distributed video coding with encoder driven fusion.** *Proceedings of the European Conference on Signal Processing (EUSIPCO '07), September 2007, Poznan, Poland*

17. Joint Bi-Level Image Experts Group http://www.jpeg.org/jbig

18. Flierl M, Girod B: **Coding of multi-view image sequences with video sensors.** *Proceedings of the International Conference on Image Processing (ICIP '06), October 2006, Atlanta, Ga, USA* 609-612.

19. Flierl M, Girod B: **Video coding with motion-compensated lifted wavelet transforms.** *Signal Processing: Image Communication* 2004,**19**(7):561-575. 10.1016/j.image.2004.05.002

20. Dufaux F, Ouaret M, Ebrahimi T: **Recent advances in multiview distributed video coding.** *Mobile Multimedia/Image Processing for Military and Security Applications, April 2007, Orlando, Fla, USA, Proceedings of SPIE* **6579:** 1-11.

21. Dufaux F, Konrad J: **Efficient, robust, and fast global motion estimation for video coding.** *IEEE Transactions on Image Processing* 2000,**9**(3):497-501.

22. Martinian E, Behrens A, Xin J, Vetro A: **View synthesis for multiview video compression.** *Proceedings of the 25th Picture Coding Symposium (PCS '06), April 2006, Beijing, China*

23. Seitz SM, Dyer CR: **View morphing.** *Proceedings of the 23rd Annual Conference on Computer Graphics and Interactive Techniques (SIGGRAPH '96), August 1996, New Orleans, La, USA* 21-30.

24. Artigas X, Tarres F, Torres L: **Comparison of different side information generation methods for multiview distributed video coding.** *Proceedings of the International Conference on Signal Processing and Multimedia Applications (SIGMAP '07), July 2007, Barcelona, Spain*

25. Ye S, Ouaret M, Dufaux F, Ebrahimi T: **Improved side information generation with iterative decoding and frame interpolation for distributed video coding.** *Proceedings of the 15th International Conference on Image Processing (ICIP '08), October 2008, San Deigo, Calif, USA* 2228-2231.

26. **AVC/H.264 software** http://iphome.hhi.de/suehring/tml

27. Dufaux F: *Multigrid Block Matching Motion Estimation for Generic Video Coding, Ph.D. thesis*. Ecole Polytechnique Federale de Lausanne, Lausanne, Switzerland; 1994.

28. Coban MZ, Mersereau RM: **Fast rate-constrained N-step search algorithm for motion estimation.** *Proceedings of the IEEE International Conference on Acoustics, Speech and Signal Processing (ICASSP '98), May 1998, Seattle, Wash, USA***5:** 2613-2616.

Chapter 2

Error Evaluation in a Stereovision-Based 3D Reconstruction System

Abdelkrim Belhaoua,1 Sophie Kohler,2 and Ernest Hirsch1

1 LSIIT (UMR CNRS-UdS 7005), Universit´e de Strasbourg, Bd S´ebastien Brant, BP 10413, 67412 Illkirch Cedex, France

2 MIPS (EA 2332), Universit´e Haute Alsace, 12, rue des fr`eres Lumi`ere, 68093 Mulhouse Cedex, France

ABSTRACT

The work presented in this paper deals with the performance analysis of the whole 3D reconstruction process of imaged objects, specifically of the set of geometric primitives describing their outline and extracted from a pair of images knowing their associated camera models. The proposed analysis focuses on error estimation for the edge detection process, the starting step for the whole reconstruction procedure. The fitting parameters describing the geometric features composing the workpiece to be evaluated are used as quality measures to determine error bounds and finally to estimate the edge detection errors. These error estimates are then propagated up to the final 3D reconstruction step. The suggested error analysis procedure for stereovision-based reconstruction tasks further allows evaluating the quality of the 3D reconstruction. The resulting final error estimates enable lastly to state if the reconstruction results fulfill *a priori* defined criteria, for example, fulfill dimensional constraints including tolerance information, for vision-based quality control applications for example.

1. INTRODUCTION

Quality control is the process applied to ensure a given level of quality for a product, especially in the automotive industry sector. Implementation of such a control at all stages of a production, from design to manufacturing, is unavoidable to guarantee a high level of quality, requiring often high measurement accuracy in order to avoid both loss of manufacturing time and material. Thus, when making use of vision-based approaches, it is necessary to develop fully automated tools for the accurate computation of 3D descriptions of the object of interest out of the acquired image contents. The latter can then be compared, taking tolerance information into account, with either ground truth or the CAD model of the object under investigation, in order to evaluate quantitatively its quality. An autonomous cognitive vision system is currently being developed for the optimal quantitative 3D reconstruction of manufactured parts, based on *a priori* planning of the task. As a result, the system is built around a cognitive intelligent sensory system using so-called situation graph trees as a planning/control tool [1]. The planning system has been successfully applied to structured light and stereovision-based 3D reconstruction tasks [2, 3, 4], with the aim to favor the development of an automated quality control system for manufactured parts evaluating quantitatively their geometry. This requires the coordination of a set of complex processes performing sequentially data acquisition, its quantitative evaluation (i.e., extraction of geometric features and their 3D reconstruction), and the comparison with a reference model (e.g., CAD model of the object) in order to evaluate quantitatively the object, including means allowing adjusting/ correcting online either data acquisition or processing.

Stereovision is a direct approach for obtaining three-dimensional information using two images acquired from two different points of view. The approach, when efficiently implemented, enables to achieve reconstruction and consequently dimensional measurements, with rather high accuracy. Thus, the method is widely used in many applications, ranging from 3D object recognition to machine inspection. In this last case, the outline of the object can be determined, based on the set of geometric contour-based features defining this outline. As a result, such a contour-based approach provides good (i.e., reasonable) reconstruction quality at low cost. However, in order to assess the quality of the results, specifically when high levels of accuracy are required, it is mandatory to carry out a thorough analysis of the errors occurring in the system. More precisely, presence of noise in the acquired data affects the accuracy of the subsequent image processing steps and, thus, of the whole reconstruction process. 3D reconstruction errors depend on the quality of the acquired images (resulting from the environment; i.e., the specific acquisition conditions used) as well as on their processing (e.g., segmentation, feature extraction, matching, and reconstruction).

The work presented in this paper deals with the performance analysis of the 3D reconstruction process of a set of geometric primitives (in our case, lines and arcs of or full ellipses) from a pair of images knowing their associated camera models. The suggested analysis focuses firstly on the error estimation affecting the edge detection process, the starting processing step for the whole reconstruction procedure. Using fitting techniques in order to describe the geometric elements and assuming that the noise is independent and uniformly distributed in the images, error bounds are established for each geometric feature that composes the outline of the object to be evaluated. The error bounds are then propagated through the following processing steps, up to the final 3D reconstruction step. Specifically devised here to enable error analysis for stereovision-based reconstruction tasks, it can be straightforwardly extended to other types of image-based features. This will then help to evaluate the quality of the 3D reconstructions obtained applying various imaging techniques, as illustrated in this paper by stereovision-based results. Lastly, the resulting final reconstruction error estimates enable to state if the reconstruction results fulfills *a priori* defined criteria including tolerance information (e.g., dimensions with their corresponding tolerances).

2. RELATED WORK

A literature survey shows that over the last years some efforts have been devoted to error analysis in stereovision-based computer vision systems, see, for example, [5, 6, 7, 8, 9, 10, 11, 12]. As an illustrative example, using a stereoscopic camera setup, Blostein and Huang in [5], have investigated the accuracy in obtaining 3D positional information based on triangulation techniques using point correspondences. In particular, they have been able to derive closed form expressions for the probability distributions of the position error along each direction (horizontal, vertical, and range) of the coordinate system associated with the stereo rig. With the same aim, a study of various types of error and of their effect on 3D reconstruction results obtained using a structured light technique has been presented by Yang and Wang in [6]. In their work, expressions have been derived for the errors observed in the 3D surface position, orientation, and curvature measurements. Similarly, Ramakrishna and Vaidvanathan [7] have proposed a new approach for estimating tight bounds on measurement errors, considering, as a starting point, the inaccuracies observed during calibration and the triangulation reconstruction step. Further, Balasuramanian et al. describe in [9] an analysis of the effect of noise (assumed to be independent and uniformly distributed) and of the geometry of the imaging setup on the reconstruction error for a straight line. Their analysis, however, relies mainly on experimental results based on simulation studies. Also, Rivera-Rios et al. [10] have analyzed the error when trying to evaluate dimensionally line entities, the errors being assumed to be mostly due to localization errors in the image planes of the stereo setup. Consequently, in order to determine optimal camera poses, a nonlinear optimization problem has been formulated, that allows to minimize the total MSE (Mean Square Error) for the line to be measured, while satisfying sensor related constraints. Lastly, the accuracy of 3D reconstruction results has been evaluated, based on a comparison with ground truth, in contributions presented by Park and Subbarao [11] and Albouy et al. [12]. More recently, Jianxi et al. [13] have presented an error analysis approach for 3D reconstruction problems taking only into account the accuracy of the camera calibration parameters. They note that the largest error appears in the z -direction, when computing 3D coordinates. Furthermore, their contribution shows that the 3D error is smaller, if one uses more calibration points (i.e., the calibration is more accurate).

In our case, the error analysis focuses on the estimation of errors bounds for the results outputted by the edge detection process, which is considered to be the starting step for the whole reconstruction procedure (and which includes indirectly the effect of the error sources related to the acquisition system). This analysis is thus of importance for evaluating the quality of the final 3D reconstruction result, as it helps to estimate the associated error bounds.

3. STEREOVISION-BASED RECONSTRUCTION SETUP

In our case, the stereovision sensor consists of a pair of cameras mounted on a metallic rig, linked to their image acquisition boards inserted in the control/processing computer. 3D reconstruction involves acquiring and processing two (left and right) images of the scene with different viewpoints using a pair of sensors (in our case, gray scale CCD cameras; with image size 640×480 pixels). The image processing software performs 3D reconstruction of previously extracted contour data. Firstly, each camera is carefully calibrated off line. For the two sensors, the calibration is performed with respect to a unique world coordinate system acting as reference coordinate system. As a result, the various sets of 3D points, obtained with the two sensors, are expressed in a common coordinate system in order to facilitate data fusion in subsequent processing steps. Figure 1 describes schematically the implied processing steps, from calibration of the stereo rig up to the final 3D reconstruction. The operation of the system (i.e., the sequence of processing steps) can be summarized as follows [2]:

a) calibration of both cameras and of their relation,

b) segmentation of the stereo pair of images (extraction of edge point, determination of contour point lists),

c) segmentation and classification of the edge point lists, in order to define geometric features,

d) contour matching based on so-called epipolar constraint matrices [2],

e) euclidian reconstruction using the calibration parameters.

The operating of the system (Figure 2) is controlled using a software kernel built around an intelligent component using situation graph trees (shortly SGTs) [1] as the planning/control tool. This component is able to manage and to adjust dynamically and online the acquisition conditions (i.e., camera positions and lighting source parameters such as their position and/or intensity), leading eventually to replanning of the process, in order to improve the quality of the image data required by the 3D reconstruction step. Specifically, treatments and reasoning about local image contexts are favored when dynamic replanning is required after failure of a given processing step. A global criterion allows in our case to acquire well-contrasted images, even though this may not necessarily guarantee success for the whole vision task. Indeed, when the illumination intensity is solely automatically adjusted, optimal 3D reconstruction cannot in all cases be ensured despite the fact that the image quality has been optimized.

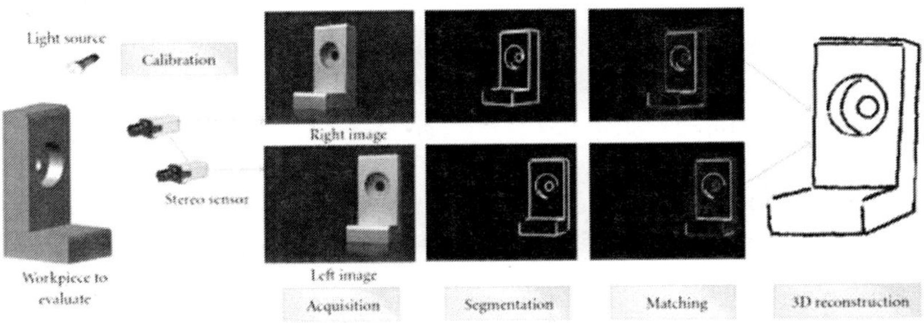

Figure 1. Processing steps of the stereovision-based 3D reconstruction procedure.

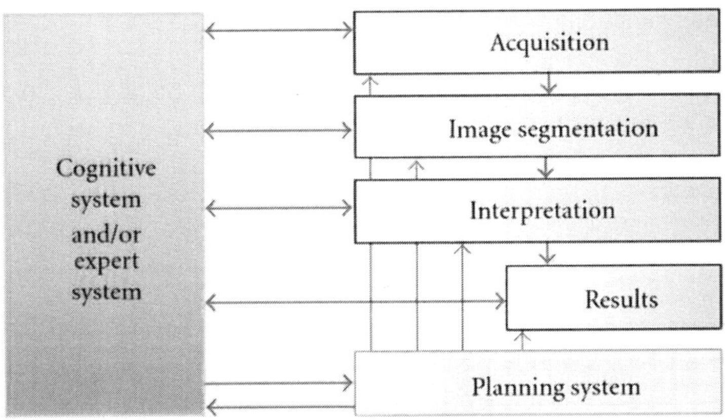

Figure 2. Block-diagram of the cognitive system developed for optimized 3D vision-based reconstruction tasks.

To solve this problem, we have chosen to analyze the placement of lighting sources moving within a virtual geodesic sphere containing the scene to be imaged, in order to define positions that allow acquisition of adequate images (i.e., well contrasted, with minimized illumination artifacts), that allow to reach, after detection of the required edges, the desired accuracy for the following 3D reconstruction step [14]. This enables to acquire best-quality images, with high contrast and minimum variance. This latter is deduced from fitting technique parameters.

4. COMMON ERROR SOURCES AFFECTING 3D RECONSTRUCTION

The stereovision-based 3D reconstruction in view of inspection tasks is sensitive to several types of error. Since uncertainty is a critical issue when evaluating the quality of a 3D reconstruction, the estimation/assessment of errors in the final reconstruction result has to be carried out carefully. In our case, the errors in obtaining the desired 3D information are estimated using expressions defined in terms of either system parameters or error source characteristics likely to be observed. In addition to this quantitative determination of errors, other likely error sources affecting both system modeling and calibration are also considered. An overview of potential error sources is given in [15]. Similarly, in [16], taking the specificities of our application into account, we were able to define three major types of error sources. These are related to camera model inaccuracies, resulting camera calibration errors and image processing errors when extracting the contour data. The 3D reconstruction results can also be affected by correspondence errors occurring during the matching process. Indeed, imprecise disparities due to noise in the images and to calibration errors (through the fundamental matrix) can be observed. As a consequence, during the standard triangulation step (i.e., the reconstruction process), these errors in disparity can sometimes be magnified when applying the projection matrices (also defined using calibration parameters).

5. ERROR EVALUATION OF THE EDGE DETECTION STEP

The extraction of edge information is the first fundamental processing step of the whole 3D reconstruction procedure. There are many ways to perform edge detection. In our case, the edge or contour point detection relies on well-known gradient-based methods. This latter convolves the image with first derivatives of a Gaussian smoothing kernel to find and locate the edge points. After evaluation of the processed images, a selection criterion is then applied to decide whether or not a pixel belongs to an edge. Edge-thinning algorithms are applied in some cases, in order to improve the results, specifically when the thickness of the primarily extracted edges is considered being too large.

One of the aims of our contributions is to develop a fully automated system (i.e., with very limited human control). Accordingly, the parameters that control the edge detection process (e.g., the width σ of the Gaussian smoothing kernel or threshold parameter values) are determined automatically. For example, the σ parameter value is determined using a measure of the amount of camera noise observed in the image and by the fine-scale texture of specific object surfaces seen in the image. In the current implementation of our approach, a fixed value ($\sigma = 1$) is used as a starting value. Following contour point extraction, chains of contour points are determined to form possibly closed contours. Each contour point list is then further subdivided into subchains defining either straight-line segments or elliptical arcs using the method described in [17]. These geometric features build the basis of the outline describing the imaged objects, as it will be exemplified later on our test workpieces.

However, these simple geometric features do not contain necessarily only true edge points. This leads for the set of edge point positions belonging to a given geometric feature to uncertainties, which are further reflected in the parameter values of the fitting equation used to describe the data. Despite this observation, the line segment and curve descriptions can be determined using more or less standard fitting technique for the edge points supposed to be on these lines or curves. For that purpose, linear or nonlinear least-squares fitting techniques are widely used. These latter minimize predefined figures of merit relying on the sum of squared errors. When using a geometric fitting approach, also known as the "best fitting" technique, the error distance is defined by the orthogonal, or the shortest, distance of a given point to the geometric feature to be fitted. Applying geometric fitting to a line segment is a linear problem, whereas its application to ellipses is a nonlinear one, which is usually solved iteratively. Gander et al. [18] have proposed a geometric ellipse fitting algorithm in parametric form, which involves a large number of fitting parameters ($n+5$ unknowns in the set of $2n$ equations to be solved, where n is the number of measurement points), each used measurement point carrying an individual angular parameter to be estimated simultaneously, together with the five ellipse parameters.

In a related contribution, for line segments, Yi et al. [19] discussed the relationship between the random perturbations of edge point positions and the variance of the least squares estimates of the corresponding line parameters. Assuming that the noise is independent and uniformly distributed, as a result, they propose an optimized fitting technique for lines. As the outline of our test workpiece is composed of simple geometric features such as lines and elliptical arcs, one can determine descriptors of these lines or arcs using fitting techniques similar to the ones described above, in order to obtain the parameters of these features. In our work, we have extended Yi's results to analyze the edge detection error for both straight line segments and elliptical arcs. The parameters of the fitted geometric features are finally used as a quality measure to estimate the 3D reconstruction error of the reconstruction procedure carried out after having matched corresponding geometric descriptors.

5.1. Error Analysis for Line Segments

The standard equations for the parameters of a line ($y = ax + b$) that best describes (x, y) data pairs, when all of the measurement error is assumed to belong to the y -axis (i.e., the x values are assumed to be error-free), are well known and easily derived. In this case, one can apply a standard least-squares method. This latter involves minimizing the sum of squared differences between the fitted line and the data points in the y -direction. However, for contour points extracted from an image, it is more reasonable to assume that the uncertainties are observed in both the x - and y -axis directions. In this case, application of a fitting procedure is somewhat more complex. Several methods have been published and discussed, as in [20, 21, 22, 23, 24, 25, 26, 27]. For example, in [27], an algorithm is developed, which copes with the problem of fitting a straight line (with the restriction that vertical lines are avoided) to data with uncertainties in both coordinates. The problem has been reduced by the authors to a one dimensional search for the minimum. Expressions for the fitting parameters (variances and covariance matrix) are derived, which are further used for the estimation of uncertainties.

In our work, based on the approach described above, we consider that a line in the $x - y$ plane is described by the following equation:

$$Ax + By + C = 0 \,. \tag{1}$$

Equation (1) represents all geometric lines in the plane, including verticals ($B = 0$) and horizontals ($A = 0$). Also, this relation ensures finiteness of the moments of the estimates of the parameters, and helps to secure numerical stability when applying the fitting procedure. The fitting line is then determined by minimizing orthogonal distances. An additional constraint (e.g., as in our case, $A^2 + B^2 = 1$) is imposed in order to ensure uniqueness of the solution, as suggested in [28] for so-called linear equality-constrained least squares (LSE) fitting methods.

To estimate the parameters A, B , and C , we have used the singular value decomposition (SVD) approach. Errors are quantified by the perpendicular distances of the edge pixels to the fitting line. These errors are interpreted as representing the error for the edge detection process in the case of straight lines.

5.2. Error Analysis for Arcs of Ellipses

For computer vision based applications such as inspection tasks, ellipses, or arcs of ellipse are a major type of geometric primitives. They are the image (perspective projections) of circles, which on workpieces can be associated with holes. Due to the importance of this kind of features, a large set of fitting methods have been suggested, as, for example, in [18, 29, 30, 31], to compute ellipse equations from data point sets. In particular, Gander et al. [18] propose a geometric ellipse fitting algorithm in parametric form. Their method achieves a good compromise between accuracy of the results and required computing time.

In this approach, an ellipse in a general position is expressed in parametric form as follows:

$$XY = \begin{bmatrix} O_x \\ O_y \end{bmatrix} + Q(\propto)\begin{bmatrix} a\cos\varphi \\ b\sin\varphi \end{bmatrix}, \qquad (2)$$

where

$$Q(\alpha) = \begin{pmatrix} \cos\alpha & -\sin\alpha \\ \sin\alpha & \cos\alpha \end{pmatrix}. \qquad (3)$$

XY are the vectors $[x\ y]^T$ and describe the set of points to be fitted, $o[o_x\ o_y]^T$ is the center of the ellipse, a and b are, respectively, the semimajor and the semiminor ellipse axis (assuming $b < a$) and α is the angle between the x -axis and the major axis of the ellipse.

Even though the ellipse could also have been described by the canonical equation $ax^2 + bxy + cy^2 + dx + ey + f = 0$, the description given by (2) is preferred, as it leads to more efficient implementations of the fitting procedure.

Ellipse fitting is performed using a nonlinear least-squares approach, minimizing the squared sum of orthogonal distances of the points to the fitting ellipse. That implies minimizing the following criterion:

$$\mathcal{F} = \begin{bmatrix} x \\ y \end{bmatrix} - \begin{bmatrix} o_x \\ o_y \end{bmatrix} - Q(\alpha)\begin{bmatrix} a\cos\varphi_i \\ b\sin\varphi_i \end{bmatrix}, \tag{4}$$

where $i = 1, \dots, n$; and $\varphi_i(0, \dots, 2\pi)$ are the n uniformly distributed unknown angles associated with the set of points to be fitted.

Here also, the sum of orthogonal distances is interpreted as representing the error for the edge detection process in the case of ellipses.

5.3. 2D Error Propagation

The error estimates, based on the distances computed as described in the previous section, are then propagated up to the 3D reconstruction step.

Stereovision refers to the ability to infer information on the 3D structure and distance of a scene from two images taken from different viewpoints, assuming that the relationship between the 3D objective world and the acquired 2D images (see Figure 5), namely the projection matrix, is known. Two main problems have to be solved: finding the correspondences and the reconstruction itself. Determining the correspondences leads to find which parts in the left and right images are projections of the same scene element, whereas the reconstruction problem determines the 3D structure from the correspondences, using additional information such as the calibration parameters if a metric reconstruction is desired.

A camera is usually described using the pinhole model and calibration enables to quantify the projection matrix. As it is well know, there exists a collineation, which maps the projective space to the camera's retinal plane: $P^3 \rightarrow P^2$. Then, the coordinates of a 3D point $\mathbf{X} = [x, y, z]^T$ in an Euclidean world coordinate system and the retinal image coordinates $\mathbf{x} = [u, v]^T$ are related by

$$\lambda \begin{bmatrix} u \\ v \\ 1 \end{bmatrix} = \begin{bmatrix} f_x & s & u_0 \\ 0 & f_y & v_0 \\ 0 & 0 & 1 \end{bmatrix} \begin{bmatrix} 1 & & & \\ & 1 & & \\ & & 1 & \end{bmatrix} \begin{bmatrix} R & T \\ 0_3^T & 1 \end{bmatrix} \begin{bmatrix} x \\ y \\ z \\ 1 \end{bmatrix}, \tag{5}$$

where λ is a scale factor, $c = [u_0, v_0]^T$ is the principal point, f_x and f_y are focal lengths, s is the skew angle, $\mathbf{R}$ and $\mathbf{T}$ are extrinsic parameters describing the attitude of the camera in the scene with respect to a reference coordinate system. $\mathbf{R}$ is a 3×3 rotation matrix, which relates the camera coordinate axes with those of the reference coordinate system. $\mathbf{T}$ is the translation in the X, Y, and Z directions representing the camera center in the reference coordinate system [32]. For stereovision, the same reference coordinate system is used for both views of the stereo couple.

Equation (5) can be expressed as

$$\lambda \mathbf{x} = \mathbf{MX}, \tag{6}$$

where $\mathbf{x} = [u, v, 1]^T$ and $\mathbf{X} = [x, y, z, 1]^T$ are the homogeneous coordinates of the corresponding spatial vectors, and $\mathbf{M}$is a 3×4 matrix, called the perspective projection matrix, representing the collineation: $P^3 \rightarrow P^2$.

If the image coordinates of the same 3D point in the two images can be obtained, the world coordinates of this point can be calculated using the two-camera geometry of Figure 6. For the two cameras, we have thus

$$\lambda^1 \mathbf{x}^1 = \mathbf{M}^1 \mathbf{X}, \qquad \lambda^2 \mathbf{x}^2 = \mathbf{M}^2 \mathbf{X}. \tag{7}$$

In the resulting linear system, the three unknowns $\mathbf{X}(x, y, z)$ can be determined, solving the system using, for example, linear least-squares methods. Exponent 1 represents the left image and exponent 2 the right image. As described in the previous section, line and ellipse fitting provides 2D error estimates ($du_i^1, dv_i^1, du_i^2, du_i^2$) for each pixel i and for each contour that compose the object of interest. The pixel coordinates can then be expressed by the following:

$$u_i^1 = \overline{u_i^1} \pm du_i^1, \qquad v_i^1 = \overline{v_i^1} \pm dv_i^1,$$
$$u_i^2 = \overline{u_i^2} \pm du_i^2, \qquad v_i^2 = \overline{v_i^2} \pm dv_i^2. \tag{8}$$

The quantities in (8) are further propagated through the 3D reconstruction process using (7), leading to the 3D measurements. Calibration and correspondence errors occurring during the calibration and the matching processes have not yet been considered.

6. RESULTS

With the objective to quantify the errors for 3D reconstruction results, we have used a quasipolyhedral test object of known size (overall size: $80 \times 50 \times 40$ mm), an example of which is shown on Figure 3(a). The images of this object are composed of straight lines, arcs, and ellipses (resulting from the perspective projection of circles from the object onto the image plane).

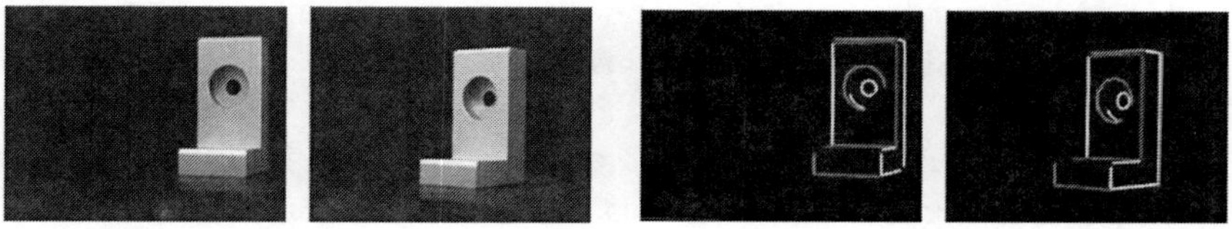

Figure 3. Representative stereo pair of images of the test piece and corresponding extracted geometric features. Left and right image of the test objectClassified geometric features

Firstly, and in order to simplify the error analysis, the experimental images are acquired under good illumination conditions in order to obtain images of good quality. Figure 3(a) shows an example of a pair of images of the object acquired, respectively, with the left and the right camera of the stereo rig.

The first image processing step in our system provides the desired edge detection results. For each line or curve of the object, the corresponding contour points have been firstly extracted using Canny's edge operator and secondly classified either as lines or ellipses. Figure 3(b) shows the results of the edge detection and classification steps, after segmentation of the lists of contour points. The same color is used in the two pictures to show the geometric features that have been associated, that is, matched. These pairs of features are the input data for the matching and the reconstruction step.

In a second step, we have then applied the fitting techniques described in Sections 5.1 and 5.2 to the edge point lists supposed to belong to either a line or a curve. However, as noted above, edge point positions are always affected by uncertainty, due to, for example, the image digitization process, the various noise sources in the system, and the nonideal behavior of the image processing steps. In [16], the encountered error sources are assumed to be independent and identically distributed. The resulting errors are statistically expressed as "confidence intervals." Such an interval is computed for each pixel belonging to the projection of either a line or ellipse on the image plane. In our case, 95% confidence intervals are calculated such as to include in the intervals at least 95% of the points predicted to belong to the associated geometric feature. Here, we compute the perpendicular distances of a given contour, defining a given geometric feature, to its corresponding geometric feature described using the parameters resulting from the fitting procedure. These distances are believed to be more significant and reliable, specifically when taking the target applications (e.g., quality control) into account.

Figure 4 shows typical computed 2D error distributions for the two types of geometric contours evaluated in this contribution, composing the object of interest and extracted from both the right and left images. Results corresponding to vertical and horizontal contour lines should exhibit error distributions with mean values of zero, as it is the case on Figures 4(a) to 4(d). The distributions of the distance measurements corresponding to elliptical features are expected to be non-Gaussian, as shown on Figures 4(e) and 4(f). These distance data are then to be propagated up to the 3D reconstruction step.

Solving the reconstruction problem involves two main steps. Firstly, the correspondence problem has to be addressed and, secondly, the depth has to be estimated. In this work, establishing correspondences (i.e., defining pairs of corresponding points belonging to matched geometric primitives) relies on matching functions based on the so-called epipolar constraint [2]. For that purpose, a dedicated similarity criterion is computed, which is based on the number of intersections of the set of epipolar lines with a given contour of each image. As a result, for each image, so-called matching matrices are obtained. The matrix *Match* (*right, left*) (resp., *Match* (*left, right*)) contains all possible matches between right and left primitives (resp., between left and right primitives). Finally, matching can be finalized by searching for corresponding maxima in the two matrices, as indicated in the algorithm given below, which summarizes the whole process (Algorithm 1).

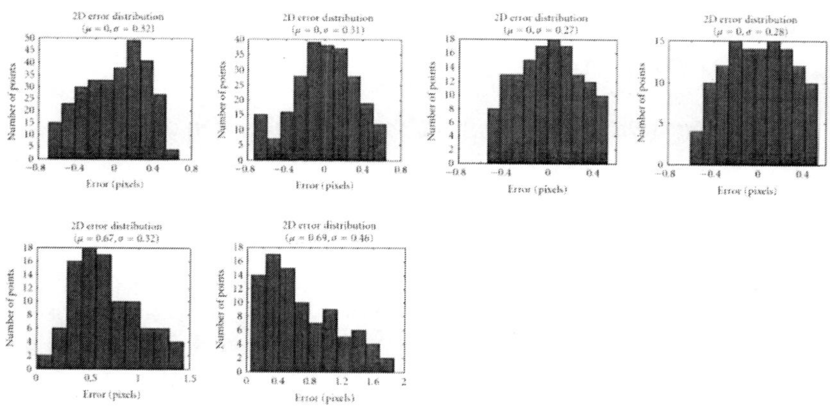

Figure 4. Error distributions for various types of matched geometric features in the left and right images of the test piece. Error distribution for a typical horizontal line in the left imageError distribution for a typical horizontal line in the right imageError distribution for a typical vertical line in the left imageError distribution for a typical vertical line in the right imageError distribution for a typical elliptical line in the left imageError distribution for a typical elliptical line in the right image

Algorithm 1: Matching procedure.

1) Estimation of the epipolar geometry

2) Determination of the candidate matches

a) *For each left primitive, computation of the number of intersections of epipolar lines with right primitives. The result is the matrix Match (left, right).*

b) *For each right primitive, computation of the number of intersections of epipolar line with left primitives in the other image. The result is the matrix Match (right, left).*

3) Finalization/validation of the matches

a) *Computation of the similarity criterion between the two matrices: searching for corresponding maxima in the two matrices.*

b) *Elimination of the matched contours according to step (c) in the two matrices*

c) *Repeat steps (a) to (d) until all contours have been processed.*

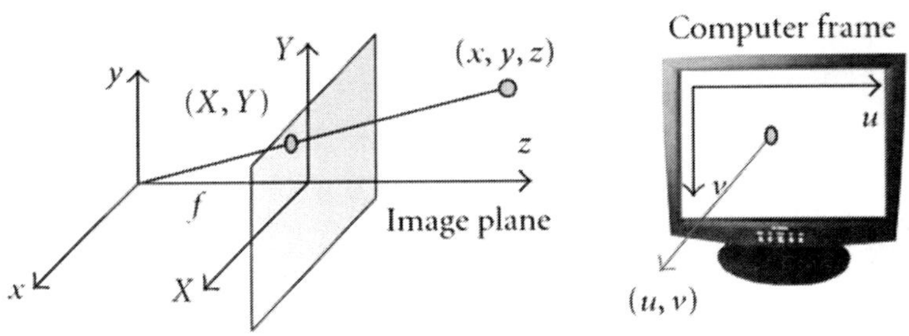

Figure 5. Projection geometry from the 3D world to the 2D image.

Estimating the 3D coordinates from each matched point pairs, leading to the desired 3D reconstruction, is routinely and easily achieved applying a simple procedure known as triangulation.

If both the intrinsic and extrinsic parameters of the camera setup are known, the resulting reconstruction is called Euclidean, that is, the reconstruction is metric.

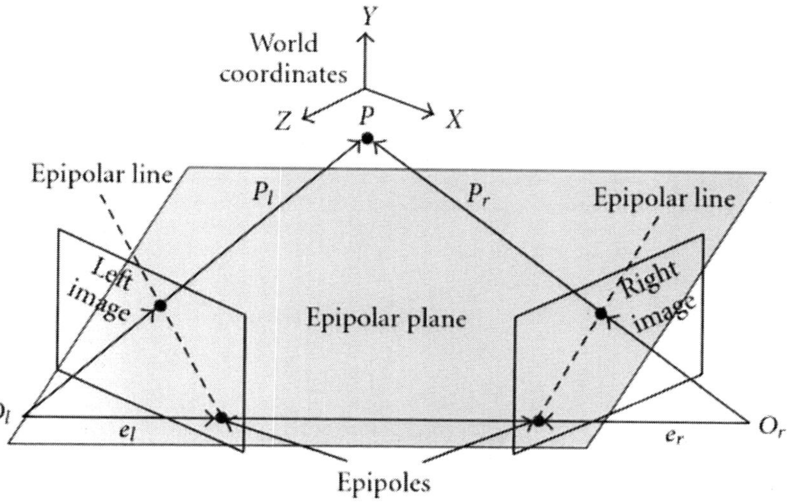

Figure 6. 3D measurement using a stereovision sensor.

As a prerequisite for applications such as inspection or quality control tasks, estimation of the error affecting the 3D reconstruction is essential in order to be able to evaluate quantitatively the dimensions of the object or to state if the reconstruction results fulfill tolerance rules.

Further, these error estimates enable also to qualify the behavior of the vision system. With this objective, we firstly evaluate the accuracy/quality of the reconstructed contours using a linear orthogonal regression procedure, carried out in the 3D space and based on a standard principal components analysis of the reconstructed geometric features. Figure 7 illustrates the resulting 3D error distributions in the X, Y, and Z directions of a reference coordinate system (here, the camera coordinate system). The mean errors μ_x, μ_y, and μ_z and associated variances σ_x, σ_y, and σ_z are also indicated, as they build the basic descriptors of the computed distributions. Application of the method is only shown here for vertical and horizontal contours. As can be seen in Figure 7, the distributions are approximately normal, with a mean value of zero and a variance which varies in the range $(0, 0.6)$ mm for a typical vertical reconstructed contour and $(0, 1.2)$ mm for a typical horizontal reconstructed contour.

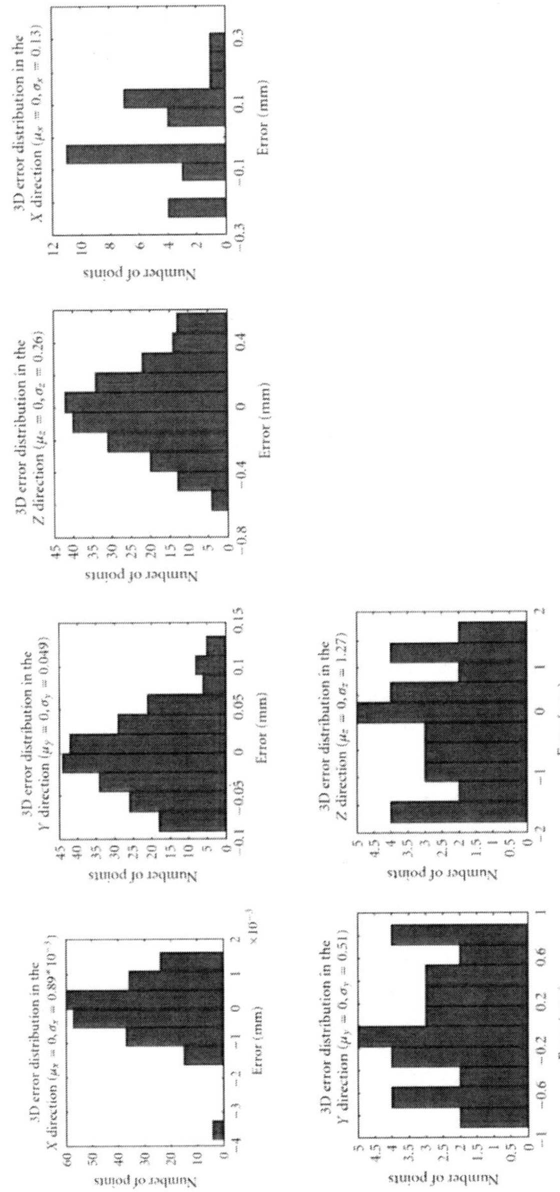

Figure 7. 3D error distribution in the *x*, *y*, and *z*-directions of a typical vertical and horizontal reconstructed contour. 3D error distribution in the *x*-direction (vertical contour)3D error distribution in the *y*-direction (vertical contour)3D error distribution in the *z*-direction (vertical contour) 3D error distribution in the *x*-direction (horizontal contour)3D error distribution in the *y*-direction (horizontal contour)3D error distribution in the *z*-direction (horizontal contour)

The difference in accuracy for a vertical edge, compared to that of a horizontal one, can be also observed in Figure8. Thus, the quality of reconstructed vertical contours is better than that for horizontal ones. This observation can be traced back to the matching problem. As a matter of fact, vertical contours are easier to match accurately than horizontal ones, due to the configuration of the cameras of the stereo rig. Usually, the optical axes of the cameras are not aligned, that is, parallel, as it is the case for the geometry used when rectifying a stereo pair of images.

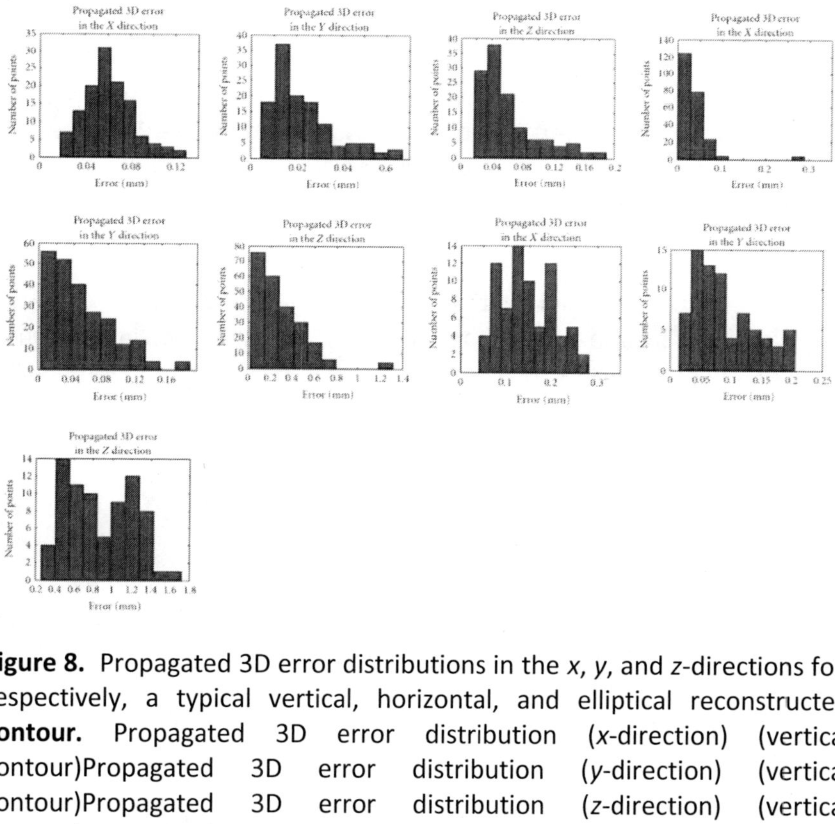

Figure 8. Propagated 3D error distributions in the *x*, *y*, and *z*-directions for, respectively, a typical vertical, horizontal, and elliptical reconstructed **contour.** Propagated 3D error distribution (*x*-direction) (vertical contour)Propagated 3D error distribution (*y*-direction) (vertical contour)Propagated 3D error distribution (*z*-direction) (vertical contour)Propagated 3D error distribution (*x*-direction) (horizontal contour)Propagated 3D error distribution (*y*-direction) (horizontal contour)Propagated 3D error distribution (*z*-direction) (horizontal contour)Propagated 3D error distribution (*x*-direction) (elliptical contour)Propagated 3D error distribution (*y*-direction) (elliptical contour)Propagated 3D error distribution (*z*-direction) (elliptical contour)

Such a configuration could be obtained by rotating the cameras from their original positions to reach alignment. An alternative is accordingly needed to rectify the stereo pair of images. As a result, matched image points corresponding to point features in a rectified image pair will lie on the same horizontal scanline and differ only in horizontal displacement. This horizontal displacement or disparity between rectified feature points is directly related to the depth of the 3D feature point. Further, the rectifying process does not require a high computation cost.

Work is currently being devoted to enhance the overall performance of the matching procedure. As could be expected (the behavior being routinely observed for stereovision-based reconstruction procedures), the error in the Z direction (i.e., range) is much higher than that in the X and Y directions (corresponding approximately to the directions of the coordinate axes of the image plane). This behavior is induced by the vergence of the cameras. Indeed, controlling the vergence of the optical axes of the cameras defines a basic tool to obtain good results when applying a matching algorithm, because the disparity values related to the object of interest can be reduced. Knowledge of the vergence also allows a distance measure of the so-called fixation point (defined as the intersection point between the focal axes and the surface of the object of interest in the scene). This measure is obtained by carrying out a triangulation involving the focal axes (i.e., their intersection). Knowing this distance enables to control the vergence by calculating the distance information of the object of interest. One can also use disparity information related to the object, according to its position in the left and right images [33].

Lastly, as a final test, we have also propagated the 2D errors observed for edge points through to the 3D computation step, in order to estimate the final 3D error for single points. Figure 8 shows the obtained 3D error distributions in the X, Y , and Z directions after propagation of the 2D errors. Again, we can observe that the error in the Z direction is much higher than in the other two directions.

Finally, Figures 9 and 10 show the partial 3D reconstructions (i.e., corresponding to the point of view of the stereo sensor) of our test object, after having applied the triangulation procedure to either the extracted 2D contours or their corresponding descriptors (i.e., the fitting equations of the contours).

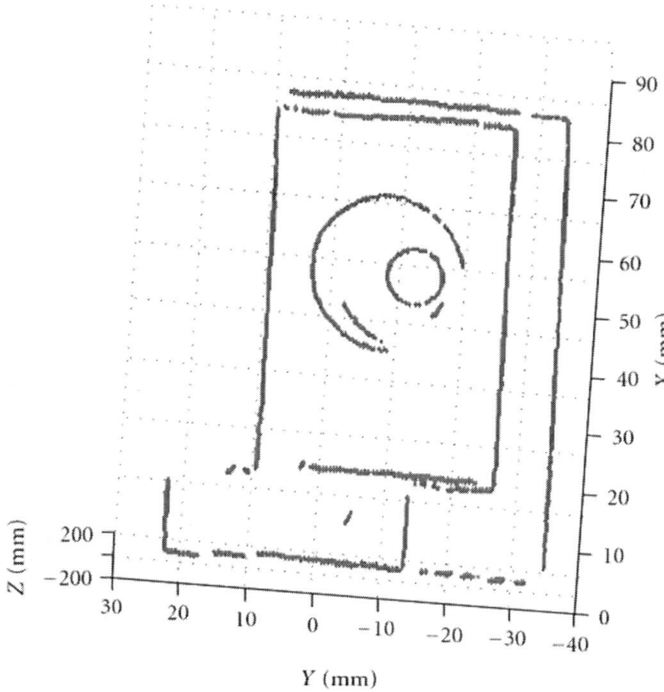

Figure 9. Partial 3D reconstruction using actually extracted contours.

The reconstruction using the descriptors shows that the object is better estimated, as the reconstruction step allows recovering parts of contours, which have not been extracted adequately (this is especially the case for the elliptical parts of the object). In Figure 11, an example of a reconstructed 3D vertical contour is shown, together with associated errors bounds drawn as ellipses. As an example, the 3D errors are shown for one contour, which is the vertical line represented in blue in Figure 3(b), in order to illustrate the method. The 2D ellipses around the contour represent the errors in the z - and y -directions. Since these errors are not the same for all points along the line, the two axes of the ellipse are different, depending on the position along the line. The reason for this change in error magnitude can be traced back to the perpendicular distance of the pixels belonging to the edge described as a line after the fitting step. We recall that this distance can be interpreted as representing the error resulting from the edge detection process for the case of straight line primitives, which cannot basically be assumed to be of the same magnitude.

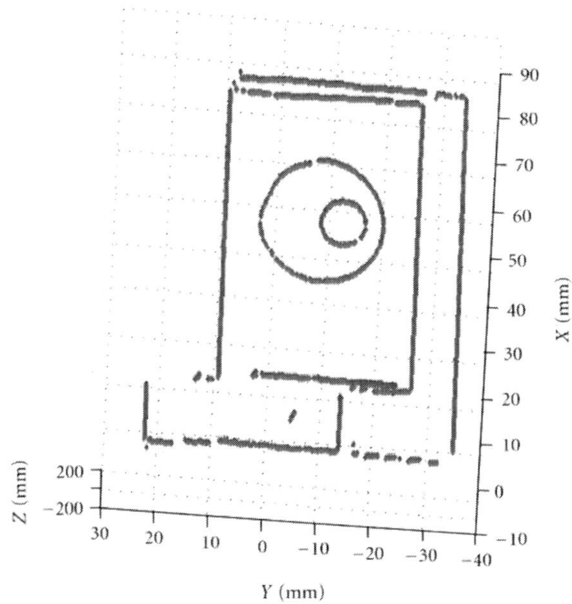

Figure 10. Partial 3D reconstruction using the fitting equations approximating the contours.

7. CONCLUSIONS AND OUTLOOK

In this paper, we have introduced a method for analyzing and evaluating the uncertainties encountered during vision-based reconstruction tasks. Specifically, the uncertainties have been estimated from the feature extraction step up to the triangulation based 3D reconstruction embedded within a cognitive stereovision system. As a result, the reconstruction process is sensitive to various types of error sources, as indicated in [16]. In this paper, we have mainly considered the errors introduced by the image segmentation procedure, their estimates being propagated through the whole reconstruction procedure.

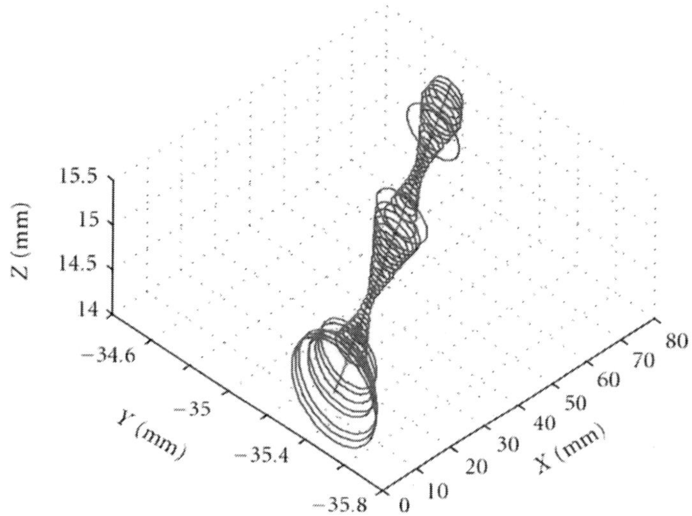

Figure 11. Example of a reconstructed 3D contour and associated error bounds drawn as ellipses; the line corresponds to the vertical line represented in blue in Figure 3(b).

Approximating the contours point lists describing the piece under evaluation using fitting results, assuming further that the various errors, specifically those related to image processing, are independent and identically distributed, we have estimated error bounds for the edges detection process. These errors are defined as being equal to the orthogonal distances of the contour pixels to the geometric feature described by the corresponding fitting parameters. These data are computed for each geometric feature being part of the object of interest. Using a dedicated error propagation scheme, the estimates have also been propagated through the whole processing chain setup for analyzing the images acquired with our stereovision system.

Since the resulting 3D reconstruction depends on image quality, the experimental images are usually acquired under good illumination conditions, in order to obtain images of sufficient quality using, for example, the approach described in [14]. Controlling the acquisition conditions allows minimizing the 3D measurement error. The experimental results presented here validate the error estimation technique and show that reconstructions of good quality with reasonable accuracy can be automatically computed. In comparison with previously obtained results, the measures presented above, with our suggested error propagation scheme, are of much higher precision and lead to reduced 3D reconstruction errors.

Generalization of the error propagation scheme is currently in progress in order to take into account all the other sources of errors, more specifically the matching errors.

REFERENCES

1. Khemmar R, Lallement A, Hirsch E: **Steps towards an intelligent self-reasoning system for the automated vision-based evaluation of manufactured parts.** *Proceedings of the Workshop on Applications of Computer Vision, in Conjunction with European Conference on Computer Vision (ECCV '06), May 2006, Graz, Austria* 136-143.

2. Far BA, Kohler S, Hirsch E: **3D reconstruction of manufactured parts using bi-directional stereovision-based contour matching and comparison of real and synthetic images.** *Proceedings of the 9th IAPR Conference on Machine Vision Applications, May 2005, Tsukuba Science City, Japan* 456-459.

3. Kohler S, Far BA, Hirsch E: **Dynamic (re)planning of 3D automated reconstruction using situation graph trees and illumination adjustment.** *Quality Control by Artificial Vision, May 2007, Le Creusot, France, Proceedings of SPIE***6356:**-11.

4. Khemmar R, Lallement A, Hirsch E: **Design of an intelligent self-reasoning system for the automated vision-based evaluation of manufactured parts.** *proceedings of 7th International Conference on Quality Control by Artificial Vision (QCAV '05), May 2005, Nagoya, Japan* 241-246.

5. Blostein SD, Huang TS: **Error analysis in stereo determination of 3D point positions.** *IEEE Transactions on Pattern Analysis and Machine Intelligence* 1987,**9**(6):752-765.

6. Yang Z, Wang Y-F: **Error analysis of 3D shape construction from structured lighting.** *Pattern Recognition*1996,**29**(2):189-206.

7. Ramakrishna RS, Vaidvanathan B: **Error analysis in stereo vision.** *Proceedings of the Asian Conference on Computer Vision (ACCV '98), 1998* **1351:** 296-304.

8. Kamberova G, Bajcsy R: *Precision of 3D points reconstructed from stereo.* Department of Computer & Information Science; 1997.

9. Balasuramanian R, Sukhendu D, Swaminathan K: **Error analysis in reconstruction of a line in 3D from two arbitrary perspective views.** *International Journal of Computer Vision and Mathematicss* 2000, **78:** 191-212.

10. Rivera-Rios AH, Shih F-L, Marefat M: **Stereo camera pose determination with error reduction and tolerance satisfaction for dimensional measurements.** *Proceedings of the IEEE International Conference on Robotics and Automation, 2005, Barcelona, Spain* 423-428.

11. Park S-Y, Subbarao M: **A multiview 3D modeling system based on stereo vision techniques.** *Machine Vision and Applications* 2005,**16**(3):148-156.

12. Albouy B, Koenig E, Treuillet S, Lucas Y: **Accurate 3D structure measurements from two uncalibrated views.** *Advanced Concepts for Intelligent Vision Systems* 2006, **4179:** 1111-1121.

13. Jianxi Y, Jianting L, Zhendong S: **Calibrating method and systematic error analysis on binocular 3D position system.***Proceedings of the 6th International Conference on Automation and Logistics, September 2008, Qingdao, China* 2310-3214.

14. Belhaoua A, Kohler S, Hirsch E: **Determination of optimal lighting position in view of 3D reconstruction error minimization.** *Proceedings of the 10th European Congress of International Society of Stereology (ISS '09), June 2009, Bologna, Italy* 408-414.

15. Egnal G, Mintz M, Wildes RP: **A stereo confidence metric using single view imagery with comparison to five alternative approaches.** *Image and Vision Computing* 2004,**22**(12):943-957.

16. Belhaoua A, Kohler S, Hirsch E: **Estimation of 3d reconstruction errors in a stereo-vision system.** In *Modeling Aspects in Optical Metrology II,*

June 2009, Münich, Germany, Proceedings of the SPIE. Volume 7390. Optical Metrology; 1-10.

17. Daul C: *Construction et utilisation de liste de primitives en vue d'une analyse dimensionnelle de pièce à géométrie simple, Ph.D. thesis.* Université Louis Pasteur, Strasbourg, France; 1989.

18. Gander W, Golub GH, Strebel R: **Least-squares fitting of circles and ellipses.** *BIT Numerical Mathematics*1994,**34**(4):558-578.

19. Yi S, Haralick RM, Shapiro LG: **Error propagation in machine vision.** *Machine Vision and Applications* 1994,**7**(2):93-114.

20. York D: **Least-squares fitting of a straight line.** *Canadian Journal of Physics* 1966, **44:** 1079-1086.

21. Lybanon M: **A better least-squares method when both variables have uncertainties.** *American Journal of Physics*1984, **52:** 22-26.

22. Reed BC: **Linear least-squares fits with error in both coordinates.** *American Journal of Physics* 1989, **58:** 642-646.

23. Gonzalez AG, Marquez A, Sanz JF: **An iterative algorithm for consistent and unbiased estimation of linear regression parameters when there are errors in both the x and y variables.** *Computers and Chemistry* 1992,**16**(1):25-27.

24. Macdonald JR, Thompson WJ: **Least-squares fitting when both variables contain errors : pitfalls and possibilities.***American Journal of Physics* 1992, **60:** 66-73.

25. Reed BC: **Linear least-squares fits with errors in both coordinates. II: comments on parameter variances.** *American Journal of Physics* 1992, **60:** 59-62.

26. York D, Evensen NM, Martínez ML, De Basabe Delgado J: **Unified equations for the slope, intercept, and standard errors of the best straight line.** *American Journal of Physics* 2004,**72**(3):367-375.

27. Krystek M, Anton M: **A weighted total least-squares algorithm for fitting a straight line.** *Measurement Science and Technology* 2007,**18**(11):3438-3442.

28. Van Huffel S, Vandewalle J: *The Total Least Squares Problem, Computational Aspects and Analysis*. Society for Industrial and Applied Mathematics, Philadelphia, Pa, USA; 1990.

29. Halir R, Flusser J: **Numerically stable direct least squares fitting of ellipses.** *Proceedings of the 6th International Conference in Central Europe on Computer Graphics and Visualization (WSCG '98), February 1998, Plzen, Czech* 125-132.

30. Ahn SJ, Rauh W, Recknagel M: **Ellipse fitting and parameter assessment of circular object targets for robot vision.***Proceedings of the International Conference on Intelligent Robots and Systems, October 1999, Kyongju, Korea* **1:** 525-530.

31. O'Leary P, Zsombor-Murray P: **Direct and specific least-square fitting of hyperbolæ and ellipses.** *Journal of Electronic Imaging* 2004,**13**(3):492-503.

32. Bouguet J-Y: *Visual methods for three-dimensional modeling, Ph.D. thesis*. California Institute of Technology, Pasadena, Calif, USA; 1999.

33. Kwon K-C, Lim Y-T, Kim N, Song Y-J, Choi Y-S: **Vergence control of binocular stereoscopic camera using disparity information.** *Journal of the Optical Society of Korea* 2009,**13**(3):379-385.

Chapter 3

A System for an Accurate 3D Reconstruction in Video Endoscopy Capsule

Anthony Kolar1, Olivier Romain1, Jade Ayoub1, David Faura1, Sylvain Viateur1, Bertrand Granado2, and Tarik Graba3

1 Departement SOC—LIP6, Universite P&M CURIE—Paris VI, Equipe SYEL, 4 place Jussieu, 75252 Paris, France

2 ETIS, CNRS/ENSEA/Universit´e de Cergy-Pontoise, 95000 Cergy, France

3 Electronique des syst`emes num´eriques complexe, Telecom ParisTech, 46 rue Barrault, 75252 Paris, France

ABSTRACT

Since few years, the gastroenterologic examinations could have been realised by wireless video capsules. Although the images make it possible to analyse some diseases, the diagnosis could be improved by the use of the 3D Imaging techniques implemented in the video capsule. The work presented here is related to Cyclope, an embedded active vision system that is able to give in real time both 3D information and texture. The challenge is to realise this integrated sensor with constraints on size, consumption, and computational resources with inherent limitation of video capsule. In this paper, we present the hardware and software development of a wireless multispectral vision sensor which allows to transmit, a 3D reconstruction of a scene in realtime. multispectral acquisitions grab both texture and IR pattern images at least at 25 frames/s separately. The different Intellectual Properties designed allow to compute specifics algorithms in real time while keeping accuracy computation. We present experimental results with the realization of a large-scale demonstrator using an SOPC prototyping board.

1. INTRODUCTION

Examination of the whole gastrointestinal tract represents a challenge for endoscopists due to its length and inaccessibility using natural orifices. Moreover, radiologic techniques are relatively insensitive for diminutive, flat, infiltrative, or inflammatory lesions of the small bowel. Since 1994, video capsules (VCEs) [1, 2] have been developed to allow direct examination of this inaccessible part of the gastrointestinal tract and to help doctors to find the cause of symptoms such as stomach pain, disease of Crohn, diarrhoea, weight loss, rectal bleeding, and anaemia.

The Pillcam video capsule designed by Given Imaging Company is the most popular of them. This autonomous embedded system allows acquiring about 50 000 images of gastrointestinal tract during more than twelve hours of an analysis. The off-line image processing and its interpretation by the practitioner permit to determine the origin of the disease. However, recent benchmark [3] published shows some limitations on this video capsule as the quality of images and the inaccuracy on the size of the polyps. Accuracy is a real need because the practitioner makes an ablation of a polyp only if it exceeds a minimum size. Actually the polyp size is estimated by practitioner's experience with more or less error for one practitioner to another. One of the solutions could be to use techniques of 3D imagery, either directly in the video capsule or on a remote computer.

This later solution is actually used in the Pillcam capsule by using the 2–4 images that are taken per second and stored wirelessly in a recorder that is worn around the waist. 3D processing is performed off-line from the estimation of the displacement of the capsule. However, the speed of video-capsule is not constant; for example, in the oesophagus, it is of 1.44 m/s, and in the stomach it is almost null and is 0.6 m/s in the intestine. Consequently, by taking images at frequencies constant, certain areas of the transit will not be rebuilt. Moreover, the regular transmission of the images by the body consumes too much energy and limits the autonomy of the video capsules to 10 hours. Ideally, the quantity of information to be transmitted must be reduced at the only pertinent information like polyps or other 3D objects. The first development necessary to the delivery of such objects relies on the use of algorithm of pattern recognition on 3D information inside the video capsule.

The introduction of 3D reconstruction techniques inside a video capsule needs to define a new system that takes into account the hard constraints of size, low power consumption, and processing time. The most common 3D reconstruction techniques are those based on passive or active stereoscopic vision methods, where image sensors are used to provide the necessary information to retrieve the depth. Passive method consists of taking at least two images of a scene at two different points of view. Unfortunately using this method, only particular points, with high gradient or high texture, can be detected [4]. The active stereo-vision methods offer an alternative approach when processing time is critical. They consist in replacing one of the two cameras by a projection system which delivers a pattern composed by a set of structured rays. In this latter case, only an image of the deformation of the pattern by the scene is necessary to reconstruct a 3D image. Many implementations based on active stereo-vision have been realised in the past [5, 6] and provided significant results on desktop computers. Generally, these implementations have been developed to reconstruct 3D large objects as building [7, 8, 9, 10, 11, 12, 13, 14].

In our research work, we have focused on an integrated 3D active vision sensor: "Cyclope." The concept of this sensor was first described in [4]. In this new article we focus on the presentation of our first prototype which includes the instrumentation and processing blocks. This sensor allows making in real time a 3D reconstruction taking into account the size and power consumption constraints of embedded systems [15]. It can be used in wireless video capsules or wireless sensor networks. In the case of video capsule in order to be comfortable for the patient, the results could be stored in a recorder around the waist. It is based on a multispectral acquisition that must facilitate the delivery of a 3D textured reconstruction in real time (25 images by second).

This paper is organised as follows, Section 2 describes briefly Cyclope and deals with the principles of the active stereo-vision system and 3D reconstruction method. In Section 3 we present our original multispectral acquisition. In Section 4 we present the implementation of the optical correction developed to correct the lens distortion. Section 5 deals with the implementation of a new thresholding and labelling methods. In Sections 6 and 7, we present the processing of matching in order to give a 3D representation of the scene. Section 8 deals with wireless communication consideration. Finally, before a conclusion and perspectives of this work, we present, in Section 9, a first functional prototype and its performances which attest the feasibility of this original approach.

2. CYCLOPE

2.1. Overview of the Architecture

Cyclope is an integrated wireless 3D vision system based on active stereo-vision technique. It uses many different algorithms to increase accuracy and reduce processing time. For this purpose, the sensor is composed of three blocks (see Figure 1).

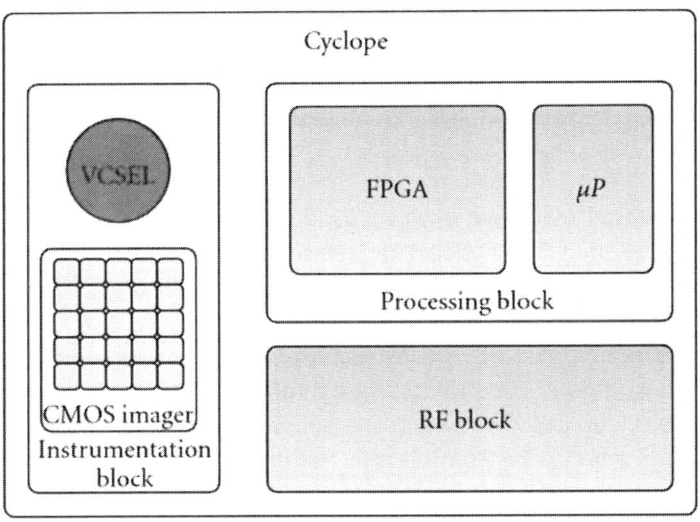

Figure 1. Cyclope Diagram.

1) Instrumentation block: it is composed of a CMOS camera and a structured light projector on IR band.

2) Processing block: it integrates a microprocessor core and a reconfigurable array. The microprocessor is used for sequential processing. The reconfigurable array is used to implement parallels algorithms.

3) RF block: it is dedicated for the OTA (Over the Air) communications.

The feasibility of Cyclope was studied by an implementation on an SOPC (System On Programmable Chip) target. These three parts will be realised in different technologies: CMOS for the image sensor and the processing units, GaAs for the pattern projector, and RF–CMOS for the communication unit. The development of such integrated "SIP" (System In Package) is actually the best solution to overcome the technological constraints and realise a chip scale package. This solution is used in several embedded sensors such as The "Human++" platform [16] or Smart Dust [17].

2.2. Principle of the 3D Reconstruction

The basic principle of 3D reconstruction is the triangulation. Knowing the distance between two cameras (or the various positions of the same camera) and defining of the line of views, one passing by the center of camera and the other by the object, we can find the object distance.

The active 3D reconstruction is a method aiming to increase the accuracy of the 3D reconstruction by the projection on the scene of a structured pattern. The matching is largely simplified because the points of interest in the image needed to the reconstruction are obtained by the extraction of the pattern; it also has the effect to increase the speed of processing.

The setup of active stereo-vision system is represented in Figure 2. The distance between the camera and the laser projector is fixed. The projection of the laser beams on a plane gives an IR spots matrix.

The 3D reconstruction is achieved through triangulation between laser and camera. Each point of the projected pattern on the scene represents the intersection of two lines (Figure 3):

1) the line of sight, passing through the pattern point on the scene and its projection in the image plan,

2) the laser ray, starting from the projection center and passing through the chosen pattern point.

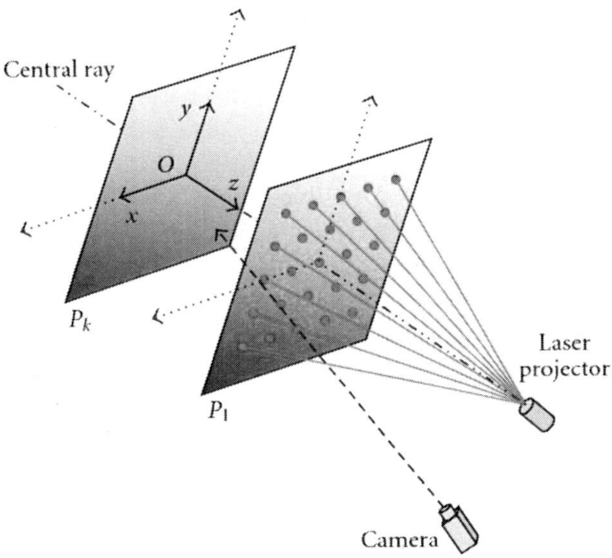

Figure 2. Active stereo-vision system.

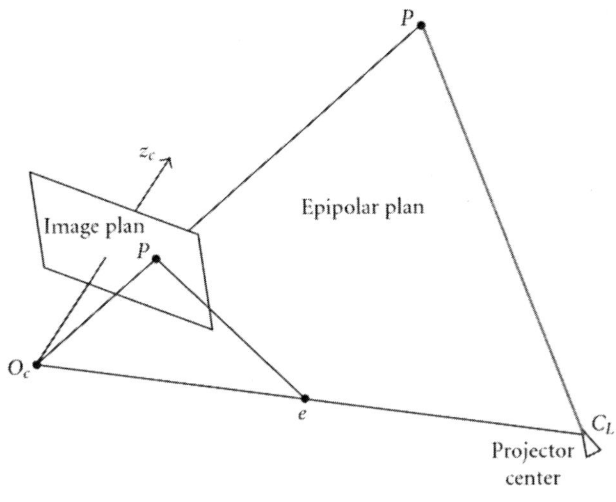

Figure 3. Epipolar projection.

If we consider the active stereoscopic system as shown in Figure 3, where p is the projection of P in the image plan and e the projection of C_L on the camera plan O_C , the projection of the light ray supporting the dot on the image plan is a straight line. This line is an epipolar line [18, 19, 20].

To rapidly identify a pattern point on an image we can limit the search to the epipolar lines.

For Cyclope the pattern is a regular mesh of points. For each point (j,k) of the pattern we can find the corresponding epipolar line:

$$v = a_{jk} \cdot u + b_{jk}, \tag{1}$$

where (u,v) are the image coordinates and the parameters (a_{jk}, b_{jk}) are estimated through an off-line calibration process.

In addition to the epipolar lines, we can establish the relation between the position of a laser spot in the image and its distance to the stereoscopic system.

On Figure 4, we consider a laser ray (5) projected on two different plans Π_1 and Π_2 located, respectively, at z_1 and z_2 , the trajectory d of the coordinates in the image will be constrained to the epipolar line.

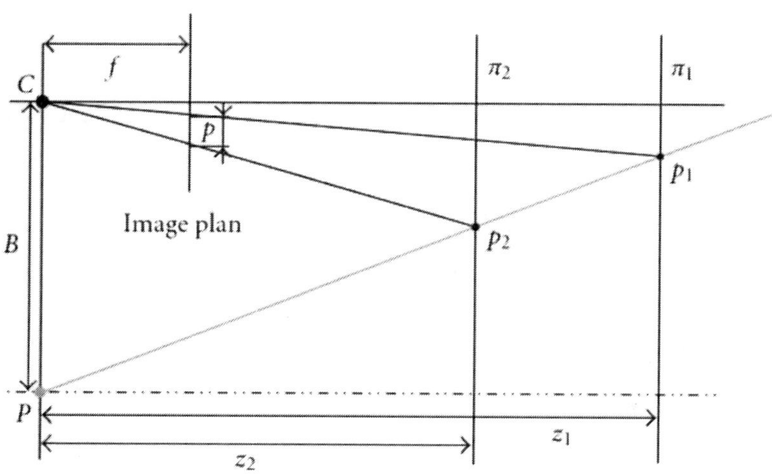

Figure 4. Spot image movement versus depth.

By considering the two triangles CPp_1 and CPp_2, we can express d as

$$d = B\left[\left(\frac{z_1 - f}{z_1}\right) - \left(\frac{z_2 - f}{z_2}\right)\right] = Bf\frac{(z_1 - z_2)}{z_1 z_2}, \tag{2}$$

where B is the stereoscopic, f the focal length of the camera and d the distance in pixels:

$$d = \sqrt{(u_1 - u_2)^2 + (v_1 - v_2)^2}. \tag{3}$$

Given the epipolar line we can express d as a function of only one image coordinates:

$$d = \sqrt{1 + a^2}\ (u_1 - u_2). \tag{4}$$

From (2) and (4), we can express, for each pattern point (j,k), the depth as a hyperbolic function:

$$z = \frac{1}{\alpha_{jk} u + \beta_{jk}}, \tag{5}$$

where the α_{jk} and β_{jk} parameters are also estimated during the off-line calibration of the system [21].

We can compute the inverse of the depth z to simplify the implementation. Two operations are only needed: an addition and a multiplication. The computation of the depth of each point is independent of the others. So, all the laser spots can be computed separately allowing the parallelisation of the architecture.

3. AN ENERGETIC APPROACH FOR MULTISPECTRAL ACQUISITION

The main problem when you design a 3D reconstruction processing for an integrated system is the limitation of the resources. However, we can obtain a good accuracy considering hard constraints by using the following method which is shown in Figure 5:

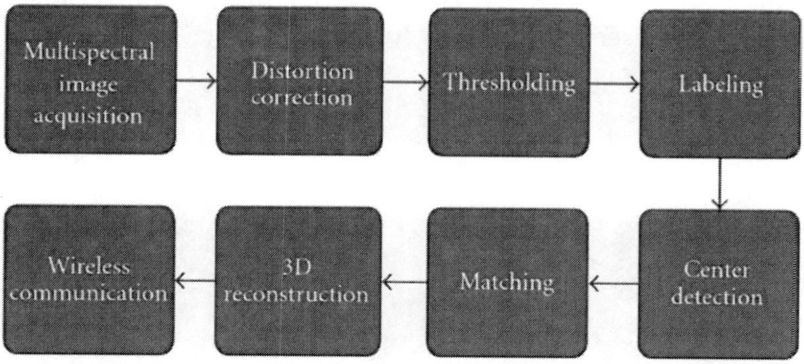

Figure 5. Acquisition and 3D reconstruction flow chart.

1) the multispectral acquisition which makes the discrimination between the pattern and the texture by an energetic method;

2) the correction of the error coordinates due to the optical lens distortion;

3) the processing before the 3D reconstruction as thresholding, segmentation, labelling, and the computation of the laser spot center;

4) the computation of the matching and the third dimension;

5) the transmission of the data with a processor core and an RF module.

The spectral response of the Silicon cuts near 1100 nm and it covers UV to near Infrared domains. This important characteristic allows defining a multispectral acquisition by grabbing on the visible band the colour texture image and, on the near infrared band, the depth information. Cyclope uses this original acquisition method, which permits to access directly at the depth information's independently from texture image processing (Figure 6).

The combination of the acquisition of the projected pattern on the infrared band, the acquisition of the texture on the visible band, and the mathematical model of the active 3D sensor makes it possible to restore the 3D textured representation of the scene. This acquisition needs to separate texture and 3D datas. For this purpose we have developed a multispectral acquisition [15]. Generally, filters are used to cut the spectral response. We used here an energetic method, which has the advantage of being generic for imagers.

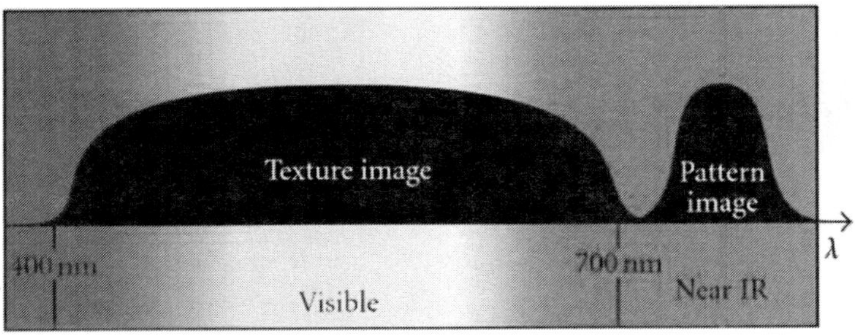

Figure 6. Multispectral image sensor.

To allow real-time acquisition of both pattern and texture, we have developed a first 64×64 pixels CMOS imager prototype in 0.6 μm for a total surface of 20 mm^2 (Figure 7). This sensor has programmable light integration and shutter time to allow dynamic change. It was designed to have large response in the visible and near infrared. This first CMOS imager prototype, which is not the subject of this article, had allowed the validation of our original energetic approach, but its small size needs to be increased to have more information. So, in our demonstrator we have used a greater CCD sensor (CIF resolution 352×288 pixels) to obtain normal size images and validate the 3D processing architecture.

The projector pulses periodically on the scene an energetic IR pattern. An image acquisition with a short integration time allows grabbing the image of the pattern with a background texture which appears negligible. A second image acquisition with a longer integration allows to grab the texture when the projector is off. Figure 8 shows the sequential scheduling of the images acquisition. To reach a video rate of 25 images/s this acquisition sequence must be done in less than 40 milisecond. The global acquisition time is given in (6) where T_{rst} is the reset time, T_{rd} is the time needed to read the entire image, and T_{intVI} and T_{intIR} are, respectively, the integration time for both visible and IR image.

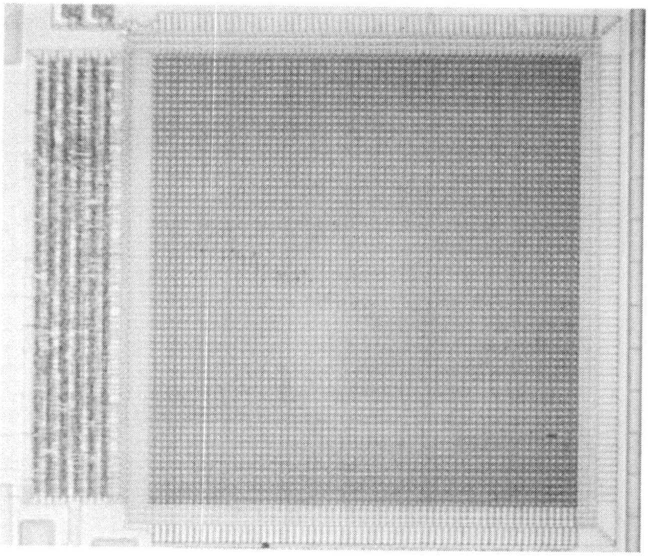

Figure 7. 64 × 64 image sensor microphotograph.

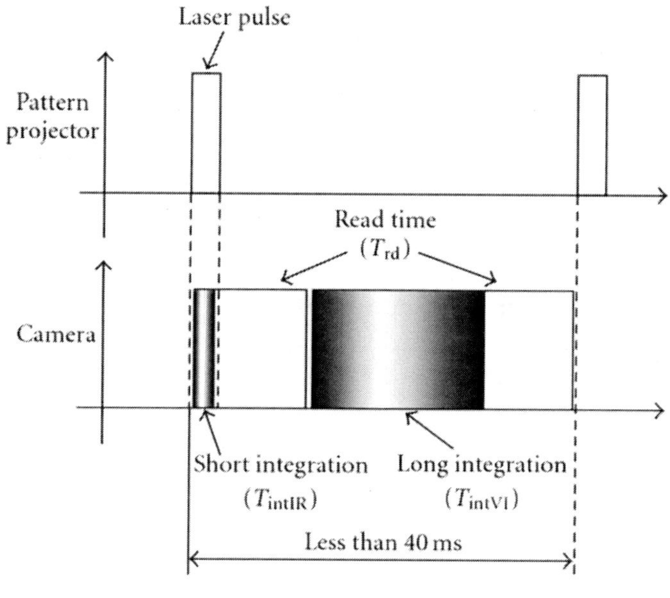

Figure 8. Acquisition sequence.

$$T_{\mathrm{total}} = 2 \cdot T_{\mathrm{rst}} + 2 \cdot T_{\mathrm{rd}} + T_{\mathrm{intVI}} + T_{\mathrm{intIR}} \cdot \tag{6}$$

The typical values are

$$\begin{aligned} T_{\mathrm{rst}} &= 0.5\,\mathrm{ms}, \\ T_{\mathrm{rd}} &= 0.5\,\mathrm{ms}, \\ T_{\mathrm{intVI}} &= 15\,\mathrm{ms}, \\ T_{\mathrm{intIR}} &= 20\,\mu\mathrm{m}. \end{aligned} \tag{7}$$

4. OPTICAL DISTORTION CORRECTION

Generally, the lenses used in the VCE introduce large deformations on acquired images because of their weak focal [22]. This distortion is manifested in inadequate spatial relationships between pixels in the image and the corresponding points in the scene. Such change in the shape of captured object may have critical influence in medical applications, where quantitative measurements in Endoscopy depend on the position and orientation of the camera and its model. The used camera model needs to be accurate. For this reason we introduce firstly the pinhole camera model and later the correction of geometric distortion that are added to enhance it. For practical purposes two different methods are studied to implement this correction, and it is up to researchers to choose their own model depending on their required accuracy level and computational cost.

Pinhole camera model (see Figure 9) is based on the principle of linear projection where each point in the object space is projected by a straight line through the projection center into the image plane. This model can be used only as an approximation of the real camera that is actually not perfect and sustains a variety of aberration [23]. So, pinhole model is not valid when high accuracy is required like in our expected applications (Endoscopes, robotic surgery, etc.). In this case, a more comprehensive camera model must be used, taking into account the corrections for the systematically distorted image coordinates. As a result of several types of imperfections in the design and assembly of lenses composing the camera's optical system, the real projection of the point P in the image plane takes into account the error between the real image observed coordinates and the corresponding ideal (non observable) image coordinates:

$$u' = u + \delta_u(u, v),$$
$$v' = v + \delta_v(u, v),$$
(8)

where (u, v) are the ideal nonobservable, distortion-free image coordinates, (u', v') are the corresponding real coordinates, and δ_u and δ_v are, respectively, the distortion along the u and v axes. Usually, the lens distortion consists of radial symmetric distortion, decentering distortion, affinity distortion, and nonorthogonally deformations. Several cases are presented on Figure 10.

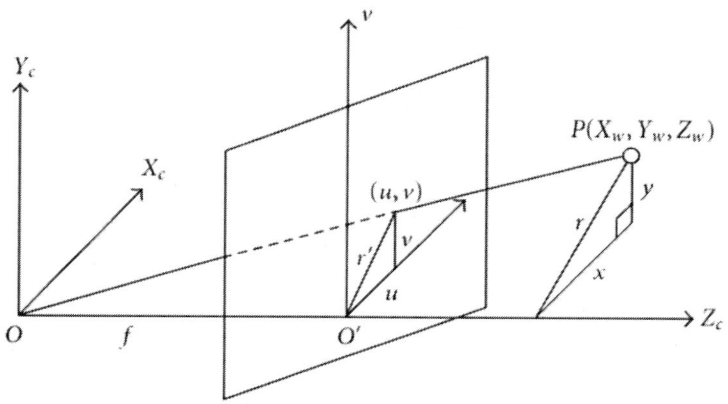

Figure 9. Pinhole camera model (X_w, Y_w, Z_w): : World coordinates; (O, X_c, Y_c, Z_c) : camera coordinates; ((O', u, v): image plane coordinates.

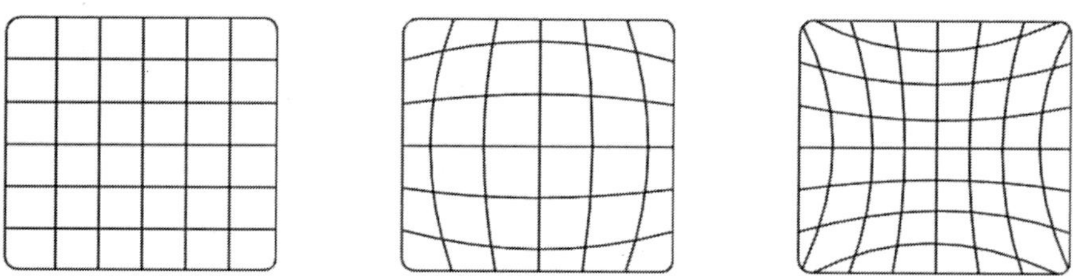

Figure 10. (a) The ideal undistorted grid. (b) Barrel distortion. (c) Pincushion distortion.

The effective distortion can be modelled by

$$\delta_u(u,v) = \delta_{ur} + \delta_{ud} + \delta_{up},$$
$$\delta_v(u,v) = \delta_{vr} + \delta_{vd} + \delta_{vp}, \quad (9)$$

where δ_{ur} represent radial distortion [24], δ_{ud} represent decentering distortion, and δ_{up} represent thin prism distortion. Assuming that only the first- and second-order terms are sufficient to compensate the distortion, and the terms of order higher than three are negligible, we obtain a fifth-order polynomials camera model (expression 8), where (u_i, v_i) are the distorted image coordinates in pixels, and $(\tilde{u}_i, \tilde{v}_i)$ are true coordinates (undistorted):

$$u_i = D_u S_u \left(k_2 \tilde{u}_i^5 + 2k_2 \tilde{u}_i^3 \tilde{v}_i^2 + k_2 \tilde{u}_i \tilde{v}_i^4 + k_1 \tilde{u}_i^3 + k_1 \tilde{u}_i \tilde{v}_i^2 + 3p_2 \tilde{u}_i^2 + 2p_1 \tilde{u}_i \tilde{v}_i + p_2 \tilde{v}_i^2 + \tilde{u}_i \right) + u_0,$$
$$v_i = D_v \left(k_2 \tilde{u}_i^4 \tilde{v}_i + 2k_2 \tilde{u}_i^2 \tilde{v}_i^3 + k_1 \tilde{u}_i^2 \tilde{v}_i + k_2 \tilde{v}_i^5 + k_1 \tilde{v}_i^3 + p_1 \tilde{u}_i^2 + 2p_2 \tilde{u}_i \tilde{v}_i + 3p_1 \tilde{v}_i^2 + \tilde{u}_i \right) + v_0. \quad (10)$$

An approximation of the inverse model is done by (11):

$$\tilde{u}_i = \frac{\breve{u}_i' + \breve{u}_i'\left(a_1 r_i^2 + a_2 r_i^4\right) + 2a_3 \breve{u}_i' \breve{v}_i' + a_4\left(r_i^2 + 2\breve{u}_i'^2\right)}{\left(a_5 r_i^2 + a_6 \breve{u}_i' + a_7 \breve{v}_i' + a_8\right) r_i^2 + 1},$$
$$\tilde{v}_i = \frac{\breve{v}_i' + \breve{v}_i'\left(a_1 r_i^2 + a_2 r_i^4\right) + 2a_4 \breve{u}_i' \breve{v}_i' + a_3\left(r_i^2 + 2\breve{v}_i'^2\right)}{\left(a_5 r_i^2 + a_6 \breve{u}_i' + a_7 \breve{v}_i' + a_8\right) r_i^2 + 1}, \quad (11)$$

where

$$\tilde{u}_i' = \frac{u_i - u_0}{D_{uSU}},$$
$$\tilde{v}_i' = \frac{v_i - v_0}{D_v},$$
$$r_i^2 = \sqrt{\tilde{v}_i'^2 + \tilde{v}_i'^2}. \quad (12)$$

The unknown parameters $a_1, \ldots, a_8$ are solved using direct least mean-squares fitting [25] in the off-line calibration process.

4.1. Off-Line Lens Calibration

There are many proposed methods that can be used to estimate intrinsic camera and lens distortion parameters, and there are also methods that produce only a subset of the parameter estimates. We chose a traditional calibration method based on observing a planar checkerboard in front of our system at different poses and positions (see Figure 11) to solve the equations of unknown parameters (11). The results of the calibration procedure are presented in Table 1.

Table 1. Calibration results.

Parameter	Value	Error
u_0 (pixels)	178.04	1.28
v_0 (pixels)	144.25	1.34
fD_{uSU} (pixels)	444.99	1.21
fD_v (pixels)	486.39	1.37
a_1	−0.3091	0.0098
a_2	−0.0033	0.0031
a_3	0.0004	0.0001
a_4	0.0014	0.0004
a_5	0.0021	0.0002
a_6	0.0002	0.0001
a_7	0.0024	0.0005
a_8	0.0011	0.0002

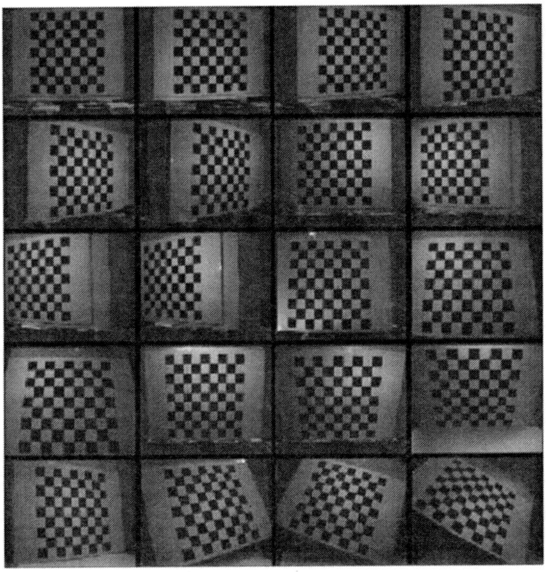

Figure 11. Different checkerboard positions used for calibration procedure.

4.2. Hardware Implementation

After the computation of parameters in (11) through an off-line calibration process, we used them to correct the distortion of each frame. With the input frame captured by the camera denoted as the source image and the corrected output as the target image, the task of correcting the source distorted image can be defined as follows: for every pixel location in the target image, compute its corresponding pixel location in the source image. Two implementation techniques of distortion correction have been compared:

Direct Computation

Calculate the image coordinates through evaluating the polynomials to determine intensity values for each pixel.

Lookup Table

Calculate the image coordinates through evaluating the polynomials correction in advance, storing them in a lookup table which is referenced at run-time. All parameters needed for LUT generation are known beforehand; therefore for our system, the LUT is computed only once and off-line.

However, since the source pixel location can be a real number, using it to compute the actual pixel values of the target image requires some form of pixel interpolation. For this purpose we have used the nearest neighbour interpolation approach that means that the pixel value closest to the predicted coordinates is assigned to the target coordinates. This choice is reasonable because it is a simple and fast method for computation, and visible image artefacts have no subject with our system.

Performance results of these two techniques are presented in terms of (i) execution time and (ii) FPGA logic resource requirements.

The proposed architectures described above have been described in VHDL in a fixed point fashion, implemented on a Xilinx Virtex II FPGA device and simulated using industry reference simulator (ModelSim). The pixel values of both the input distorted and the output corrected images use an 8-bit word length integer number. The coordinates use an 18-bit word length.

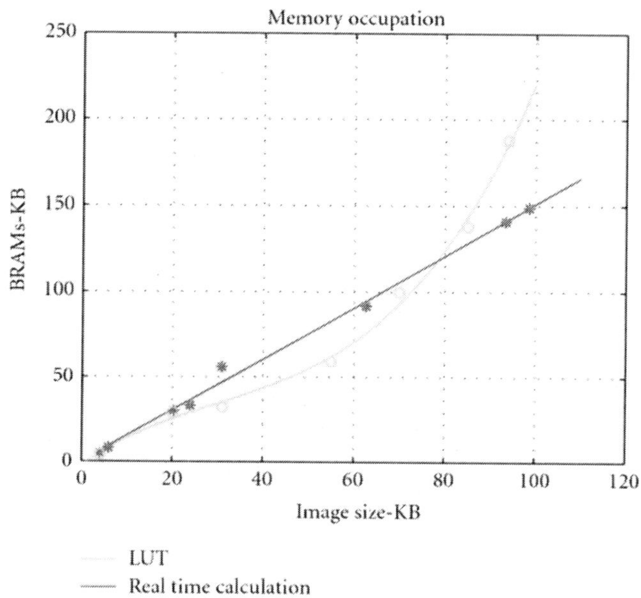

Figure 12. Block Memory occupation for both direct computation and LUT-based approaches.

The results are presented in Figures 12 and 13 and Table 2.

Table 2. Area and Clock characteristics of two approaches.

Implementation	Area (%)	Clock (MHz)
Direct Computation	58	10
Look Up Table	6	24

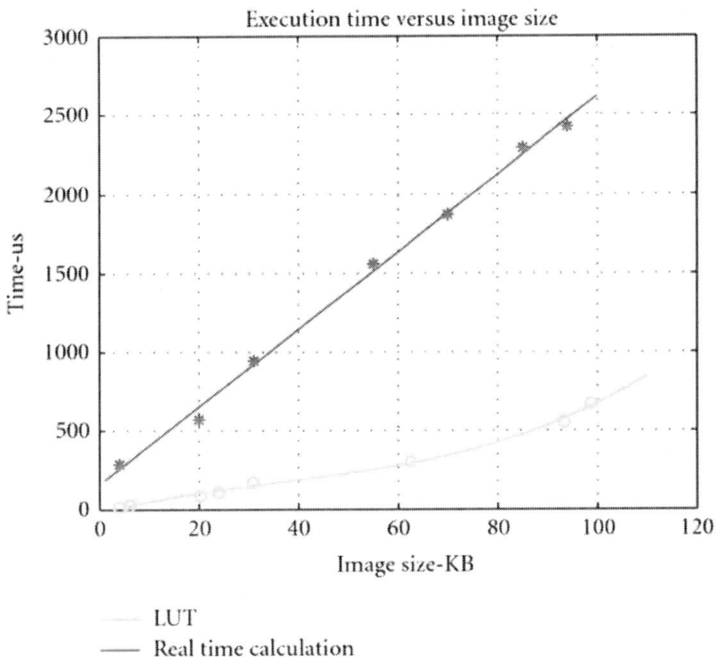

Figure 13. Execution time for both direct computation and LUT-based approaches.

The execution time for the direct computation implementation is comparatively very slow. This is due to the fact that the direct computation approach consumes a much greater amount of logic resources than the

Look-up Table approach. Moreover the slow clock cycle (10 MHz) could be increased by splitting the complex arithmetic logic into several smaller stages. The significant difference between these two approaches is that the direct computation approach requires more computation time and arithmetic operations, while the LUT approach requires more memory accesses and more RAM Blocks occupation. Regarding latency, both approaches can be executed with respect to real-time constraint of video cadence (25 frames per second). Depending on the applications, the best compromise between time and resources must be chosen by the user. For our application, arithmetic operations are intensively needed for later stages in the preprocessing block, while memory blocks are available; so we chose to use the LUT approach to benefit in time and resources.

5. THRESHOLDING AND LABELLING

After lens distortion correction, the laser spots projected must be extracted from the gray level image for delivering a 3D representation of the scene. Laser spots on the image appear with variable sizes (depending on the absorption of the surface and the projection angle). At this level, a preprocessing block has been developed and hardware implemented to make an adaptive thresholding in order to give a binary image and a labelling to classify each laser spot to compute later their center.

5.1. Thresholding Algorithm

Several methods exist from a static threshold value defined by user up to dynamic algorithm as Otsu method [26].

We have chosen to develop a new approach less complex than Otsu or others well-known dynamic methods in order to reduce the processing time [27]. The simple method is described in (Figure 14):

1) building the histogram of grey-level image,

2) finding the first maxima of the Gaussian corresponding to the Background; compute its mean μ and standard deviation σ,

3) calculating the threshold value with (13):

$$\text{Threshold} = \sigma \cdot \alpha + \mu, \tag{13}$$

where α is an arbitrary constant. A parallel architecture of processing has been designed to compute the threshold and to give a binary image. Full features of this implementation are given in [28].

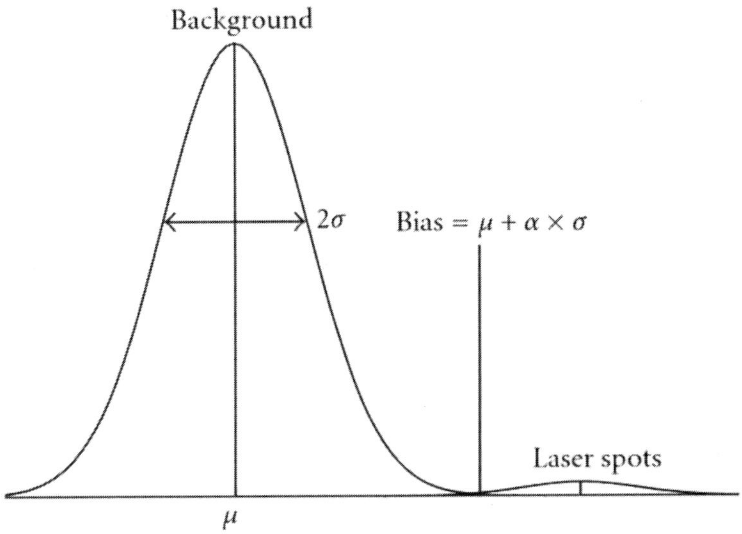

Figure 14. Method developed in Cyclope.

5.2. Labeling

After this first stage of extraction of spot laser from the background, it is necessary to classify each laser spot in order to compute separately their center. Several methods have been developed in the past. We chose to use a classical two passes component connected labeling algorithms with an 8-connectivity. We designed a specific optimized Intellectual Property in VHDL. This intellectual property uses fixed point number.

6. COMPUTATION OF SPOTS CENTERS

The threshold and labeling processes applied to the captured image allow us to determine the area of each spot (number of pixels). The coordinates of center of these spots could be calculated as follows:

$$u_{gI} = \frac{\sum_{i \in I} u_i}{N_I},$$
$$v_{gI} = \frac{\sum_{i \in I} v_i}{N_I}, \tag{14}$$

where u_{gI} and v_{gI} and the abscissa and ordinate of I th spot center. u_i and v_i are the coordinates of pixels constructing the spot. N_I is the number of pixels of I th spot (area in pixels).

To obtain an accuracy 3D reconstruction, we need to compute the spots centers with higher possible precision without increasing the total computing time to satisfy the real-time constraint. The hardest step in center detection part is the division operations A/B in (14). Several methods exist to solve this problem.

6.1. Implementation of a Hardware Divider

The simplest method is the use of hardware divider but they are computationally expensive and consume a considerable amount of resources. This not acceptable for a real-time embedded systems. Some other techniques are used to compute the center of laser spots avoiding the use of hardware dividers.

6.2. Approximation Method

Some studies suggest approximation methods to avoid implementation of hardware dividers. Such methods like that implemented in [29] replace the active pixels by the smallest rectangle containing this region and then replace the usual division by simple shifting (division by 2):

$$u^*_{gI} = \frac{\text{Max}(u_i)+\text{Min}(u_i)}{2},$$
$$v^*_{gI} = \frac{\text{Max}(v_i)+\text{Min}(v_i)}{2}. \qquad (15)$$

This approach is approximated in (15), where (u_i, v_i) are the active pixel coordinates, and (u^*_{gI}, v^*_{gI}) are the approximated coordinates of the spot center.

The determination of rectangle limits needs two times scanning of the image, detecting in every scanning step, respectively, the minimum and maximum of pixels coordinates. For each spot, we should compare the coordinates of every pixel by last registered minimum and maximum to assign new values to U_m, U_M, V_m, and V_M. (m : Minimum; M : maximum). While N_p is the average area of spots (number of pixels), we can estimate the number of operations needed to calculate the center of each spot by $4N_p + 6$. And in global, $N_{\text{op}} \approx 25 * N * (4N_p + 6)$ operations are needed to calculate the centers of N spots (video-cadence of 25 fps). Such approximation is simple and easy to use but still needs considerable time to be calculated. Beside, the error is not negligible. The error in such method is nearly 0.22 pixel, and the maximum error is more than 0.5 pixel [29]. Taking the spot of Figure 15 as an example of inaccuracy of such a method, the real center position of these pixels is (4.47; 6.51). But when applying this approximation method, the center position will be (5; 6). This inaccuracy will result mismatching problem that affects the measurement result when reconstructing object.

6.3. Our Method

The area of each spot (number of pixels) is always a positive integer, while its value is limited in a predeterminate interval $[N_{\text{min}}, N_{\text{max}}]$, where N_{min} and N_{max} are, respectively, the minimum and maximum areas of laser spot in the image. The spot areas depend on object illumination, distance between object and camera, and the angle of view of the scene. Our method consists in a memorisation of $1/N$ where N represent the spot pixel number and can take value in $[1, N_{\text{limit}}]$. N_{limit} represent the maximum considered size, in pixels, of a spot.

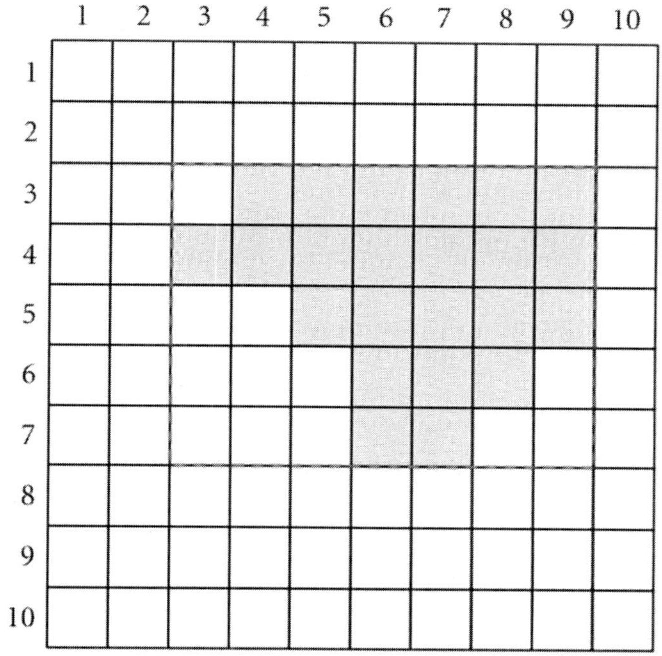

Figure 15. Smallest rectangle containing active pixel.

In this case we need only to compute a multiplication, that is resume here:

$$u_{gI} = (u_1 + u_2 + \cdots + u_I) * \frac{1}{N_I},$$
$$v_{gI} = (v_1 + v_2 + \cdots + v_I) * \frac{1}{N_I}. \tag{16}$$

The implementation of such a filter is very easy, regarding that the most of DSP functions are provided for earlier FPGAs. For example, Virtex-II architecture [30] provides an 18×18 bits Multiplier with a latency of about 4.87 ns at 205 MHz and optimised for high-speed operations. Additionally, the power consumption is lower compared to a slice implementation of an 18-bit by 18-bit multiplier [31]. For N luminous spots source, the number of operations needed to compute the centers coordinates is $N_{op} \approx 25 * N * N_p$, and N_p is the average area of spots. When implementing our approach to Virtex II Pro FPGA (XC2VP30), it was clear that we gain in execution time and size. Comparison of different implementation approaches is described in the next section.

7. MATCHING ALGORITHM

The set of parameters for the epipolar and depth models are used during run time to make point matching (identify the original position of a pattern point from its image) and calculate the depth using the coordinates of each laser spot center.

For this purpose we have developed a parallel architecture visible in Figure 16, described in detail in [32].

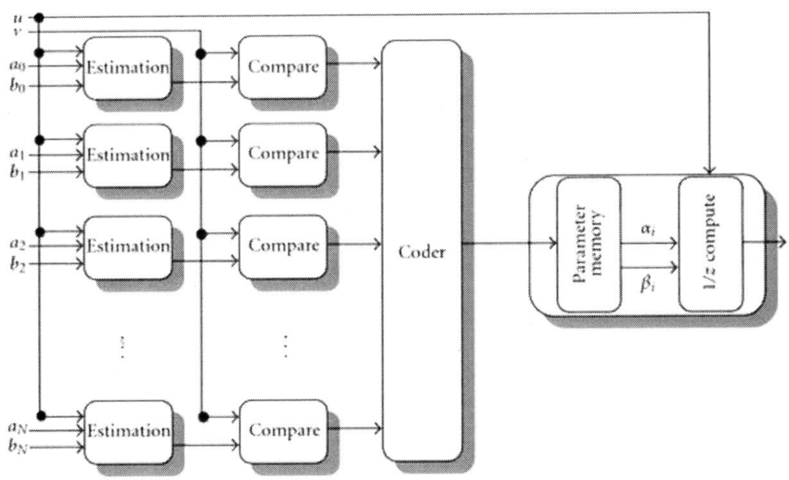

Figure 16. 3D unit.

Starting from the point abscissa (u) we calculate its estimated ordinate $(\tilde{v})$ if it belongs to a epipolar line. We compare this estimation with the true ordinate (v).

These operations are made for all the epipolar line simultaneously. After thresholding the encoder returns the index of the corresponding epipolar line.

The next step is to calculate the z coordinate from the u coordinate and the appropriate depth model parameters(α,β)

These computation blocs are synchronous and pipelined, allowing, thus, high processing rates.

7.1. Estimation Bloc

In this bloc the estimated ordinate is calculated $\tilde{v} = a \cdot u + b$. The (a,b) parameters are loaded from memory.

7.2. Comparison Bloc

In this bloc the absolute value of the difference between the ordinate v and its estimation $\tilde{v}$ is calculated. This difference is then thresholded.

The thresholding avoids a resource consuming sort stage. The threshold was a priori chosen as half the minimum distance between two consecutive epipolar lines. The threshold can be adjusted for each comparison bloc.

This bloc returns a "1" result if the distance is underneath the threshold.

7.3. Encoding Bloc

If the comparison blocs return a unique "1" result, then the encoder returns the corresponding epipolar line index.

If no comparison bloc returns a "true" result, the point is irrelevant and considered as picture noise.

If more than one comparison blocs returns "1", then we consider that we have a correspondence error and a flag is set.

The selected index is then carried to the next stage where the z coordinate is calculated. It allows the selection of the right parameters to the depth model.

We compute $(1/z)$, rather than z as we said earlier, to have a simpler computation unit. This computation bloc is then identical to the estimation bloc.

8. WIRELESS COMMUNICATION

Finally, after computation, the 3D coordinates of the laser dots accompanied by the image of texture are sent to an external reader. So, Cyclope is equipped with a block of wireless communication which allows us to transmit the image of texture, the coordinates 3D of the centers of the spots laser, and even to remotely reconfigure the digital processing architecture (an Over The Air FPGA). While attending the IEEE802.15 Body Area Network standard [33], the frequency assigned for implanted device RF communication is around 403 MHz and referred to as the MICS (Medical Implant Communication System) band due to essentially three reasons:

1) a small antenna,

2) a minimum losses environment which allows to design low-power transmitter,

3) a free band without causing interference to other users of the electromagnetic radio spectrum [34].

In order to make rapidly a wireless communication of our prototype, we chose to use Zigbee module at 2.45 GHz available on the market contrary to modules MCIS. We are self-assured that later frequency is not usable for the communication between the implant and an external reader, due to the electromagnetic losses of the human body. Two Xbee-pro modules from the Digi Corporation have been used. One for the demonstrator and the second plugged on a PC host where a human machine interface has been designed to visualise in real-time the 3D textured reconstruction of the scene.

Communication between wireless module and the FPGA circuit is performed by a standard UART protocol. this principle is shown on Figure 17. To make this communication we integrated a Microblaze softcore processor with UART functionality. The Softcore recovers all the data stored in memory (texture and 3D coordinates) and sends them to the wireless module.

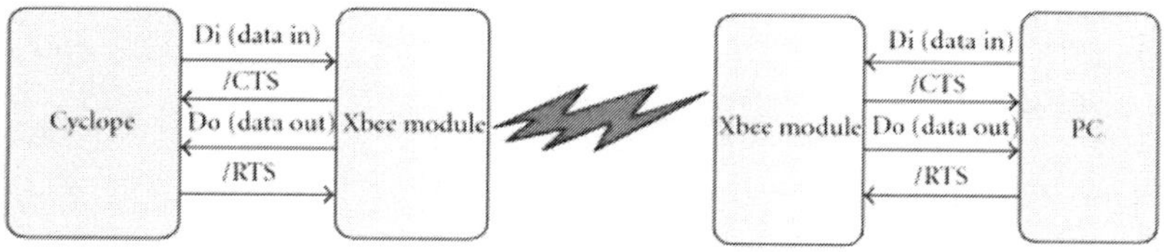

Figure 17. Wireless communication.

9. DEMONSTRATOR, TESTBENCH AND RESULTS

9.1. Experimental Demonstrator

To demonstrate the feasibility of our system, a large-scale demonstrator has been realised. It uses an FPGA prototyping board based on a Xilinx Virtex2Pro, a pulsed IR LASER projector [35] coupled with a diffraction network that generates a 49-dot pattern and a CCD imager.

Figure 18 represents the experimental set. It is composed of a standard 3 mm lens, the CCD camera with an external 8 bits DAC, a projector IR pattern, and a Virtex2pro prototyping board.

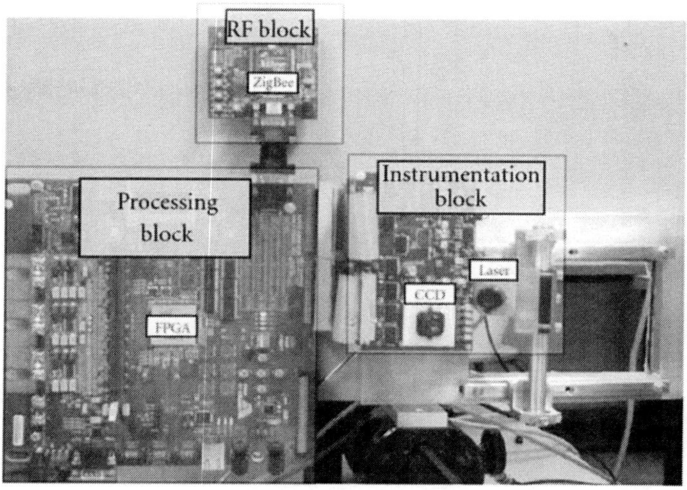

Figure 18. Demonstrator

FPGA is used mainly for computation unit but also to control image acquisition, laser synchronisation, analog-to-digital conversion, and image storage and displays the result through a VGA interface.

Figure 19 shows the principal parts of the control and storage architecture as set in the FPGA. Five parts have been designed:

1) a global sequencer to control the entire process,

2) a reset and integration time configuration unit,

3) a VGA synchronisation interface,

4) a dual port memory to store the images and to allow asynchronous acquisition and display operations,

5) a wirless communication module based on the ZigBee protocol.

A separated pulsed IR projector has been added to the system to demonstrate the system functionality.

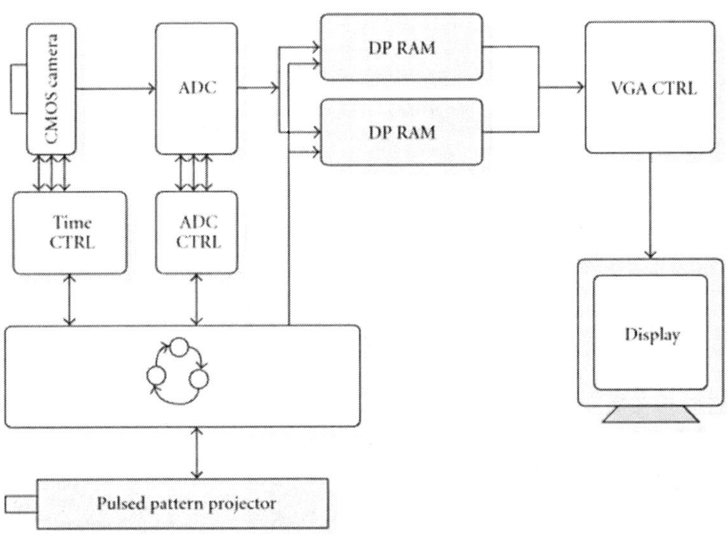

Figure 19. Implementation of the control and storage architecture.

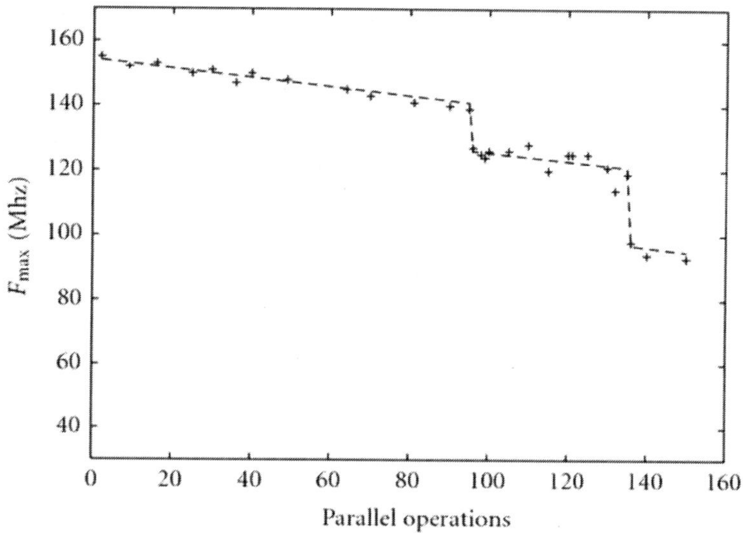

Figure 20. FPGA working frequency evolution.

The computation unit was described in VHDL and implemented on FPGA XilinX VirtexIlpro (XC2VP30) with 30816 logic cells and 136 hardware multipliers [31]. The synthesis and placement were achieved for 49 parallel processing elements. We use here 28% of the LUTs and 50 hardware multipliers, for a working frequency of 148 Mhz.

9.2. Architecture Performance

To estimate the evolution of the architecture performances, we have used a generic description and repeat the synthesis and placement for different pattern sizes (number of parallel operations). Figure 20 shows that in every case our architecture mapped on an FPGA can work at least at almost 90 Mhz and then obtain a real time constraint of 40 milliseconds.

9.3. Error Estimation of the Optical Correction

The implementation results of distortion correction method are summarised in Table 3. In this table we have implemented the correction model only to the active light spots. However, Figure 21 present an image before and after our lens distortion correction.

Table 3. Performances of the distortion correction.

Slices	1795 (13%)
Latency	11.43 ms
Error	< 0.01 pixels

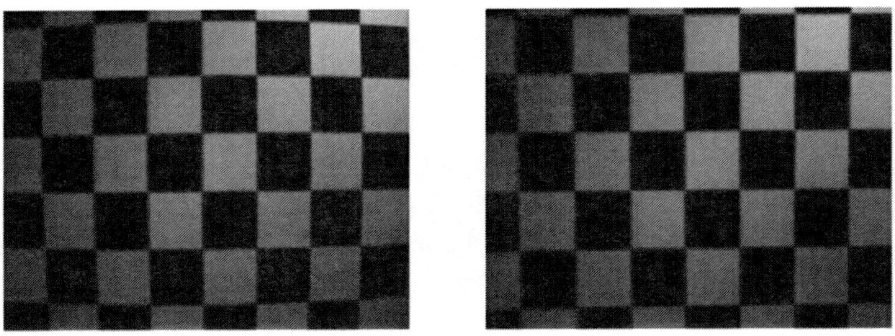

Figure 21. (a) Checkerboard image before distortion correction. (b) Checkerboard image after correction.Image without correctionImage with correction

Regarding size and latency, it is clear that the results are suitable for our application.

Comparing our used method to compute the spots centers with two other methods (see Table 4), it is clear that our approach has higher accuracy and smaller size than approximation method. Since it has nearly the same accuracy as method using hardware divider, it still uses less resources. Regarding latency, the results of all three approaches respect real time constraint of video cadence (25 frames per second). Comparing many measures on the depth estimation before and after the implementation of our improvements, the results indicate that the precision of the system increased, so that the residual error is reduced about 33% (Figure 22).

Table 4. Centers computation performances.

Method	Slices	Latency (μs)	Error (pixel)
Approximation	287	4.7	0.21
Hardware divider	1804	1.77	0.0078
Our approach	272	2.34	0.015

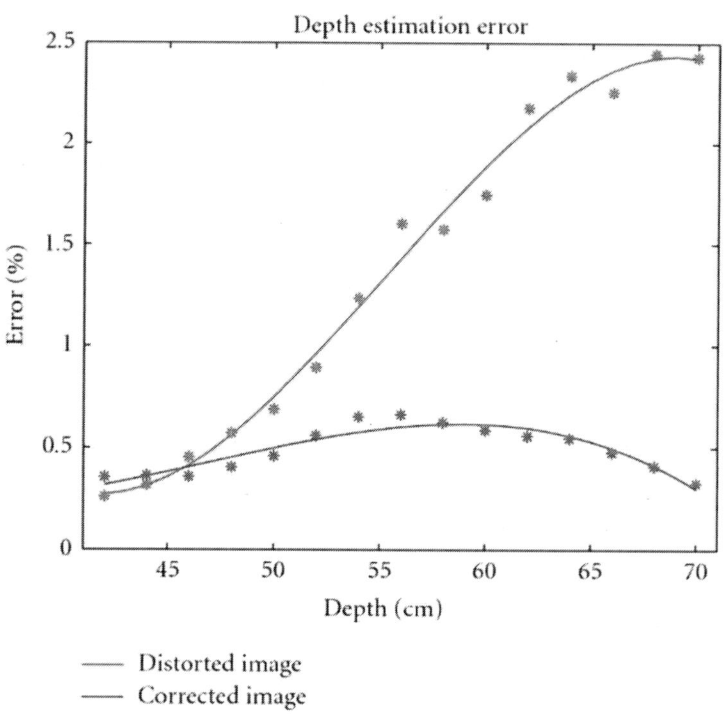

Figure 22. Error comparison before and after applying distortion correction and centers recomputing.

These results were interpolated with a scale factor to measure the error lens in the case of integration inside a video capsule, and the results can be shown in Figure 23. This scaling was calculated with a distance between the laser projector and the imager of 1 cm. It is the maximal distance that can be considered for endoscopy. This distance corresponds to the diameter of the PillCam video capsule. We can show that the correction of the distortion produced by the lens increases the accuracy of our sensor.

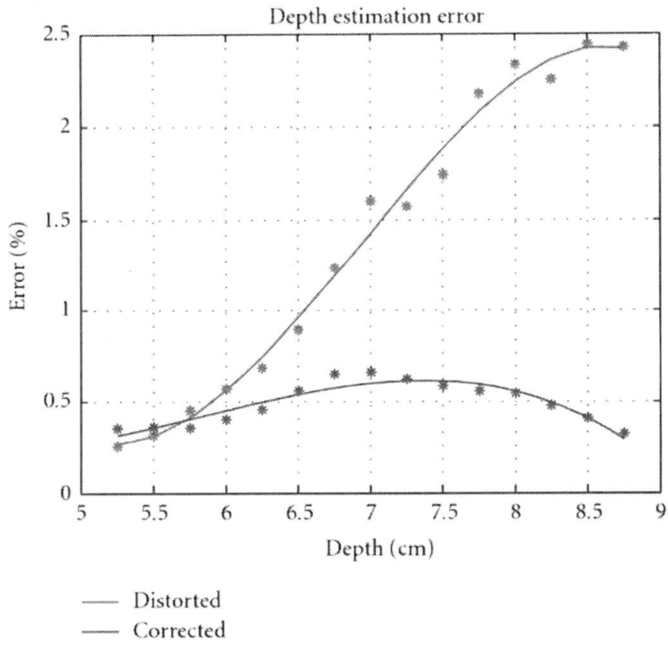

Figure 23. Error comparison before and after applying distortion correction and centers recomputing after scaling for integration.

9.4. Error Estimation of the 3D Reconstruction

In order to validate our reconstruction architecture, we have compared the results obtained with the synthesised IP (Table 5) and those obtained from a floating point mathematical model which was already validated by experimentation. As we can see, the calculation error margin is relatively weak in comparison with the distance variations and shows that our approach to translate a complex mathematical model into a digital processing for embedded system is valid.

Table 5. Results Validation.

Coordinates couples abscise/ordinate (pixel)	Model results (meter)	IP results (meter)
401/450	1.57044	1.57342
357/448	1.57329	1.57349
402/404	1.57223	1.57176
569/387	1.22065	1.21734
446/419	1.11946	1.11989
478/319	1.07410	1.07623
424/315	1.04655	1.04676
375/267	1.03283	1.03297
420/177	1.03316	1.03082

Table 6 shows the error of reconstruction for different distances and sizes of the stereoscopic base. We can see that for a base of 5 mm we are able to have a 3D reconstruction with an error above to 4% at a distance of 10 cm. This precision is perfectly enough in the context of the human body exploration and an integration of a stereoscopic base with a such size is relatively simple.

Table 6. Precision versus the size of the stereoscopic base.

Base of 0.5 cm		Base of 1.5 cm	
Distance (cm)	Error (%)	Distance (cm)	Error (%)
5	1.8	5	0.61
10	3.54	10	1.21
50	15.52	50	5.77
100	26.87	100	10.91

9.5. Example of Reconstruction

We have used the calibration results to reconstruct the volume of an object (a 20 cm diameter cylinder). The pattern was projected on the scene and the snapshots were taken.

The pattern points were extracted and associated to laser beams using the epipolar constraint. The depth of each point was then calculated using the appropriate model. The texture image was mapped on the reconstructed object and rendered in an VRML player.

We have created an application written in C++ for visualising the Cyclope's results (Figure 24). The application gets the textural information and the barycenter spatial position of the 49 infrared laser spots from a wireless communication module. After the result reception, it draws the texture of three binary maps representing the location of the 49 barycenters on a 3D coordinates system (XY, ZX, and ZY).

The recapitulation of the hardware requirement is presented Table 7. We can observe that the design is small and if we make an equivalence in logics gates, it should be integrated in a small area chip like IGLOO AGL 1000 device from Actel. Such a device has a size of 10×10 mm^2 and its core can be integrated in a VCE which has a diameter around 1 cm. At this moment, we did not make implementation on this last platform. It is a feasibility study but the first results prove that this solution is valid if we consider the needed ressources.

We present also an estimation of the energetic consumption which was realised with two tools. This estimation is visible in Table 8. The first tool is XPE (Xilinx Power Estimation) from Xilinx to evaluate the power consumption of a Virtex, and the second is IGLOOpowercalculator from Actel to evaluate the power consumption of a low power consumption FPGA.

These two tools use the processing frequency, the number of logic cells, the number of D flip-flop, and the amount of memory of the design to estimate the power consumption. To realise our estimation, we use the results summarised in Table 7. Our estimation is made with an activity rate of 50% that is the worst case.

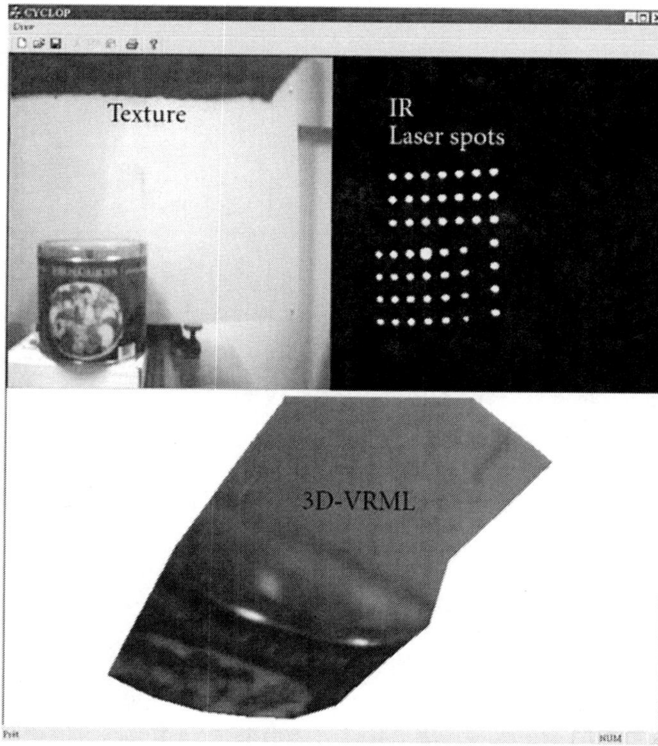

Figure 24. Visualisation of the results by our application.

Table 7. Recapitulation of the performances.

Architecture	Clb slices	Latches	LUT	RAM
Camera	309	337	618	4
Optical correction*	92/94	8/8	176/190	32/56
Thresholding	107	192	214	1
Labelling	114	102	227	0
Matching	1932	3025	3864	0
Communication	170	157	277	3
Total used*	2323/2325	3821	1555/1569	40/64
Total free	13693	29060	27392	136

* Direct computation/Look up table.

Table 8. Processing block power consumption estimation.

Device	Power consumption	Duration	
		1 battery	3 battery
Virtex	1133 mW	29 min	1h 26 min
IGLOO	128,4 mW	4 hours	12 hours

To validate the power consumption estimation in an embedded context, we consider that a 3V-CR1220 battery (3V-CR1220 is a 3 Volt battery, its diameter is of 1.2 cm, and its thickness is of 2 mm) which has a maximum of 180 mAh power consumption, that is to say an ideal power of 540 mWh. This battery is fully compatible with a VCE like the Pillcam from Given Imaging.

As we can see, the integration of a Virtex in a VCE is impossible because of the SRAM memory that consumes too much energy. If we consider the IGLOO technology based on flash memory, we can observe that its power consumption is compatible with a VCE. Such technology permits four hours of autonomy with only one battery, and twelve hours of autonomy if we used three 3V-CR1220 in the VCE. This result is encouraging because at this time the mean duration of an examination is ten hours.

10. CONCLUSION AND PERSPECTIVES

We have presented in this paper Cyclope, a sensor designed to be a 3D video capsule.

We have explained a method to acquire the images at a 25-frame/s video rate with a discrimination between the texture and the projected pattern. This method uses an energetic approach, a pulsed projector, and an original 64×64 CMOS image sensor with programmable integration time. Multiple images are taken with different integration times to obtain an image of the pattern which is more energetic than the background texture. Our CMOS imager validates this method.

Also we present a 3D reconstruction processing that allows a precise and real-time reconstruction. This processing which is specifically designed for an integrated sensor and its integration in an FPGA-like device has a low power consumption compatible with a VCE examination.

The method was tested on a large scale demonstrator using an FPGA prototyping board and a 352×288 pixels CCD sensor. The results show that it is possible to integrate a stereoscopic base which is designed for a integrated sensor and to keep a good precision for a human body exploration.

The next step to this work is the chip level integration of both the image sensor and the pattern projector. Evaluate the power consumption of the pulsed laser projector considering the optical efficiency of the diffraction head.

The presented version of Cyclope is the first step toward the final goal of the project. After this, the goal is to realise a real-time pattern recognition with processing-like support vector machine or neuronal network. The final issue of Cyclope is to be a real smart sensor that can realize a part of a diagnosis inside the body and then increase its fiability.

REFERENCES

1. Iddan G, Meron G, Glukhovsky A, Swain P: **Wireless capsule endoscopy.** *Nature* 2000,**405**(6785):417-418.

2. Rey J-F, Kuznetsov K, Vazquez-Ballesteros E: **Olympus capsule endoscope for small and large bowel exploration.***Gastrointestinal Endoscopy* 2006,**63**(5):AB176.

3. Gay M, *et al.*: **La vidéo capsule endoscopique: qu'en attendre?** CISMEF, http://www.churouen.fr/ssf/equip/capsulesvideoendoscopiques.html

4. Graba T, Granado B, Romain O, Ea T, Pinna A, Garda P: **Cyclope: an integrated real-time 3d image sensor.***Proceedings of the 19th International Conference on Design of Circuits and Integrated Systems, 2004*

5. Marzani F, Voisin Y, Voon LLY, Diou A: **Active sterovision system: a fast and easy calibration method.** *Proceedings of the 6th International*

Conference on Control Automation, Robotics and Vision (ICARCV '00), 2000

6. Li W, Boochs F, Marzani F, Voisin Y: **Iterative 3d surface reconstruction with adaptive pattern projection.** *Proceedings of the 6th IASTED International Conference on Visualization, Imaging, and Image Processing (VIIP '06), August 2006* 336-341.

7. Lavoie P, Ionescu D, Petriu E: **A high precision 3d object reconstruction method using a color coded grid and nurbs.** *Proceedings of the International Conference on Image Analysis and Processing, 1999*

8. Oike Y, Shintaku H, Takayama S, Ikeda M, Asada K: **Real-time and high resolution 3-d imaging system using light-section method and smart CMOS sensor.** *Proceedings of the IEEE International Conference on Sensors (SENSORS '03), October 2003* **2:** 502-507.

9. Ullrich A, Studnicka N, Riegl J, Orlandini S: **Long-range highperformance time-of-flight-based 3d imaging sensors.***Proceedings of the International Symposium on 3D Data Processing Visualization and Transmission, 2002*

10. Mansouri A, Lathuiliére A, Marzani FS, Voisin Y, Gouton P: **Toward a 3d multispectral scanner: an application to multimedia.** *IEEE Multimedia* 2007,**14**(1):40-47.

11. Bernardini F, Rushmeier H: **The 3d model acquisition pipeline.** *Computer Graphics Forum* 2002,**21**(2):149-172.

12. Zhang S: **Recent progresses on real-time 3d shape measurement using digital fringe projection techniques.** *Optics and Lasers in Engineering* 2010,**48**(2):149-158.

13. Depiero FW, Triverdi MM: **3d computer vision using structured light: design, calibration, and implementation issues.** *Journal of Advances in Computers* 1996, 243-278.

14. Hemayed EE, Ahmed MT, Farag AA: **CardEye: a 3d trinocular active vision system.** *Proceedings of the IEEE Conference on Intelligent Transportation Systems (ITSC '00), October 2000, Dearborn, Mich, USA* 398-403.

15. Kolar A, Graba T, Pinna A, Romain O, Granado B, Belhaire E: **Smart Bi-spectral image sensor for 3d vision.***Proceedings of the 6th IEEE Conference on SENSORS (IEEE SENSORS '07), October 2007, Atlanta, Ga, USA* 577-580.

16. Gyselinckx B, Van Hoof C, Ryckaert J, Yazicioglu RF, Fiorini P, Leonov V: **Human++: autonomous wireless sensors for body area networks.** *Proceedings of the IEEE Custom Integrated Circuits Conference, 2005* 12-18.

17. Warneke B, Last M, Liebowitz B, Pister KSJ: **Smart dust: communicating with a cubic-millimeter computer.** *Computer*2001,**34**(1):44-51.

18. Horaud R, Monga O: *Vision par Ordinateur*. Hermès; 1995.

19. Faugeras O: *Three-Dimensional Computer Vision, a Geometric Viewpoint*. MIT Press, Cambridge, Mass, USA; 1993.

20. Batlle J, Mouaddib E, Salvi J: **Recent progress in coded structured light as a technique to solve the correspondence problem: a survey.** *Pattern Recognition* 1998,**31**(7):963-982.

21. Woo S, Dipanda A, Marzani F, Voisin Y: **Determination of an optimal configuration for a direct correspondence in an active stereovision system.** *Proceedings of the IASTED International Conference on Visualization, Imaging, and Image Processing, 2002*

22. Mang O-Y, Huang S-W, Chen Y-L, Lee H-H, Weng P-K: **Design of wide-angle lenses for wireless capsule endoscopes.***Optical Engineering, October 2007* **46:**

23. Heikkilä J, Silvén O: **A four-step camera calibration procedure with implicit image correction.** *Proceedings of the IEEE Computer Society Conference on Computer Vision and Pattern Recognition, 1997, San Juan, Puerto Rico, USA* 1106-1112.

24. Hwang K, Kang MG: **Correction of lens distortion using point correspondence.** *Proceedings of the IEEE Region 10 Conference (TENCON '99), 1999* **1:** 690-693.

25. Heikkilä J: *Accurate camera calibration and feature based 3-D reconstruction from monocular image sequences, Ph.D. dissertation*. University of Oulu, Oulu, Finland; 1997.

26. Otsu N: **A threshold selection method from gray level histogram.** *IEEE Transactions on Systems, Man, and Cybernetics* 1979,**9**(1):62-66.

27. Kapur JN, Sahoo PK, Wong AKC: **A new method for gray-level picture thresholding using the entropy of the histogram.** *Computer Vision, Graphics, & Image Processing* 1985,**29**(3):273-285.

28. Faura D, Graba T, Viateur S, Romain O, Granado B, Garda P: **Seuillage dynamique temps réel dans un système embarqué.** *Proceedings of the 21ème Colloque du Groupe de Recherche et d'Étude du Traitement du Signal et des l'Image (GRETSI '07), 2007*

29. Graba T: *Etude d'une architecture de traitement pour un capteur intégré de vision 3d, Ph.D. dissertation*. Université Pierre et Marie Curie; 2006.

30. Adhiwiyogo M: **Optimal pipelining of the I/O ports of the virtex-II multiplier.** XAPP636, vol. 1.4, June 2004

31. Xilinx : **Virtex-II Pro and Virtex-II Pro Platform FPGA: Complete Data Sheet.** October 2005.

32. Kolar A, Graba T, Pinna A, Romain O, Granado B, Ea T: **A digital processing architecture for 3d reconstruction.***Proceedings of the International Workshop on Computer Architecture for Machine Perception and Sensing (CAMPS '06), August 2006, Montreal, Canada* 172-176.

33. ieee802 http://www.ieee802.org/15/pub/TG6.html

34. Yuce MR, Ng SWP, Myo NL, Khan JY, Liu W: **Wireless body sensor network using medical implant band.** *Journal of Medical Systems* 2007,**31**(6):467-474.

35. Laser2000 http://www.laser2000.fr/index.php?id=368949&L=2

Chapter 4

Robust video super resolution algorithm using measurement validation method and scene change detection

Minjae Kim1 , Bonhwa Ku1 , Daesung Chung1 , Hyunhak Shin1 , David K Han2 and Hanseok Ko1*

1 School of Electrical Engineering, Korea University, Anam-dong, Seongbuk-Gu, Seoul 136-701, Korea

2 Office of Naval Research, Arlington, VA, USA

ABSTRACT

Explicit motion estimation is considered a major factor in the performance of classical motion-based super resolution (SR) algorithms. To reconstruct video frames sequentially, we applied a dynamic SR algorithm based on the Kalman recursive estimator. Our approach includes a novel measurement validation process to attain robust image reconstruction results under inexplicit motion estimation. In our method, the suitability for high-resolution pixel estimation is determined by the accuracy of motion estimation. We measured the accuracy of the image registration result using the Mahalanobis distance between the input low-resolution frame and the motion compensated high-resolution estimation. We also incorporate an effective scene change detection method dedicated to the proposed SR approach for minimizing erroneous results when abrupt scene changes occur in the video frames. According to the ratio of well-aligned pixels (i.e., motion is compensated accurately) to the total number of pixels, we are able to detect sudden changes of scene and context in the input video. Representative experiments on synthetic and real video data show robust performance of the proposed algorithm in terms of its reconstruction quality even with errors in the estimated motion.

1. INTRODUCTION

In imaging devices and applications, we often have to deal with degraded low resolution (LR) images due to because of the theoretical and practical limits of imaging devices. In visual surveillance and satellite imaging systems, certain regions of interest in the input video must be magnified for more detailed analyses. However, it is difficult to obtain satisfactory images using conventional image zooming techniques and the interpolation methods. Expensive imaging devices capable of capturing images of higher resolution or higher quality may not be desirable for higher cost.

Nowadays, the super resolution (SR) algorithm has been considered one of the most promising methods to overcome the limits of imaging devices since it does not induce any additional expensive hardware. The SR algorithm is an image processing technique that can recover an HR image from multiple LR images.

Researchers have investigated a variety of SR approaches over the past last two decades in an attempt to achieve better image reconstruction results [1, 2]. SR algorithms can be divided into two broad categories. The first is *motion-based* SR which considers movement between the LR image frames as a cue [3, 4, 5, 6, 7, 8, 9]. By making certain assumptions in the image acquisition model, this approach becomes straightforward and easy to implement. In this scheme, however, precise motion estimation and compensation are very important to reconstruct the HR image. Since the estimation of complex motions of multiple objects in LR video is difficult and time-consuming, new approaches have recently been developed to avoid the high dependency of motion-based SR on accurate motion estimation [10, 11, 12, 13, 14]. These approaches constitute the second category of SR algorithms and are referred to as *motion-free* SR [15]. Instead of directly estimating the motion, motion-free SR obtains spatial enhancement by incorporating cues such as blur.

Among the various motion-free SR approaches, the example-based SR algorithm [11] is one of the most promising methods. This method involves the concept of prior information to reconstruct HR image. They use learned data sets of image patches capturing the relationship between LR and HR images and find appropriate patches for estimating an HR image. However, because a large amount of training data is required to obtain a robust reconstruction results, example- or learning-based SR incurs an enormous computational load.

Daniel et al. [12] tried to handle this problem by combining the motion-based SR and example-based SR. Based on an assumption that patches in a single natural image tend to recur many times in an image, their approach uses LR/HR pairs of patches within and across the scales of a single image. However, the quality of the reconstructed image still depends on the accuracy of motion estimation when compensating motions of the patches. In addition, the desired LR/HR pairs of patches might be insufficient when the observed image is small or severely degraded. This makes it hard to apply their approach to practical applications such as video surveillance systems.

For the point of view of estimation criteria, SR algorithms may be divided into *static* and *dynamic* SR [8]. Static SR fuses multiple LR images to reconstruct a single HR image at a specific time point, while dynamic SR exploits the temporal evolution which reconstructs the HR image sequence. Dynamic SR requires relatively lower memory and numbers of computations than static SR, and is therefore regarded as being a more appropriate approach for real-time applications.

In this article, we propose a robust dynamic motion-based SR algorithm for LR video input. Our approach iteratively fuses the pixel data from an LR image sequence to estimate the pixel data of the HR image sequence based on the Kalman recursive estimation [8]. To deal with the performance degradation because of the inexplicit motion estimation, we suggest a validation process to filter out the irregularly registered pixels caused by inaccurate motion estimation. By implementing the proposed validation method, our SR approach was able to show robust HR image reconstruction results, even when the motion estimates were not accurate at the sub-pixel level. Moreover, abrupt changes in the scene input video can be detected in this validation process, so the fusion of pixels from two different scenes can be prevented. Since the quality of the reconstructed images is stable even with inaccurate motion estimation with low memory usage (requires only two frame memory) because of the sequential estimation, and each updated HR frame can be viewed during the estimation process, our approach is suitable for practical applications, especially in visual surveillance systems.

The remainder of this article is structured as follows. In Section 2, we describe the image acquisition modeling and basic concept of the dynamic SR process using the Kalman filter framework. In Section 3, we describe the proposed validation method for observed image data, and in Section 4 the scene change detection process developed for the robust sequential estimation of HR video has been described. In Section 5, we demonstrate both synthetic and real real-data experiments. Section 6 concludes this effort and discusses future study.

2. DYNAMIC SR

In this section, we review the dynamic SR approach proposed in [8], which is based on the Kalman recursive estimation. The main contribution of our approach will be described in Sections 3 and 4.

2.1. Image acquisition modeling

Among the many different image acquisition models, the following linear dynamic model is the most general and well represents the process of obtaining an LR image sequence:

$$\underline{X}(t) = M(t)\underline{X}(t-1) + \underline{U}(t), \tag{1}$$

$$\underline{Y}(t) = DB\underline{X}(t) + \underline{W}(t). \tag{2}$$

We used the underscore notation to indicate a vector derived from an image scanned in lexicographic order [8]. Thus, the HR frame at time t, $X(t)$ with a size of $[r^2MN \times 1]$ is the warped version of the previous HR frame where r is the resolution-enhancement factor, since $M(t)$ with a size of $[r^2MN \times r^2MN]$, indicates the existing motions between the two neighboring frames. The $[r^2MN \times 1]$ vector, $U(t)$, can be explained as the system noise that represents the accuracy of the motion estimation. In Equation 2, $Y(t)$

with a size of $[MN \times 1]$ is the observed LR image at time t, and the $[r^2MN \times r^2MN]$ matrix, B, describes the blur operations resulting from the sensor's point spread function. The $[MN \times r^2MN]$ matrix, D, reflects the downsample operation in the image acquisition and saving. The $[MN \times 1]$ vector $W(t)$ is the measurement noise.

To apply Kalman filtering for estimating X from Y, we constrain the model with the following assumptions:

1) Only translational (planar) motion is considered in the input video.

2) The blur and downsampling operation are invariant in time. This is why there are no time indices in B and D.

3) Both the system and measurement noise are assumed to be additive white Gaussian noise.

By substituting $Z(t) = B\,X(t)$, we first estimate the *blurred version* of the HR image, $Z(t)$, with a size of $[r^2MN \times 1]$ and then deblur it to obtain the final clear HR image, $X(t)$. The following two equations reflect the changes resulting from incorporating the blurred operation B to generate the measurement$Z(t)$ into Equations 1 and 2, where the $[r^2MN \times 1]$ vector $V(t)$ is the colored version of the measurement noise $U(t)$:

$$\underline{Z}(t) = M(t)\underline{Z}(t-1) + \underline{V}(t), \tag{3}$$

$$\underline{Y}(t) = D\underline{Z}(t) + \underline{W}(t). \tag{4}$$

2.2. Kalman recursive for data fusion

Kalman filtering is the optimal method of estimating the dynamic state in linear modeling as described above [16]. The state to be estimated is the blurred HR image, i.e., $Z(t)$. By means of the Kalman filtering theories [16, 17], the *update* equations for the state vector and covariance matrix can be derived as follows:

$$\begin{aligned}\hat{\underline{Z}}(t) &= \underbrace{\hat{\underline{Z}}^M(t)}_{prediction} + \underbrace{K(t)}_{gain}\underbrace{[\underline{Y}(t) - D\hat{\underline{Z}}^M(t)]}_{innovation} \\ &= M(t)\hat{\underline{Z}}(t-1) + K(t)[\underline{Y}(t) - DM(t)\hat{\underline{Z}}(t-1)],\end{aligned} \tag{5}$$

$$\begin{aligned}\mathrm{Cov}(\hat{\underline{Z}}(t)) &= \underbrace{P(t)}_{prediction} - K(t)\underbrace{S(t)}_{innovation}K^T(t) \\ &= [\mathbf{I} - K(t)D]P(t),\end{aligned} \tag{6}$$

$$\begin{aligned}K(t) &= P(t)D^T S^{-1}(t) \\ &= P(t)D^T[DP(t)D^T + C_w(t)]^{-1},\end{aligned} \tag{7}$$

where $\hat{\underline{Z}}(t)$ denotes the estimated state vector, i.e., the blurred HR image. Equation 5 indicates that the final estimate of the blurred HR image is the sum of the *prediction* $\hat{\underline{Z}}^M(t)$ (i.e., motion compensated version of the previous estimate, $M(t)\hat{\underline{Z}}(t-1)$ and *innovation* or *measurement residual* (i.e., the difference between the new observation, $Y(t)$, and prediction) multiplied by $K(t)$, which is the *Kalman gain* defined as the ratio of the *prediction covariance* $P(t)$ to the *innovation covariance* $S(t)$. Analogously, the updated covariance of $\hat{\underline{Z}}(t)$ can be derived as in Equation 6.

The procedures used to compute $P(t)$ and $S(t)$ are shown in Equations 8 and 9, respectively. The prediction covariance $P(t)$ in Equation 8 reflects the accuracy of the prediction for original HR image, $\hat{\underline{Z}}^M(t)$. The innovation covariance $S(t)$ in Equation 9 reflects the accuracy of prediction for an LR observation image, $D\hat{\underline{Z}}^M(t)$.

$$\begin{aligned}P(t) &= E\{[\underline{Z}(t) - \hat{\underline{Z}}^M(t)][\underline{Z}(t) - \hat{\underline{Z}}^M(t)]^T\} \\ &= M(t)\mathrm{Cov}(\hat{\underline{Z}}(t-1))M^T(t) + C_v(t),\end{aligned} \tag{8}$$

$$\begin{aligned}S(t) &= E\{[\underline{Y}(t) - D\hat{\underline{Z}}^M(t)][\underline{Y}(t) - D\hat{\underline{Z}}^M(t)]^T\} \\ &= DP(t)D^T + C_w(t).\end{aligned} \tag{9}$$

Since the inversion of the covariance matrix in Equation 7 is very cumbersome and requires substantial computation and memory, further assumptions are needed to achieve a faster implementation. As proven in [8], if the covariance matrix of $V(t)$ denoted as $C_v(t)$ and the initial covariance $\mathrm{Cov}(\dot{\underline{Z}}(0))$ are *diagonal*, *P*(*t*) and $\mathrm{Cov}(\dot{\underline{Z}}(t))$ become diagonal for all *t*. This enables a pixel-by-pixel implementation, so all of the procedures from Equations 1 to 9 can be computed as a single scalar value (i.e., single pixel). A more detailed description can be found in [8].

Once the covariances of the noise components $C_w(t)$, $C_v(t)$, and $\mathrm{Cov}(\dot{\underline{Z}}(0))$ are initialized at time t = 0, they are used to calculate *P*(*t*), *S*(*t*), and *K*(*t*). After *K*(*t*) is calculated, the estimation of the HR image $\dot{\underline{Z}}(t)$ and its covariance $\mathrm{Cov}(\dot{\underline{Z}}(t))$ is calculated recursively by the Kalman filter*update* equations in Equations 5 and 6. Since all of the covariance matrices are diagonal, we can convert them into general image matrices (not lexicographic ordered) to compute the Kalman gain on a pixel-by-pixel basis. The graphical procedures of Equations 7-9 are illustrated in Figure 1. The additions, multiplication, and inversion in Figure 1 are element-wise operations. Only *MN* elements of*K*(*t*) have non-zero values, because of the up-sampling (zero-filling) of the innovation covariance,*S*(*t*). This means that only *MN* pixels are updated in Equation 5 when the new input image frame *Y*(*t*) is measured.

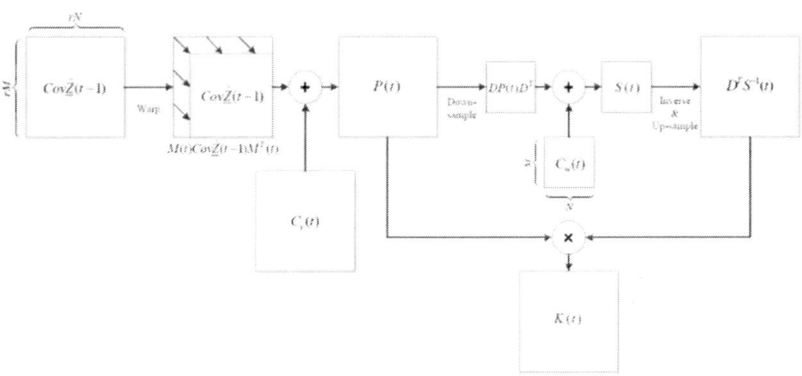

Figure 1. Graphical illustration of computing Kalman gain.

To estimate and compensate the motions existing among the input frames modeled by *M*(*t*), we adopt the image registration method in frequency-domain [18] since it is simple and accurate for translational motions. It estimates the horizontal and vertical shifts in spatial domain by computing the phase shift in the frequency domain. Moreover, the frequency-domain approach benefits when the aliasing effect exists in input LR frames.

To handle color video input, we apply the same Kalman filtering process to each RGB channel. Once the blurred HR image, $\hat{\underline{Z}}(t)$, is estimated, the final clear HR image, $\hat{\underline{X}}(t)$, is reconstructed by the deblurring method. The flow chart of the conventional dynamic SR algorithm is illustrated in Figure 2.

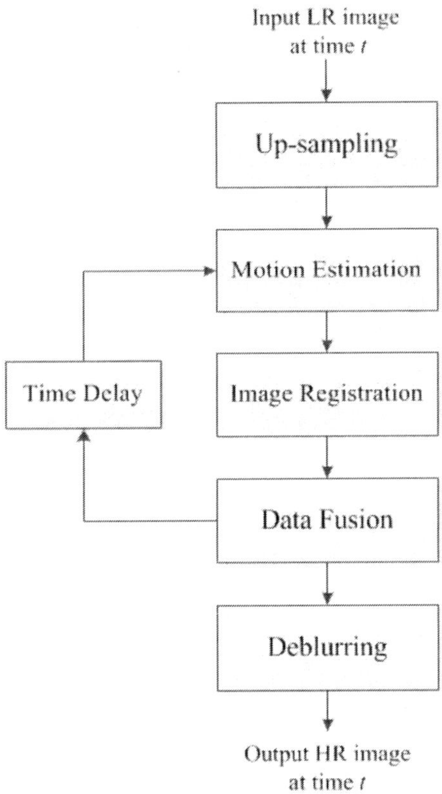

Figure 2. Flow chart of conventional dynamic SR algorithm.

3. MEASUREMENT VALIDATION

Explicit motion estimation is a major factor that affects the performance of the motion-based SR algorithm as mentioned in [13, 14]. Various research efforts have been dedicated to enable precise (sub-pixel accuracy) motion estimation; however, the methods developed are insufficient to guarantee perfect motion compensation and, even though perfect motion estimation is potentially possible, it usually requires a large amount of computation.

Some novel approaches not involving accurate motion estimation were recently suggested in [10, 11,12, 13, 14], but they are not suitable for practical real-time surveillance system applications because of their computation requirements. In this article, we added a validation method in the sequential estimation process to enhance erroneous reconstructed HR images caused by inexplicit motion estimations.

When the motion estimation result is inaccurate (i.e., the reference and target frames are misaligned), the difference in the pixel intensity between the two corresponding frames will be increased as depicted in Figure 3. With the dynamic linear modeling described in Section 2, this difference in the pixel intensity can be represented by the distance in Equation 10:

$$d^2(t) = [\underline{Y}(t) - D\hat{\underline{Z}}^{M}(t)]^{T} S^{-1}(t)[\underline{Y}(t) - D\hat{\underline{Z}}^{M}(t)]. \tag{10}$$

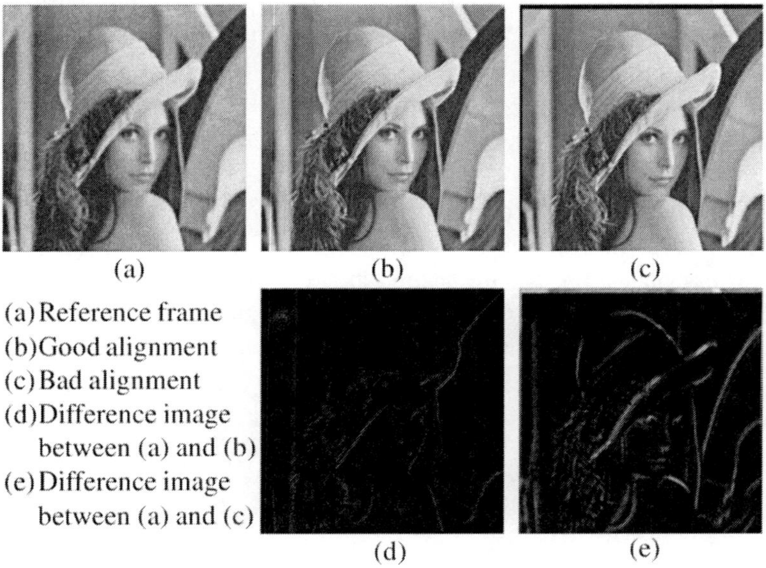

Figure 3. Pixel intensity difference increases when misalignment occurs.

$$d^2(t) = \sum_{k=1}^{MN} d_k^2,$$

$$\text{where } d_k^2(t) = [y_k(t) - D_k\hat{\underline{Z}}^M(t)]^T S_k^{-1}(t)[y_k(t) - D_k\hat{\underline{Z}}^M(t)] \quad (11)$$

Since we assume that all covariance matrices including $S(t)$ are diagonal, computing the distance of one measured frame at time t, $d(t)$ which is referred to as the *'Mahalanobis distance'* or *'Statistical distance'*, is the same as computing the sum of the distances of each pixel in that frame, $d_k(t)$, in Equation 11. $y_k(t)$ is the k th pixel in a measured frame $Y(t)$ and $S_k(t)$ is the k th diagonal element of$S(t)$. D_k is the k th row of the downsampling operator D size of $[1 \times r^2 MN]$.

When the Kalman filter has at least been initialized and the state vector is being estimated, the true observation at time t, given the measurements $Y^{t-1} = \{Y(1), \cdots, Y(t-1)\}$,, is normally distributed.

$$p[\underline{Y}(t)|\underline{Y}^{t-1}] = N[D\hat{\underline{Z}}^M(t), S(t)]. \quad (12)$$

$Y(t)$ in Equation 12 is the measurement at time t and $Y^{t-1}$is the sequence of measurements from the initial time to time t - 1. Thus, Equation 12 represents that the conditional probability of $Y(t)$ given the measurements up to time t - 1, namely $Y^{t-1}$is normally distributed with the mean equal to the predicted measurement $D\hat{\underline{Z}}^M(t)$ and the covariance equal to the innovation covariance $S(t)$. The theoretical description for this can be found in the sections on the Kalman filter in [16, 17].

In the proposed SR algorithm, we attempt to detect any *'misalignment'* at the pixel level but not at the frame level, meaning that we want to exclude only those pixels that are misaligned in the measured frame, not all of the pixels in the measured frame that are misaligned. By incorporating the concept from [17] and from the ideas of the validation methods or data association for target tracking field in [19, 20], we may define a *validation region* $V(\gamma)$ for a measured pixel as in Equation 13:

$$V(\gamma) = \{y_k(t) : d_k^2(t) \leq \gamma\}, \quad k = 1, 2, \ldots, MN. \quad (13)$$

By fixing the threshold γ at all times for every pixel, the validation region $V(\gamma)$ is dependent only on the threshold γ, but not on the time t or pixel index k. Whenever the pixel data from the input LR image at each time instant (i.e., $y_k(t)$ for all k) are observed, we compute each distance $d_k(t)$ in Equation 11 and filter out the pixels falling out of the region in Equation 13. In other words, only those pixels whose distance is below the threshold are considered *valid*. So, this procedure regards the pixels that lie outside of the validation region as outliers, i.e., misaligned, hence they are excluded from the data fusion process. This is the so-called *'Measurement Validation'* method and it is applied right before the pixel data fusion process in Equations 5 and 6 in our SR approach illustrated in Figure 4.

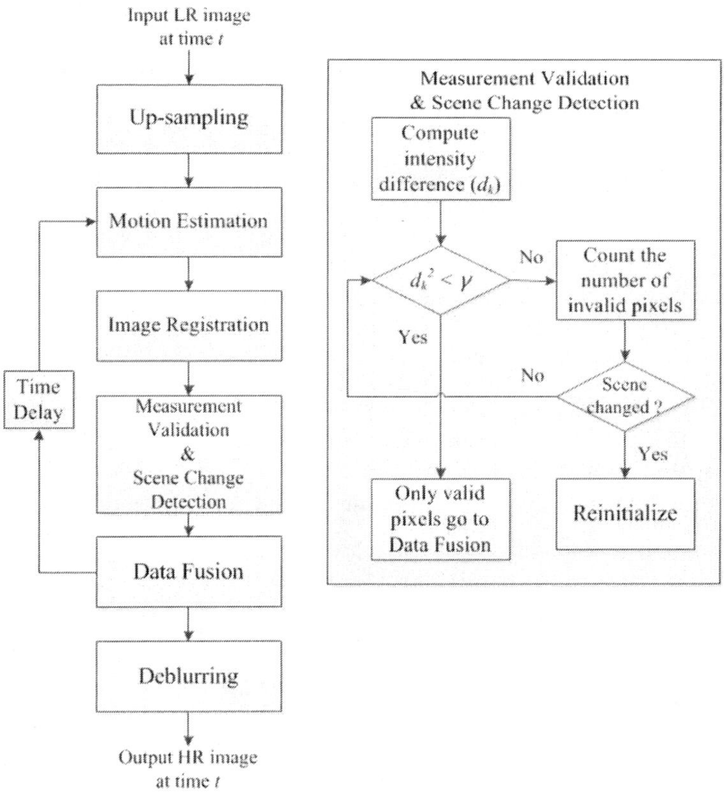

Figure 4. The flow chart of the proposed dynamic SR algorithm.

As represented in Equations 5 and 6, $K(t)$ determines the amount of updates required for estimating $\dot{\underline{z}}(t)$ and $Cov(\dot{\underline{Z}}(t))$. In the proposed measurement validation method, only valid pixel values should be used in the update equations. When $K(t)$ is equal to zero, no updates will be made in Equations 5 and 6, thus the estimations for $\dot{\underline{Z}}(t)$ and $\mathrm{Cov}(\dot{\underline{Z}}(t))$ are only dependent on the prediction terms. In our implementation, after the new measurement is obtained, i.e., *MN* pixels are observed at time *t*, each pixel is investigated to determine whether or not it falls inside the validation region in Equation 13. After we determine the misaligned pixels among *MN* pixels, we can prevent them from being used in the update equations by setting those elements of *K*(*t*), whose indices correspond to the indices of misaligned pixels, to zero.

Under the Gaussian assumption, the validation region *V*(γ) is *chi-square* distributed with the number of degrees of freedom equal to the dimension of the measurement. The chi-square distribution table gives the probability mass:

$$P(\gamma) = p\{y_k(t) \in V(\gamma)\}, \quad k = 1, 2, \ldots, MN. \tag{14}$$

P(γ) is the probability that the measurement will fall inside the validation region for various values of γ and dimensions of $y_k(t)$. Since the degree of freedom (DoF) for a single pixel is one, we can select the threshold γ in Table 1. Therefore, we can control the range of the valid region by varying the threshold value, γ, obtained from the chi-square table for the desired confidence level [17]. For example, if we set γ to 2.71,[a] the probability that the measurement falls inside of the validation region will be 90%. In the proposed method, the threshold is set to 15.1 which means that there is a 99.99% chance that d2k(t)$d_k^2(t)$ will be less than or equal to 15.1. So, the threshold value is not directly related to the image dynamic range, but to the range of the statistical distance of the image pixel. The bigger the threshold that is selected, the wider the validation region. In other words, the probability that the measured pixels are determined as misaligned will decrease as the threshold becomes larger.

Table 1. Chi-square distribution table

DoF	*P* = 0.9	*P* = 0.99	*P* = 0.999	*P* = 0.9999
1	2.71	6.63	10.8	15.1
2	4.61	9.21	13.8	18.4
10	16.0	23.2	29.6	35.6
100	118	136	149	161

4. SCENE CHANGE DETECTION

Since the dynamic SR algorithm recursively fuses the pixel data from the sequentially observed images, it is highly likely for an erroneous HR estimation result to occur when the scene or contents of two adjacent frames are totally different. This problem arises frequently when the input LR video contains many different scenes or the motions in it are too large to be estimated. There is no possible motion between different frames from different scenes and, hence, these frames can never be aligned correctly. Even though the measurement validation method can detect and filter out misaligned pixels, fusing pixels from two different scenes is not a desired situation.

Instead of applying one of the conventional scene change detection methods [21, 22], we suggest a simple but effective way to detect a sudden change of scene in the input LR video by exploiting the statistical distance already discussed in the previous section.

The proposed method detects abrupt scene changes between adjacent frames by computing the proportion of invalid pixels with respect to the total number of pixels in the observed LR frame of size [$M \times N$]:

$$\frac{1}{MN}\sum_{k=1}^{MN} I(d_k(t)) \geq Th, \text{ where } I(d_k(t)) = \begin{cases} 1 & \text{if } d_k^2(t) > \gamma, \\ 0 & \text{otherwise.} \end{cases} \tag{15}$$

In this article, we set the threshold value, *Th* to 0.3, which means that about 30% of the pixels from the current input LR frame are different from those of the previous frame. This threshold value is determined experimentally with more than ten real video data containing scene changes. If a sudden scene change is detected with this method, we reset the estimation process (i.e., reinitialize the Kalman filter). The procedure is summarized in Figure 4.

5. EXPERIMENTAL RESULTS

We evaluated the performance of the proposed dynamic SR algorithm with synthetic and real video data. The threshold for measurement validation was set to 15.1 for all experiments, which represents that a confidence probability of 99.99% according to the chi-square distribution table. For the deblurring method in the last step of the proposed SR algorithm, we used the classical but effective*Wiener filter* approach with a constant noise-to-signal ratio (NSR) to reduce the computation complexity. The parameter NSR for the Wiener filter was tuned to obtain the best performance in all experiments.

5.1. Synthetic video data test

In this experiment, we tested the proposed algorithm with synthetic LR video data. We generated LR color videos by simulating the image acquisition procedure described in Section 2.1. The test video in Figure 5 was downloaded from the website of the author in [8][b] and the test videos in Figures 6 and 7were captured by a commercial surveillance camera, SHC-730N, courtesy of Samsung Techwin Co., Ltd., Korea. We downsampled the original videos by a factor of two after blurring them with a 3 × 3 Gaussian kernel whose variance was equal to 1. Finally, we generated LR videos by adding Gaussian noise to achieve its signal-to-noise ratio (SNR) of 30 dB. The size of all three LR videos was 160 × 120 and they contained only global translational motions. The test LR videos are super-resolved by a factor of two through the proposed algorithm and the method in [8].

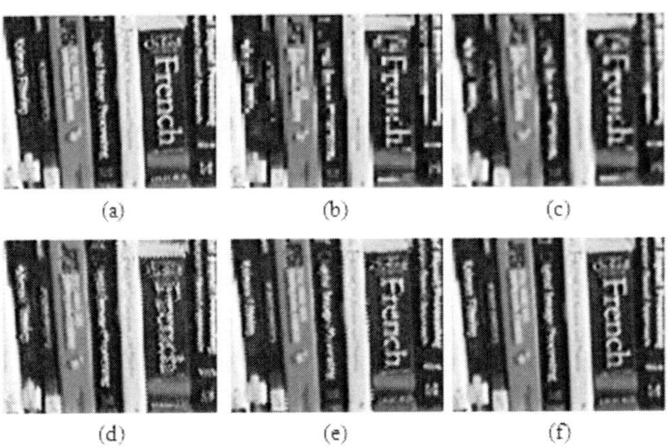

Figure 5. The synthetic webcam video data result**: (a)** Original frame. **(b)** LR frame. **(c)** Bicubic interpolated frame. **(d)** Reconstructed HR frames by applying the method in [8] with the image registration algorithm in [23]. **(e)** Reconstructed HR frames by applying the method in [8] with the image registration algorithm in [18]. **(f)** Reconstructed HR frames by applying the proposed method.

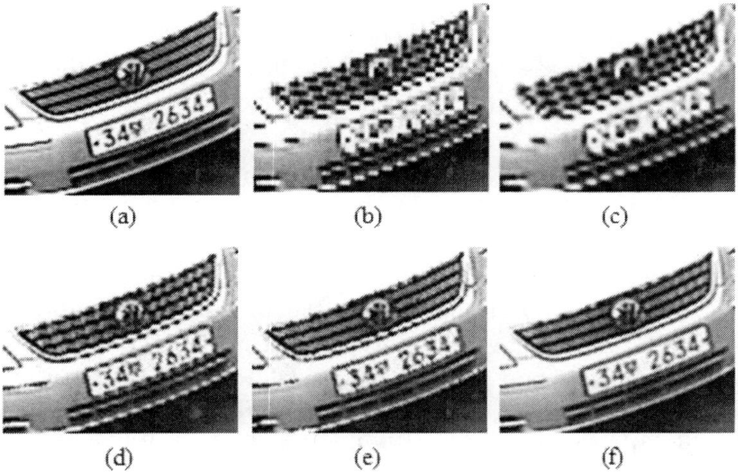

Figure 6. The synthetic surveillance video data result**:** **(a)** Original frame. **(b)** LR frame. **(c)** Bicubic interpolated frame. **(d)** Reconstructed HR frames by applying the method in [8] with the image registration algorithm in [23]. **(e)** Reconstructed HR frames by applying the method in [8] with the image registration algorithm in [18]. **(f)** Reconstructed HR frames by applying the proposed method.

The method in [8] was implemented directly from the MATLAB GUI (http://users.soe.ucsc.edu/~milanfar/software/superresolution.html). According to [8], they used the image registration algorithm in [23] which is different from the algorithm we exploited. As mentioned in the earlier sections and previous related studies, the major factor contributing to the reconstruction image result of the multi-frame SR algorithm is the accuracy of the image registration. Thus, if a different image registration algorithm is used in the reference method, we cannot say that the improved HR image result is completely because of the proposed measurement validation. For a fair comparison, we also implemented the method in [8] using the frequency-domain image registration algorithm [18] which is used in the proposed method. Therefore, we compared the proposed method with two reference methods, one from the author's website and the other from our own implementation by modifying the image registration part. In addition, we applied the Wiener filter to the method in [8], instead of the bilateral-total variation (BTV) regularization to see the effect of the measurement validation only. The quality of the reconstructed HR image is evaluated quantitatively with the PSNR[c] (Peak SNR) metric.

We enlarged the 100 × 80 sections of the original, simulated LR, bicubic interpolated, and reconstructed video frames for better visual quality evaluation. The images in Figure 5 are the 90th frames and the images in Figure 6 are the 60th frames of each input video. In the reconstructed HR frames in Figures 5 and 6, there are some artifacts because of the motion estimation error, such as periodic teeth along horizontal and vertical lines or stair-case phenomena along diagonal lines. The motion estimation error may become large when the size of an image is too small, or the motion is too large. Because the only difference between the methods in Figure 5d,e is the image registration algorithm, the slightly better quality of Figure 5e can be attributed to the better performance of the algorithm in [18]. As shown in Figures 5f and 6f, the image quality of the HR result with the proposed method is enhanced more than the results in Figures 5e and 6e. The corresponding PSNR values are listed in Table 2. When compared to the results obtained with the method in [8], the jaggedness of the edges and corners is substantially reduced. Even though the same image registration algorithm was used for the results in Figure 5e,f, the result obtained with the proposed method is visually superior. This demonstrates the effectiveness of the proposed measurement validation method. Analogously, the same analysis can be applied to the results in Figure 6.

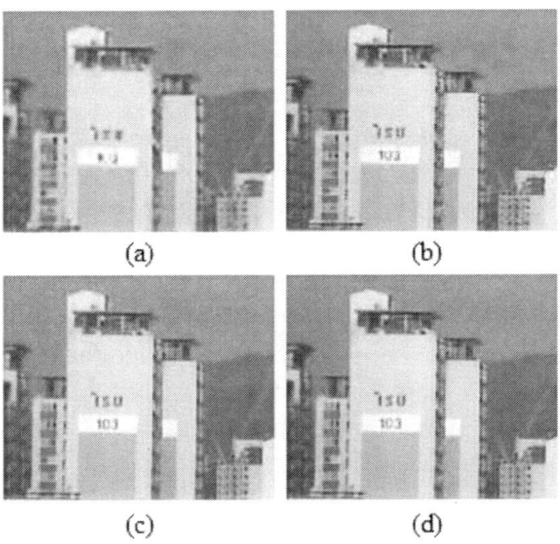

Figure 7. The synthetic video data result: **(a)** Bicubic interpolated frame. **(b)** Reconstructed 90th HR frame using the method in [8, 23]. **(c)** Reconstructed 90th HR frame using the method in [8, 18]. **(d)**Reconstructed 90th HR frame using the proposed method. The PSNR are 19.91, 21.09, 23.94, and 24.02 dB, respectively.

Table 2. PSNR of experiment in Figures 5 and 6.

Output size	Bicubic interpolation	Farsiu [8] + [21](without MV)	Farsiu [8] + [17](without MV)	Proposed (with MV)
320 × 240	5(c), 19.44 dB	5(d), 19.33 dB	5(e), 18.84 dB	5(f), 23.95 dB
	6(c), 19.79 dB	6(d), 20.98 dB	6(e), 21.56 dB	6(f), 24.73 dB

In the experiment corresponding to the results in Figure 7, we enhanced the spatial resolution of the LR video by a factor of two. In Figure 7, only 160 × 130 zoomed sections of the results are depicted. There is little difference in performance between the results obtained with and without the measurement validation (Figure 7c,d, respectively) because the image registration was quite accurate. To test the performance of the measurement validation, we intentionally added alignment errors to the aligned LR frames beyond the 60th frame. The HR image at the 90th frame without the measurement validation in Figure 8a was significantly degraded because of the registration errors. On the contrary, the resulting HR image obtained with the measurement validation was less affected by the registration errors as shown in Figure 8b. In Figure 8c, one can see that the number of misaligned pixels determined by the threshold in Equation 13 increases after the 60th frame. This tells us that the measurement validation method becomes more effective when a large amount of image registration errors occurs.

5.2. Real video data test

In the next experiment, our algorithm is evaluated with real video data captured by a surveillance camera, courtesy of Adyoron Intelligent Systems Ltd., Tel Aviv, Israel. We increased the spatial resolution of the real LR video by a factor of two in the vertical and horizontal directions. The input size of the video frame was 138 × 115 and, therefore, the resulting size of the reconstructed video frame is 276 × 230, as shown in Figure 9. Figure 9d demonstrates the superior performance of the proposed algorithm compared to the conventional methods in Figure 9b,c. Especially, the jagged edges because of the wrong translational motion estimation are clearly reduced in Figure 9c. This is the contribution of the measurement validation process.

In the case of a small input size, the effect of filtering misaligned pixels becomes more remarkable, as shown in the experimental results of Figure 10. In general, precise motion estimation is more difficult when the input image is small, since the number of pixels, i.e., *features* or *information* is insufficient to achieve a good alignment. The visual quality of the results without the measurement validation in Figure 10c,g is worse than the Bicubic interpolated results in Figure 10b,f.

Figure 8. The synthetic video data result**:** **(a)** Reconstructed 90th HR frame using the method without measurement validation. **(b)** Reconstructed 90th HR frame using the method with measurement validation. **(c)** The number of misaligned pixels for each frame. **We artificially added registration errors from the 60 to 90th frames**.

Assuming that a sufficient number of LR frames are available and the proper image registration algorithm is used for compensating the motions existing among the LR frames, multi-frame SR generally outperforms the single image interpolation method. In the extreme case where we do not register the LR frames at all, the estimated HR image result will be worse than the Bicubic interpolation result. However, if we apply the measurement validation while still not registering all LR frames, the HR image result will be almost the same as the initial estimated HR image since most of the unregistered LR pixels will be regarded as *invalid*. Thus, if we set the initial estimated HR image as the Bicubic interpolated one of the initial LR frames, the HR image result obtained with the proposed method cannot be worse than the Bicubic interpolation result even though most of the LR data are excluded.

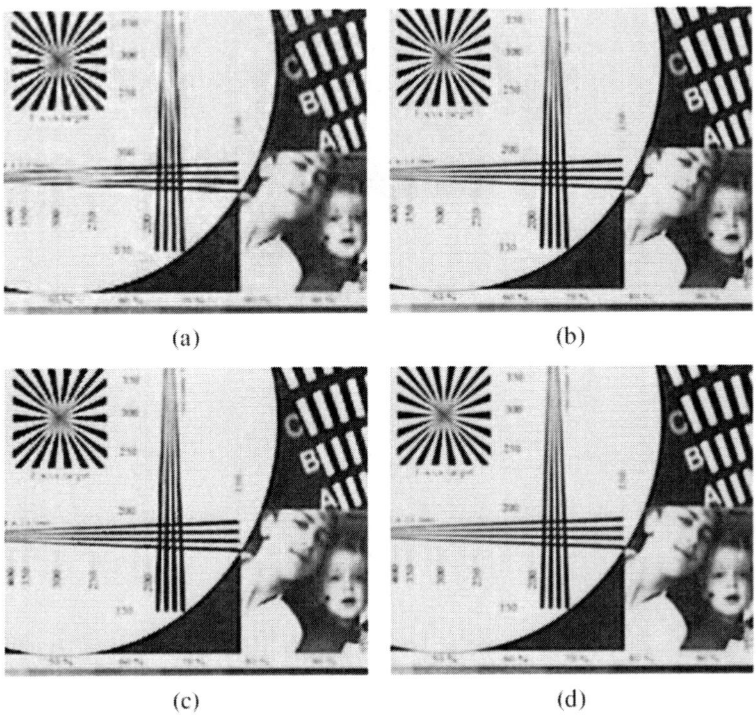

Figure 9. Real video data result**:** **(a)** Bicubic interpolated frame. **(b)** Reconstructed 40th HR frame using the method in [8, 23]. **(c)** Reconstructed 40th HR frame using the method in [8, 18]. **(d)** Reconstructed 40th HR frame using the proposed method. Note that the artifact because of misalignment around the edges are effectively removed in **(d)**.

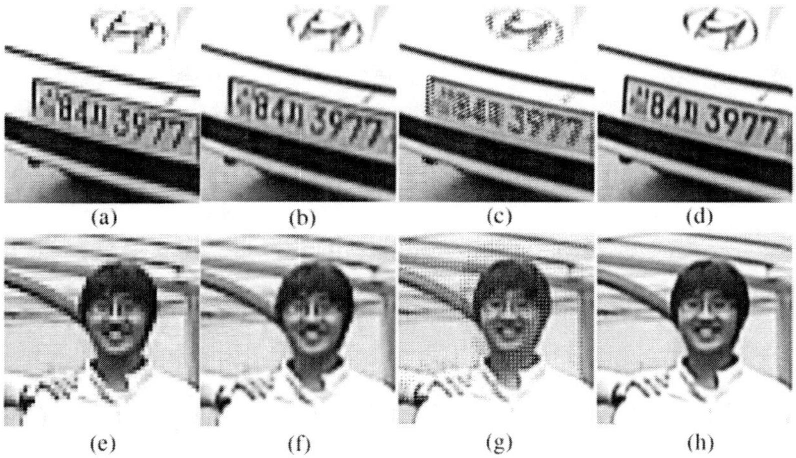

Figure 10. Small size real video data result**: (a, e)** 90th LR frames with sizess of 50 × 50. **(b, f)** Bicubic interpolated frames. **(c, g)** Super-resolved by a factor of four with the methods in [8, 23]. **(d, h)**Reconstructed frames using the proposed method.

If all of the frames are aligned perfectly or well enough to fall in the preset validation region, all of the measured pixel values will contribute to the HR image estimation process. The benefit of the measurement validation process is that it prevents the misaligned pixel values from contributing to the HR image estimation. By setting the confidence level for the image registration result (i.e., the threshold for the validation region), we can exclude undesired updates of the pixel values. Thus, it becomes more beneficial when there is a higher possibility of misalignment because of the poor performance of the image registration algorithm or because of the existence of LR frames with fast motion. This is the reason why the results obtained with the proposed method in Figure 10d,h show more robust performance when large motion estimation errors occur frequently.

5.3. Scene change detection performance test

In this experiment, we evaluate the proposed scene change detection method. We created LR videos containing four different scenes. The input size is 50 × 50 and the spatial resolution ratio was increased by a factor of four. The upper images in Figure 11 are 30 frames after the scene change occurred without using the proposed scene change detection method. When the incoming frames are different from the previously reconstructed frame, two different scenes are overlapped with each other. This artifact can easily be addressed by resetting the SR process when the current input frame belongs to a different scene. In this case, most of the pixels from the changed scene will be considered as invalid ones by the proposed measurement validation method. Consequently, the ratio of invalid pixels will cross the preset threshold with high probability.

Figure 11. Effect of scene change detection method: **(a-c)** 120, 270, and 390th reconstructed frames without the scene change detection method, respectively. **(d-f)** Well-reconstructed frames exploiting proposed scene change detection method.

The lower images in Figure 11 are the reconstructed frames at the same time instant as the upper ones. The scene change was detected when the ratio of invalid pixels is below the threshold value, *Th*, in Equation 15 which was set to 0.3; hence, the SR process was reinitialized. The artifact in Figure 11a-c is eliminated by fusing the pixel data from the same scene. In Figure 12, the blue line represents the number of invalid pixels for the input video frames and the red line is the preset threshold. The scene changes abruptly three times at frames #91, #241, and #361.

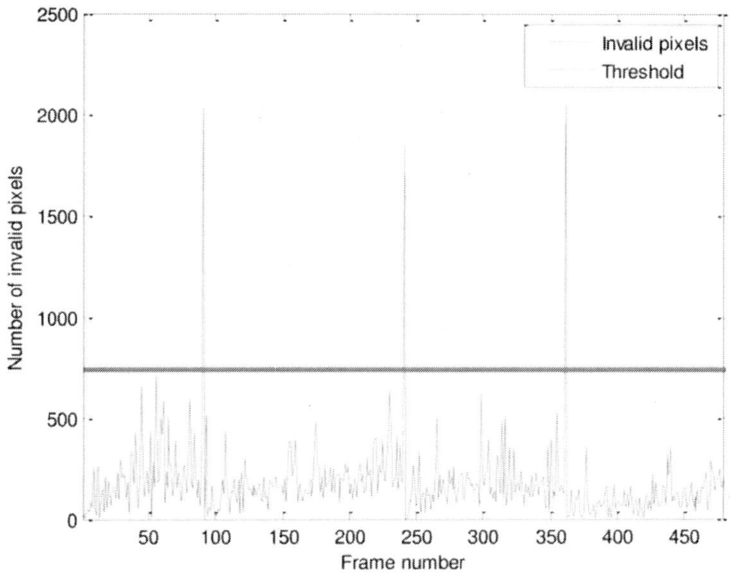

Figure 12. Invalid pixels of each input frame**.** Scene changes occurr at the 90, 241, and 361th frames.

6. CONCLUSIONS

In this article, we proposed a robust dynamic SR algorithm to alleviate the performance degradation because of inaccurate motion estimation and sudden scene changes. We adopted the dynamic SR algorithm based on the Kalman filter approach, because of its effectiveness when applied to real-time applications. When the size of the output super-resolved image is about 200 × 200, the proposed dynamic SR algorithm estimates the HR images sequentially at a speed of over 20 fps while necessitating a memory size corresponding to only two frames.

In the case of misalignment caused by motion estimation error, the proposed measurement validation method determines whether each of the pixels is suitable for data fusion or not with the statistical distance of intensity. It is preferable to set the pixels with a large distance as invalid and filter them out after the estimation process enters the steady state. Otherwise, the estimated HR pixels tend to remain the same as the previous LR pixel since every input pixel with a large intensity difference would be filtered out and, hence, the update process in Kalman filtering would be prevented. The starting point of the measurement validation and the appropriate threshold remain as an ongoing research topic.

In addition, we developed a scene change detection method to handle various input videos containing one or more scene changes. By virtue of the proposed scene change detection method, we can handle input video containing more than one scene. Adaptive threshold setting for the scene change detection method is preferable for robust detection performance, and so this remains as a future study. Throughout this study, we fixed, defined a relatively large validation region, $V(\gamma)$, whose threshold is equal to 15.1, because we assumed that the image registration algorithm performs well enough to align most of the LR frames correctly. If we can predict the accuracy of image registration, we can control the validation region by varying the threshold, γ.

As shown in the several representative experiments, a considerable degree of enhancement and the restoration of the deteriorated visual information can be achieved by the proposed SR algorithm. Especially, for input images of small size, such as human face and license plate images, the proposed SR algorithm is appropriate for real-time visual surveillance applications considering the processing speed and the visual quality of the reconstructed image.

ENDNOTES

[a]The threshold value has no digital unit since $d(t)$ is a normalized random variable (i.e., statistical distance). [b]The test video can be downloaded from http://users.soe.ucsc.edu/~milanfar/software/sr-datasets.html. [c]The PSNR of two images $\underline{X}$ and $\underline{Y}$ of size M by N is defined as $\mathrm{PSNR(dB)} = 10\log_{10}((255^2 \times MN)/\|\underline{X}-\underline{Y}\|_2^2)$.

ACKNOWLEDGEMENTS

This research was supported by the Seoul R&BD Program (WR080951).

REFERENCES

1. Park SC, Park MK, Kang MG: **Super-resolution image reconstruction: a technical overview.** *IEEE Signal Proc. Mag* 2003,**20**(3):21-36.

2. Elad M, Feuer A: **Restoration of a single superresolution image from several blurred, noisy, and undersampled measured images.** *IEEE Trans. Image Process* 1997,**6**(12):1646-1658.

3. Elad M, Hel-Or Y: **A fast super-resolution reconstruction algorithm for pure translational motion and common space-invariant blur.** *IEEE Trans. Image Process* 2001,**10**(8):1187-1193

4. Farsiu S, Robinson D, Elad M, Milanfar P: **Fast and robust multiframe super resolution.** *IEEE Trans. Image Process* 2004,**13**(10):1327-1344.

5. Elad M: **A fast super-resolution reconstruction algorithm for pure translational motion and common space-invariant blur.** *IEEE Trans. Image Process* 2001,**10**(8):1187-1193.

6. Farsiu S, Elad M, Milanfar P: **Multiframe demosaicing and super-resolution of color images.** *IEEE Trans. Image Process* 2006,**15**(1):141-159.

7. Elad M, Feuer A: **Super-resolution reconstruction of image sequences.** *IEEE Trans. Pattern Anal. Mach. Intell* 1999,**21**(9):817-834.

8. Farsiu S, Elad M, Milanfar P: **Video-to-video dynamic super-resolution for grayscale and color sequences.** *EURASIP J. Appl. Signal Process* 2006, 1-15. **Article ID 61859**

9. Narayanan B, Hardie RC, Barner KE, Shao M: **A computationally efficient super-resolution algorithm for video processing using partition filters.** *IEEE Trans. Circuits Syst. Video Technol* 2007,**17**(5):621-634.

10. Protter M, Elad M, Takeda H, Milanfar P: **Generalizing the nonlocal-means to super-resolution reconstruction.** *IEEE Trans. Image Process* 2009,**18**(1):36-51.

11. Freeman W, Jones T, Pasztor E: **Example-based super-resolution.** *Comput. Graph. Appl* 2002,**22**(2):56-65.

12. Glasner D, Bagon S, Irani M: **Super-resolution from a single image.** *International Conference on Computer Vision (ICCV)* 2009.

13. Protter M, Elad M: **Super resolution with probabilistic motion estimation.** *IEEE Trans. Image Process*2009,**18**(8):1899-1904.

14. Takeda H, Milanfar P, Protter M, Elad M: **Super-resolution without explicit subpixel motion estimation.** *IEEE Trans. Image Process* 2009,**18**(9):1958-1975.

15. Chaudhuri S, Manjunath J: *Motion-free Super-Resolution*. Springer; 2005.

16. Louis L: *Statistical Signal Processing*. Scharf, Addison-Wesley Pub. Co; 1991.

17. Bar-Shalom Y, Fortmann TE: *Tracking and Data Association*. Academic Press, Inc; 1988.

18. Vandewalle P, Susstrunk S, Vetterli M: **A frequency domain approach to registration of aliased images with application to super-resolution.** *EURASIP J. Appl. Signal Process* 2006, 1-14. Article ID 71459

19. Ku BH, Lee YH, Hong WY, Ko H: **Suppressing ghost targets via gating and tracking history in Y-shaped passive linear array sonars.** *IEEE Trans. AES* 2011,**47**(3):1605-1616.

20. Ko H, Lee IK, Lee JH, Han D: **Effective multi-vehicle tracking in nighttime condition using imaging sensors.** *IEICE Trans-Inform. Syst* 2003,**E86-D**(9):1887-1895.

21. El-Qawasmeh E: **Scene change detection schemes for video indexing in uncompressed domain.***Informatica* 2003,**14**(1):19-36.

22. Ngo C, Pong T, Chin R, Zhang H: **Motion-based video representation for scene change detection.** *Int. J. Comput. Vis* 2002,**50**(2):127-142.

23. Bergen JR, Anandan P, Hanna KJ, Hingorani R: **Hierarchical model-based motion estimation.***Proceedings of European Conference on Computer Vision (ECCV '92), 237-252., Santa Margherita Ligure, Italy* 1992.

Chapter 5

Adaptive dualISO HDR reconstruction

Saghi Hajisharif*, Joel Kronander and Jonas Unger

Linköping University, Norrköping, Sweden

ABSTRACT

With the development of modern image sensors enabling flexible image acquisition, single shot high dynamic range (HDR) imaging is becoming increasingly popular. In this work, we capture single shot HDR images using an imaging sensor with spatially varying gain/ISO. This allows all incoming photons to be used in the imaging. Previous methods on single shot HDR capture use spatially varying neutral density (ND) filters which lead to wasting incoming light. The main technical contribution in this work is an extension of previous HDR reconstruction approaches for single shot HDR imaging based on local polynomial approximations (Kronander et al., Unified HDR reconstruction from raw CFA data, 2013; Hajisharif et al., HDR reconstruction for alternating gain (ISO) sensor readout, 2014). Using a sensor noise model, these works deploy a statistically informed filtering operation to reconstruct HDR pixel values. However, instead of using a fixed filter size, we introduce two novel algorithms for adaptive filter kernel selection. Unlike a previous work, using adaptive filter kernels (Signal Process Image Commun 29(2):203–215, 2014), our algorithms are based on analyzing the model fit and the expected statistical deviation of the estimate based on the sensor noise model. Using an iterative procedure, we can then adapt the filter kernel according to the image structure and the statistical image noise. Experimental results show that the proposed filter de-noises the noisy image carefully while well preserving the important image features such as edges and corners, outperforming previous methods. To demonstrate the robustness of our approach, we have exploited input images from raw sensor data using a commercial off-the-shelf camera. To further analyze our algorithm, we have also implemented a camera simulator to evaluate different gain patterns and noise properties of the sensor.

KEYWORDS

HDR reconstruction, Single shot HDR, imaging, DualISO, Statistical image filtering

1. INTRODUCTION

The range of radiance intensities found in most real-world scenes, spanning from the sun or direct light sources to areas in shadow, typically exceeds, by orders of magnitude. It is very difficult to accurately capture this wide range using a digital sensor in a single image or video frame. This limitation has spurred the development of techniques for capture of *high dynamic range* (HDR) images and video; for an overview, see [26].

We present two algorithms for HDR image reconstruction based on a single input image where the pixel gain is varied over the sensor [4, 10]. Similar to [34, 35], we use the per-pixel gain of the analog signal, pixel measurements, to increase the dynamic range in the captured image. The analog pixel gain is proportional to the *ISO* setting found on most cameras. The input to our algorithm is a RAW sensor image consisting of pixels with either a high or a low gain setting, for example, varying the gain by every other two rows. The low gain setting enables the capturing of high-intensity region without saturation, while the high-gain setting enables us to capture image with a high signal-to-noise ratio in darker areas of the scene. Without loss of generality, we assume that color is captured using a *color filter array* (CFA), e.g., a Bayer pattern overlaid on the image sensor. Figure 1 illustrates two different distributions of per-pixel gain settings overlaid onto a raw CFA image. This approach to HDR capture is very robust and can be applied to off-the-shelf consumer cameras [4]. It does not suffer from, e.g., the various motion blurs or ghosting artifacts found in the commonly used exposure bracketing methods [7, 12]. Compared to multi-sensor cameras, e.g., [16, 31], it does not require costly specialized hardware and removes the requirement of careful geometric sensor calibration and the risk of misalignment between the exposures.

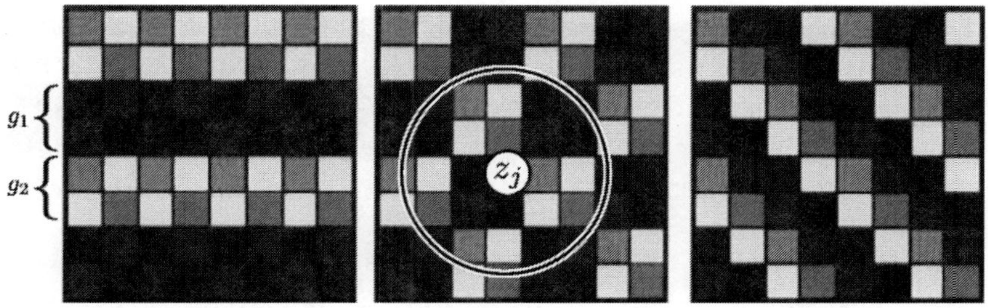

Figure 1. Illustrates three different gain patterns, with two different gain settings (ISO), for a sensor with a Bayer pattern CFA, and (*middle*) how the multiple gain pixels are filtered to reconstruct the HDR output valuez_j at pixel location X_j. The different gains, g_1 and g_2, corresponding to, e.g., 1× and 16×, amplification of the analog readout enables the capture of a wider range of intensities and extends the dynamic range in the final image

The main contribution in this paper is an extension of the previous statistical reconstruction method for dualISO data developed in [10, 15], using two novel algorithms for adapting the scale of the filtering window. In contrast to previous works [10, 15], the window support is adapted both to the statistical properties of the image noise as well as the underlying signal structure contained in the image. We show that the novel scale selection results in increased image quality in several examples.

2. BACKGROUND

Since the seminal work by Devebec and Malik [7], a large body of work has developed more robust and higher quality HDR capture and reconstruction methods; for a complete overview, see, e.g., [23,26]. In this section, we give an overview of the previous work most closely related to the methods proposed in this paper.

2.1 HDR capture

High-quality HDR capture using off-the-shelf image sensors can currently be performed with three distinct approaches.

The traditional approach captures a sequence of images with varying exposure times and then merges these into an HDR image [7, 12]. For dynamic scenes, non-rigid registration of the individual exposures is necessary; and for moving objects, general de-ghosting algorithms are necessary to apply for high-quality results. While there has been a large body of work improving these approaches, see, e.g., the survey [33], they still cannot robustly handle moving cameras and objects in general scenes.

The second approach to HDR capture is based on using beam splitters to project incident light onto multiple sensors with different exposures. The different exposures can be achieved by using varying neutral density (ND) filters in front of the sensors [1, 8, 16, 19] or by clever setups of semi-transparent beam splitter arrangements [31]. These systems offer a major advantage over exposure time fusion methods in that they robustly handle motion of the camera and objects in the scene by using the same exposure time for each sensor.

The third approach, which is most closely related to this work, is spatial multiplexing of the image to achieve HDR capture. Here, a single sensor image is used where the response to incident light varies over the sensor. Most previous works achieved this by placing a spatially varying array of ND filters in front of the sensor [2, 24, 25, 27]. Its most familiar application is color imaging via a color filter array (e.g., the Bayer pattern [6]). By avoiding the need for more than one sensor, this design provides a cost-effective solution to achieve robust HDR capture. However, most existing methods still suffer from noise as large portions of the incident light are wasted in the ND filters. By instead focusing on spatially multiplexing the response to incident light using the gain/ISO setting, we can use the entire incident light for high-quality HDR reconstruction.

2.2 HDR reconstruction

To reconstruct HDR images from a set of images with different exposures, the traditional method is to compute a per-pixel weighted average of the low dynamic range (LDR) measurements. The weights, often based on heuristics, are chosen to suppress image noise and remove saturated values from processing [3, 7, 20]. Mann and Picard [20] assigned weights according to the derivative of the inverse camera response, and later Debevec and Malik [7] used a simple double ramp function that excludes values close to the saturation point or the black level. Later work derived weight functions based on more sophisticated camera noise models. Mitsunaga and Nayar [22] derived a weight function that maximizes SNR assuming signal-independent additive noise, and Kirk and Andersen [13] derived a weight function inversely proportional to the temporal variance of the digital LDR values. Granados et al. [9] extended this approach to include both spatial and temporal camera noises. While most previous methods consider only a single pixel at a time from each LDR exposure, Tocci et al. [31] presented an algorithm that incorporates a neighborhood of LDR samples in the reconstruction.

The vast majority of previous HDR reconstruction algorithms treat the complete imaging pipeline from raw pixel measurements to a full HDR image in a series of steps [7, 9, 31], either performing demosaicing after or before HDR fusion and denoising. In this work, we instead treat all of these operations in a single joint filtering operation. This enables us to take sensor noise into account in a systematic fashion while also improving the reconstruction speed. Recently, Heide et al. [11] proposed a framework for joint demosaicing, denoising, and HDR assembly by solving an inverse problem with different global image priors and regularizers using convex optimization methods. While providing impressive results, their method does not incorporate a well-founded model of the heterogeneous sensor noise, and despite GPU implementations, their implementation is still computationally expensive which requires solving a global optimization problem. Instead, we take a local approach, enabling rapid parallel processing, while also incorporating a well-founded statistical noise model.

Our statistically motivated locally adaptive filtering framework is inspired by recent methods in image processing. The last two decades have seen an increased popularity of image processing operations using locally adaptive filter weights, for applications in, e.g., interpolation, denoising, and upsampling. Examples include normalized convolution [14], the bilateral filter [32], and moving least squares [17]. Recently, deep connections have been shown [21, 29] between these methods and traditional non-parametric statistics [18]. In this paper, we extend the earlier framework for HDR reconstruction developed in [10, 15, 16] based on fitting local polynomial approximations (LPA) [5] to irregularly distributed samples around output pixels using a localized maximum likelihood estimation [30] to incorporate the heterogeneous noise of the samples. In contrast to the previous works [10, 15, 16], we propose a novel adaptation of the filter kernel size that allows the filter extent to adapt not only to local image structure but also the sensor noise in the region.

3. DUALISO CAPTURE AND RECONSTRUCTION—OVERVIEW

The goal of the algorithm presented in this paper is to generate an HDR image based on input data in which the per-pixel gain (ISO) is varying over the sensor. This means that the analog readouts are amplified differently between segments of pixels on the sensor. Figure 1 illustrates three different gain patterns with two different gain values, g_1 and g_2, using a sensor with a Bayer pattern *color filter array* (CFA). The unity gain, g_1, pixel segments capture the high-intensity regions in the scene while the amplified segments, g_2, capture low-intensity regions. g_2 pixels may lie well below the acceptable noise floor for g_1 pixels.

The key benefit of using a varying per-pixel gain, g_i, is that the dynamic range in the final output will be extended using a single image as an input [10, 11]. However, accurate reconstruction of the output HDR image is a challenging filtering problem. The different gain settings lead to a loss of data in the spatial domain due to the fact that the amplified pixels, using gain g_2, saturate faster. For high-quality reconstruction, it is also necessary to take into account the heterogeneous image noise, which for a specific camera and exposure setting, varies with both intensity and the choice of gain settings.

The method presented here extends the statistical HDR reconstruction developed by [15, 16] to include reconstruction kernels which adapts to both the image content and the heterogeneous measurement noise. We assume that the input data is a raw CFA sensor image with per-pixel gain settings varying between pixel segments as described in Fig. 1 (middle). Each pixel value, z_j, at a pixel coordinate, X_j, in the output HDR image is, for each color channel, reconstructed by filtering the input pixels within a neighborhood around X_j. Our statistical approach first estimates the variance, or measurement noise, for each input sample in the raw image using a noise model. The input samples are then weighted using the estimated variances and an adaptive Gaussian kernel in the spatial domain. The weights, computed from the variances, ensure that low noise samples are weighted higher than noisy samples, and the Gaussian filter gives lower weights to samples further away from the reconstruction point, X_j. The HDR pixel value z_j at location X_j is then reconstructed iteratively by adjusting the shape of the Gaussian kernel to the weighted input samples. In the first iteration, the Gaussian kernel is very small. The spatial support of the kernel is gradually increased until a statistically informed threshold based on the variances and image content is reached. The final HDR pixel value, z_j, is then estimated by fitting a polynomial to the weighted input samples. Our method performs noise reduction, color interpolation, and HDR fusion in a single operation.

The detailed presentation of the algorithm is laid out as described below. Section 4 first describes the camera noise model used to estimate sample variances, and Section 5 describes how each HDR pixel value is reconstructed using our statistical HDR reconstruction framework. The novel methods for filter scale selection for HDR reconstruction are presented in Section 6. Finally, in Section 7, we describe how the parameters for the noise model are calibrated and in Section 8, we show example results and evaluation of our reconstruction method.

4. SENSOR NOISE MODEL

The camera sensor electronics convert the incident radiant power *f*, which for convenience we express as the number of photo-induced electrons collected per unit time, to a measured digital valuey_i at a pixel *i*. The samples, y_i, contain measurement noise that is dependent on sensor characteristics such as readout noise, gain/ISO setting, and the inherent Poisson shot noise in the incident illumination.

To model the dependence of the measured digital pixel value on the incident radiant power and the camera parameters, we use a well-established radiometric model derived from previous works [9,15]. Using this model, the non-saturated pixel values are modeled as random variables following a normal distribution:

$$y_i \sim N\left(g_i a_i t f_i + \mu_R, g^2{}_i a_i t f_i + \sigma_R^2(g_i)\right), \qquad (1)$$

where t is the exposure time, g_i is the pixel gain/ISO, a_i is a pixel non-uniformity, μ_R is the mean of the read out noise, and σ2R is the variance of the read out noise. An example showing the standard deviation of the read out noise, σ_R, for varying gain/ISO using a Canon Mark III sensor (saturation around 1600) is shown in Fig. 2.

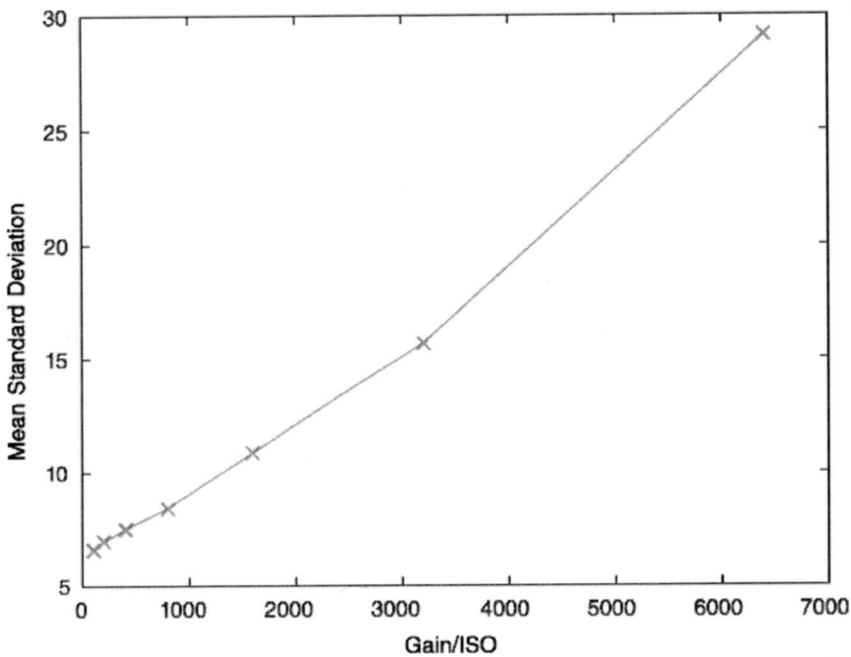

Figure 2. Mean standard deviation versus gain/ISO of the 14-bit Canon Mark III sensor. The ISO settings are 100, 200, 400, 800, 1600, 3200, and 6400

In order to compute an estimate of the incident radiant power, f^if^i, from the noisy digital input sample values y_i, we use the following estimator:

$$\hat{f}_i = \frac{y_i - b_i}{g_i t a_i}, \tag{2}$$

where b_i is obtained from a bias frame captured with no light reaching the sensor.

Similarly, we approximate the variance of this estimator by

$$\hat{\sigma}^2_{\hat{f}_i} = \frac{g_i^2 t a_i \hat{f}_i + \hat{\sigma}_R^2(g_i)}{g_i^2 t^2 a_i^2}, \tag{3}$$

where g_i, a_i, and σˆ2R(gi)σ^R2(gi) are found through calibration; see Section 7. We do not include the effect of pixel cross-talk, and the variances, σˆ2fˆi, are assumed to be independent of each other.

5. ADAPTIVE HDR RECONSTRUCTION

To estimate an HDR pixel value z_j at a location X_j on the sensor, we use a LPA [5] to fit the observation samples of the incident radiant power in the local neighborhood. The same framework is also known as kernel regression [29].

5.1 Local polynomial approximation

To estimate the radiant power, $f(x)$, at an output pixel, we use a generic local polynomial expansion of the radiant power around the output pixel location $X_j = [x_1, x_2]^T$. Assuming that the radiant power$f(x)$ is a smooth function in a local neighborhood around the output location X_j, an Mth order Taylor series expansion is used to predict the radiant power at a point X_i close to X_j as follows:

$$\tilde{f}(X_i) = C_0 + C_1(X_i - X_j) + C_2 tril\{(X_i - X_j)(X_i - X_j)^T\} + \ldots, \tag{4}$$

where *tril* lexicographically vectorizes the lower triangular part of a symmetric matrix and

$$C_0 = f(X_j) \tag{5}$$

$$C_1 = \nabla f(X_j) = \left[\frac{\partial f(X_j)}{\partial x_1}, \frac{\partial f(X_j)}{\partial x_2}\right] \tag{6}$$

$$C_2 = \frac{1}{2}\left[\frac{\partial^2 f(X_j)}{\partial x_1^2}, 2\frac{\partial^2 f(X_j)}{\partial x_1 \partial x_2}, \frac{\partial^2 f(X_j)}{\partial x_2^2}\right]. \quad (7)$$

Given the fitted polynomial coefficients, $C_{1:M}$, we can thus estimate the radiant power and the HDR pixel value, z_j, at the output location X_j by $z_j = C_0 = f(X_j)$.

5.2 Maximum localized likelihood fitting

To estimate the coefficients, we maximize a localized likelihood function [30] defined using a Gaussian smoothing window centered around X_j

$$\mathcal{W}_h(X_j) = \frac{1}{2\pi h^2} \exp\left\{\frac{-(X_k - X_j)^T (X_k - X_j)}{h}\right\}. \quad (8)$$

where h is a local scale parameter (see Section 6) which determines the shape of the filtering kernel. In Section 6, we discuss how the size of the window function can be selected adaptively depending on the features at each location in the image.

We denote the observed pixel samples (radiant power estimates, f^i(Xj) at position X_j) in the support of the local neighborhood window by f_k with a linear index $k = 1 \ldots K$. Note that these are obtained from the digital pixel values using Eq. 2 derived from the sensor noise model.

Using the assumption of normally distributed radiant power estimates, f_k, the polynomial coefficients,C~C~, maximizing the localized likelihood function is found by the weighted least squares estimate

$$\tilde{C} = \left(\Phi^T W \Phi\right)^{-1} \Phi^T W \bar{f}. \quad (9)$$

where

$$\bar{f} = [f_1, f_2, \ldots f_K]^T$$

$$W = \text{diag}\left[\frac{\mathcal{W}_h(X_1)}{\hat{\sigma}^2_{f_1}}, \frac{\mathcal{W}_h(X_2)}{\hat{\sigma}^2_{f_2}}, \ldots, \frac{\mathcal{W}_h(X_K)}{\hat{\sigma}^2_{f_K}}\right]$$

$$\Phi = \begin{bmatrix} 1 & (X_1-X_j) & tril^T\left\{(X_1-X_j)(X_1-X_j)^T\right\} & \ldots \\ 1 & (X_2-X_j) & tril^T\left\{(X_2-X_j)(X_2-X_j)^T\right\} & \ldots \\ \vdots & \vdots & \vdots & \vdots \\ 1 & (X_K-X_j) & tril^T\left\{(X_K-X_j)(X_K-X_j)^T\right\} & \ldots \end{bmatrix}. \quad (10)$$

The operator *tril* lexicographically vectorizes the lower triangular part of a symmetric matrix.

Using this maximum likelihood approach, we can efficiently solve for the polynomial coefficients $C_{1:M}$ and estimate the final HDR pixel value z_j at a pixel location X_j for a given smoothing parameter$h$. However, in order to enable a good trade-off between bias and variance, i.e., between image sharpness and noise reduction, it is necessary to locally adapt the smoothing parameter h to image features and image noise. If h is globally fixed over the image, reconstruction may lead to a noisy final image for small h and blurry result for a high h value. The best trade-off between image sharpness and denoising is achieved by adapting the smoothing parameter h to local image features.

In the next section, we describe the iterative reconstruction method and two algorithms for selecting the locally best smoothing parameter, h, for each HDR pixel estimate, z_j, individually.

Algorithm 1 Adaptive HDR reconstruction

procedure HDR RECONSTRUCTION
  for each color channel in R, G, B **do**
    for each HDR pixel estimate z_j **do**
      $h_l = h_{min}$
      z_j = estimate $\hat{z}_{j,h_l}$ using LPA with degree M
      for each $h_l < h_{max}$ **do**
        $h_l = h_l + h_{inc}$
        estimate $\hat{z}_{j,h_l}$ using LPA with degree M
        estimate $\hat{z}_{j,h_l}$ variance $\tilde{\sigma}_{\hat{z}_{j,h_l}}$ and the reconstruction error ϵ (for EVS)
        apply update rule (ICI or EVS) based on $\hat{z}_{j,h_l}$ and
        if variation in $\hat{z}_{j,h_l}$ can be explained by $\tilde{\sigma}_{\hat{z}_{j,h_l}}$ **then**
          $z_j = \hat{z}_{j,h_l}$
        else
          break
        end if
      end for
    end for
  end for
end procedure

6. ADAPTIVE SCALE SELECTION

The size of the window function introduces a trade-off between bias and variance. A large window will reduce the variance but can lead to overly smoothed images (bias). Ideally, it is desirable to have large window supports in regions where the smooth polynomial model, used for the reconstruction, is a good fit to the underlying signal, while keeping the window size small close to the edges or important image features. The size of the smoothing window is determined by the smoothing parameter *h*. Figure 3 illustrates how a signal value, the black point, is being estimated using a kernel with a gradually increasing smoothing parameter, *h*. When the smoothing parameter *h* is increased from h_0, the h_1, i.e., a higher degree of smoothing, the variance in the estimated value can be explained by the signal variance. When the smoothing parameter is increased from h_1 to h_2, the kernel reaches the step in the signal and the estimation at the black point can no longer be explained by the signal variance. Smoothing parameter h_1 thus produces a better estimate.

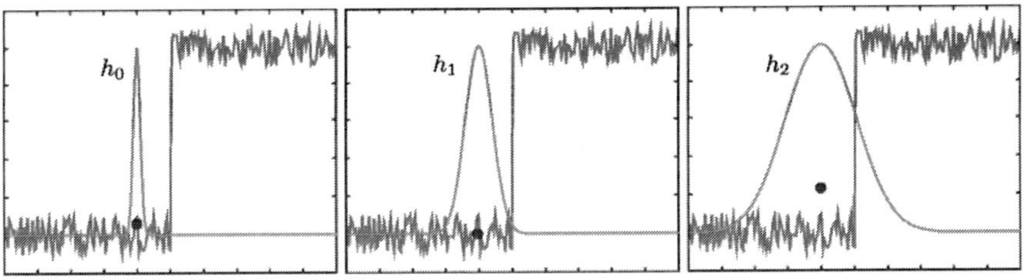

Figure 3. Illustrating how a signal value, the *black point*, is estimated using a kernel with an iteratively increasing smoothing parameter, *h*. Increasing from h_0 to h_1, i.e., a higher degree of smoothing, the variance in the estimated value can be explained by the variance in the original signal. However, when the smoothing parameter is increased from h_1 to h_2, the kernel reaches the step in the signal and the estimate at the black point can no longer be explained by the signal variance

The adaptation of the smoothing parameter, *h*, scale selection is carried out iteratively. The goal of the adaptation is to gradually increase *h*, and find an optimal *h* such that the variation in the estimated value between iterations can be explained by the signal variance and the smoothing applied. Denoting each iteration by *I* and the corresponding smoothing parameter by h_1, Algorithm 1 describes the outline of the HDR pixels z_j reconstructed by adapting the smoothing parameter h_1. In each iteration, we estimate the signal value and its variance. We then apply an update rule which determines whether the h value used is valid or not. This is repeated until the update rule does not hold or the maximum h value, h_{max}, is reached. In Sections 6.1 and 6.2, we describe how the variance of the pixel is estimated in detail with the two different update rules.

6.1 Update rule 1: error of estimation versus standard deviation (EVS)

The first update rule is built on the intuition that if the weighted mean reconstruction error is larger than the weighted mean standard deviation, i.e., the difference between the data and the fit cannot be explained by the expected signal variation due to noise, the polynomial model does not provide a good fit to the underlying image data. As described in Algorithm 1, the smoothing parameter, h_1, is iteratively increased with an increment h_{inc}. In each iteration, l, the EVS update rule computes the weighted reconstruction error e_1 as

$$e_l = \sqrt{\sum_k W^2(k,k)(\tilde{f}(X_k) - \hat{f}_k)^2}, \tag{11}$$

where k indexes the pixels in the neighborhood and W is the weights including both the variance of the original pixels and the spatial Gaussian kernel as described in Eq. 10. The weighted standard deviation, σ~z^j,hiσ~z^j,hi, of this estimate can be obtained from the covariance matrix M_C for the fitted polynomial coefficients, C~C~, which is given by

$$M_C = (\Phi^T W \Phi)^{-1} \Phi^T W \Sigma W^T \Phi (\Phi^T W^T \Phi)^{-1}, \tag{12}$$

where Σ=diag[σ2f1,σ2f2,...,σ2fk is the variance of the observation. The variance of estimated radiant power z_j, σ~f^j, at the output location X_j, is thus given by the element σ~z^j,hi=MC(0,0) inM_C. During the iterations, the smoothing parameter, h_l, is updated to $h_{l+1} = h_l + h_{inc}$ as long as the weighted reconstruction error, ϵ_l, is smaller than the standard deviation ϵl<Γσ~z^j,hi, where Γ is a user-specified parameter controlling the trade-off between levels of denoising applied by the kernel.

6.2 Update rule 2: intersection of confidence intervals (ICI)

The second update rule is based on the ICI algorithm [5]. The main purpose of this algorithm is to obtain the largest scaling parameter in the local neighborhood of the estimation point under the constraint that the polynomial model remains a likely fit to the underlying data. As described in Algorithm 1, the smoothing parameter, $h_{min} \leq h_l \leq h_{max}$, is iteratively increased. For each iteration, l, the ICI rule determines a confidence interval, $D_l = [L_l, U_l]$:

$$L_l = \hat{z}_{j,h_l}(x) - \Gamma\tilde{\sigma}_{\hat{z}_{j,h_l}}, \tag{13}$$

$$U_l = \hat{z}_{j,h_l}(x) + \Gamma\tilde{\sigma}_{\hat{z}_{j,h_l}}, \tag{14}$$

where z^j,hl(x) is the estimated radiant power given the scaling parameter h_l and σ~z^j,hl is the weighted standard deviation of this estimate computed using Eq. 12. Γ is a scaling parameter controlling how wide the intersection interval is. During adaptation, h_l is increased as long as there is an overlap between the confidence intervals, i.e., h_l is updated to $h_{l+1} = h_l + h_{inc}$ if there is an overlap between D_l and D_{l+1}. In practice, we utilize Γ as a user parameter, enabling an intuitive trade-off between image sharpness and denoising. A detailed overview of the ICI rule and its robustness can be found in [28].

7. CAMERA PARAMETER CALIBRATION

The variance of the readout noise, the sensor gain, bias, and the sensor saturation point are calibrated once for each sensor. The bias frame, *b*, and readout noise variance, Var[$r_i(g_i, t)$], are calibrated as the per-pixel mean and the variance, respectively. This calibration is done over a set of black images captured with the lens covered, so that no photons reach the sensor. The sensor gain,g_i, can be calibrated using the relation,

$$\frac{\mathrm{Var}[y_i]-\mathrm{Var}[b_i]}{E[y_i]-E[b_i]}=\frac{g_i^2\mathrm{Var}[e_i]}{g_iE[e_i]}=g_i, \quad (15)$$

where the second equality follows from e_i being Poisson distributed shot noise with $E[e_i] = \mathrm{Var}[e_i]$. In addition, $E[y_i]$ and $E[b_i]$ can be estimated by averaging flat fields and the bias frame, respectively, and $\mathrm{Var}[b_i]$ as described above. The per-pixel non-uniformity, a_i, can be estimated using a flat field image computed as the average over a large sequence of non-saturated images.

8. RESULTS AND EVALUATION

The proposed algorithm has been evaluated on two different sets of images. One synthetic image data set with known ground truth computed using a camera simulator and one set of images captured using a Canon 5D Mark III running the Magic Lantern firmware with the dualISO module installed. The synthetic data is generated using a camera simulation framework which takes a noise-free HDR image as input and applies noise based on the camera noise model described in Section 4. The camera parameters estimated from real cameras as described in Section 7 are used for simulating dualISO sample data. The noise-free HDR images (ground truth) were captured as a set of carefully calibrated exposure brackets one *f*-stop apart covering the dynamic range of the scene. Each of the different exposures in the bracketing sequence was captured as the average of 100 calibrated RAW images with the same exposure settings. The test images used exhibit a very large dynamic range, were selected to be representative for challenging scenes, and include features such as dark and bright image regions, high- and low-frequency regions, image noise, and strong local contrasts. In our evaluation, we compare three different gain patterns as shown in Fig. 1. We have tested our algorithm for a polynomial degree of $M = 0, 1, 2$ and a range of different parameter settings for Γ. In all tests (except for the non-adaptive fixed h comparisons), the smoothing parameter, h, is allowed to vary between $h = 0.6$ and $h = 5.0$. Figure 4 shows an image captured with a Canon 5D Mark III running the Magic Lantern dualISO module and reconstructed by the proposed method. The image shows that our algorithm performs well in the reconstruction by keeping image sharpness while allowing high-quality noise reduction.

Figure 4. Reconstructed from dualISO data with ISO100–1600 captured with Canon 5D Mark III. Reconstructed with ICI $M = 2$, $h \in [0.6, 5.0]$, and $\Gamma = 1.0$

Figure 5 shows a high contrast scene simulating a Canon 5D camera with dualISO settings of ISO100 and ISO1600 alternating in pairs of rows on the sensor as shown in Fig. 1 (left). Figure 5shows the input raw CFA Bayer image, and three images in the bottom row show the locally adapted$h$ values for the red, green, and blue color channels, respectively. The EVS update rule adapts the smoothing parameter h to both the image features and the image noise. The parameter h becomes smaller as we get closer to edges and textured regions and larger in homogeneous areas.

In Figs. 6 and 7, we focus on the trade-off between image sharpness and denoising. We compare our algorithm using both the ICI and EVS update rules to LPA using non-adaptive filtering kernels, [10], with $h = 0.6, 1.4$, and 5.0, and the widely used steering kernel regression (SKR) method [29]. The images compare two cutout regions of the lamp scene from Fig. 5. The two regions have been chosen to display the performance of our algorithm in a dark region, Fig. 6, and a highlight region, Fig. 7. The ground truth reference images of the cutouts are displayed in Fig. 8. In both images, the comparisons are ordered as follows: (a) non-adaptive LPA $M = 2$ from left to right with $h = 0.6, 1.4,$ and5.0, (b) SKR [29] $M = 2$ from left to right with $h = 0.6, 1.4,$ and5.0, (c) our method with ICI rule for local adaptation of scale parameter, $M = 2$, from left to right: $\Gamma = 0.6, 1.0,$ and1.4, and (d) our method with EVS rule, $M = 2$, from left to right: $\Gamma = 0.6, 1.0,$ and1.4. From Fig. 6, it is evident that the non-adaptive method in (a) [10] does not perform well. SKR produces good results for $h = 1.4$ but cannot fully adapt the smoothing parameter as artifacts from the noise filtering are visible (zoom in). Both ICI- and EVS-based algorithms keep sharpness while reducing the image noise more than the other methods. In Fig. 7, SKR with $h = 1.4$ produces a sharp image without color artifacts; however, it also smooths the reflection on the red toy. ICI and EVS produce a similar result, but EVS leads to less smoothing around the highlight areas of the scene compared to ICI. The images show that our algorithms using ICI and EVS update rules produce high-quality images. In general, the EVS update rule allows for a higher degree of smoothing and denoising while keeping higher contrast edges intact. However, in dark regions, the EVS update leads to a loss of detail compared to ICI rule. Another important difference is that although the EVS update rule may produce better results in some cases, it is built on the heuristic argument that the reconstruction error should be smaller than the standard deviation in the filtered region. While ICI rule is statistically motivated and designed to minimize the estimate variance.

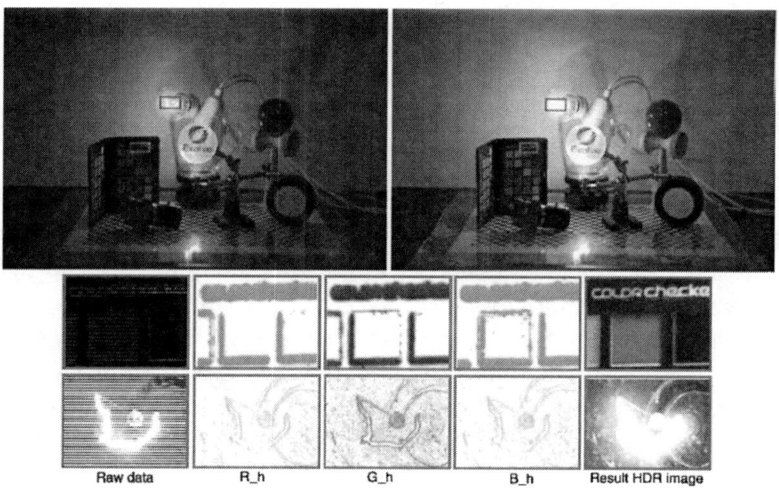

Figure 5. Reconstruction process of one sample raw image. *Top left* shows the raw input image with CFA Bayer pattern and dualISO row pattern. *Top right* indicates the resulted tone mapped HDR reconstructed image with EVS rule. *Bottom rows* extracted images from *left* to *right*: cutout of the raw image, scaling parameter image for R, G, B color channels with $\Gamma = 1.0$, and the cutout of the reconstructed HDR image

Figure 6. Lamp scene with different methods for comparison: **a** LPA $M = 2$ from *left* to *right*: $h = 0.6, 1.4$, and5.0;**b** SKR $M = 2$ from *left* to *right* $h = 0.6, 1.4$, and5.0; **c** our method with ICI $M = 2$ from *left* to *right* $\Gamma = 0.6, 1.0$, and1.4; **d** our method with EVS $M = 2$ from *left* to *right* $\Gamma = 0.6, 1.0$, and1.4

In Fig. 9, we demonstrate how our algorithms perform using the three different gain patterns illustrated in Fig. 1. This particular image region is selected as it contains slanted edges in different directions. The comparisons show that the block pattern and diagonal pattern in some cases produce better results. However, the reconstruction quality depends on how the image features are oriented and the statistically optimal configuration of the gain pattern is out of scope of this paper. Figure 10shows a cutout of the lamp scene simulated with row pattern and reconstructed using a varying polynomial degree of $M = 0, 1$, and 2. As expected, $M = 0$ produces a blocky result, and $M = 1$ and $M = 2$ produce increasingly more accurate reconstructions.

In Figs. 11 and 12, we show the effect of increasing the ISO separation in the dualISO image using a simulated 14-bit Canon 5D sensor. The dualISO settings are varied from ISO100–ISO200 to ISO100–ISO25600. As the separation between the ISO settings increase, the number of overlapping bits in the two exposures decrease. The image shows that our algorithm works well up to ISO100–ISO6400, i.e., a separation of six *f*-stops and an overlap of 8 bits. By increasing the separation further, artifacts start to appear along the edges.

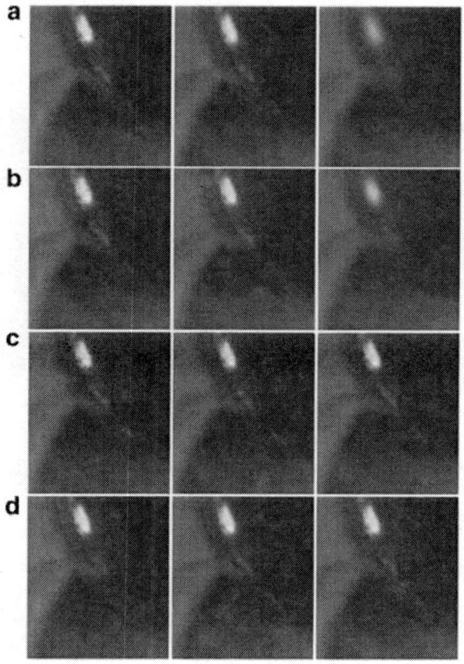

Figure 7. Another comparison of a cutout of the simulated lamp scene for different methods: **a** LPA $M = 2$ from*left* to *right*: $h = 0.6, 1.4$, and 5.0; **b** SKR $M = 2$ from *left* to *right* $h = 0.6, 1.4$, and 5.0; **c** our method with ICI $M = 2$ from *left* to *right* $\Gamma = 0.6, 1.0$, and 1.4; **d** our method with EVS $M = 2$ from *left* to *right* $\Gamma = 0.6, 1.0$, and 1.4

9. CONCLUSIONS

In this paper, we presented a novel approach for adaptive unified HDR image reconstruction that includes the sensor noise model and error of the estimation for a more robust and accurate reconstruction of single shot spatial multiplexing raw data. The method handles severe noise, especially in the darker regions while it keeps the error of the estimation low to prevent over-smoothing of the image. To the best of our knowledge, none of the previous methods have considered sensor noise model and estimated error and variance in order to adapt the reconstructed kernel for each local region of the image. The robustness of our approach for noise reduction and HDR reconstruction has been experimentally verified on both real data and simulated camera images. While being a simple method to implement, our results demonstrate a relatively good performance.

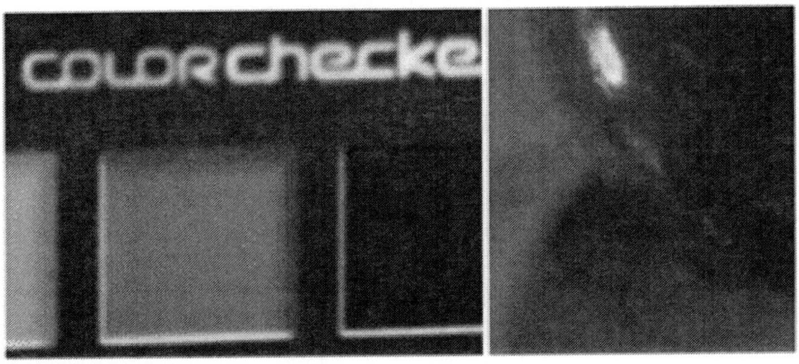

Figure 8. The ground truth reference images for the cutouts compared in Figs. 6 and 7

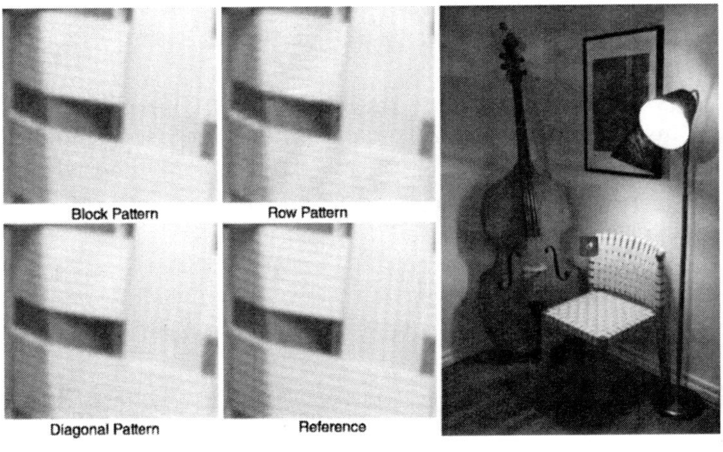

Figure 9. Living room scene. Comparison of our method with EVS rule $M = 2$; $\Gamma = 1.0$ for different gain patterns: block pattern, row pattern, and diagonal pattern

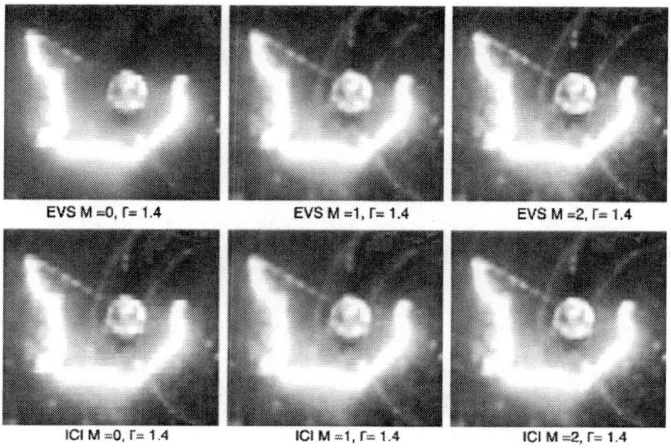

Figure 10. Lamp scene, evaluation of EVS, and ICI method for different degrees of polynomial for dualISO 100–1600 with row pattern from *left* to *right* with $M = 0$, 1, and 2

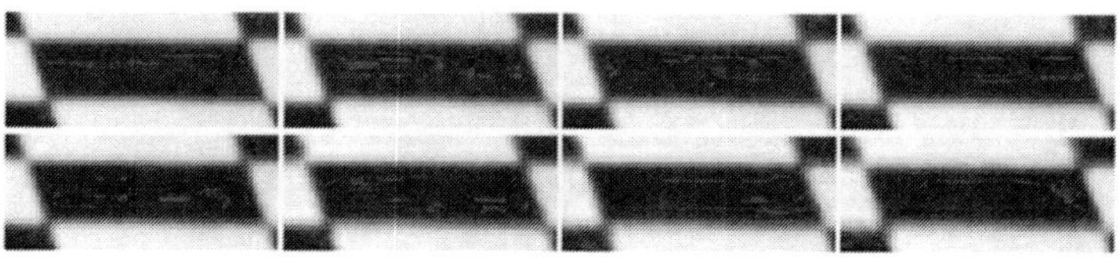

Figure 11. Cutouts of the checkerboard in the lamp scene, evaluation of ISO settings for EVS $M = 2$, $\Gamma = 1.0$. (*Top row*) From *left* to *right*: reference, dualISO 100–400, dualISO 100–800, and dualISO 100–1600. (*Bottom row*) From *left* to *right*: dualISO 100–3200, dualISO 100–6400, dualISO 100–12800, and dualISO 100–25600

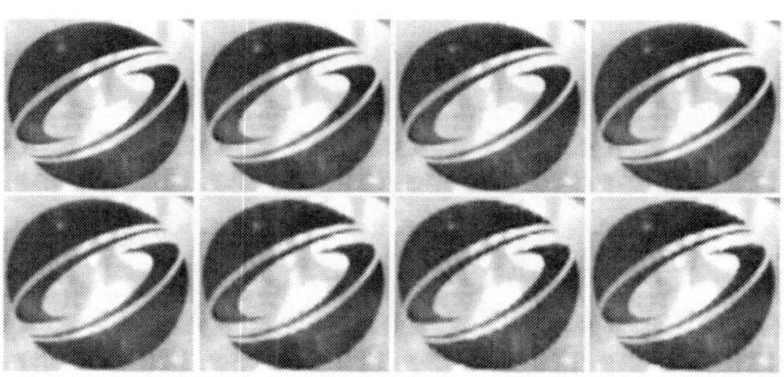

Figure 12. Cutouts of the glass in the lamp scene, evaluation of ISO settings for EVS $M = 2$, $\Gamma = 1.0$. (*Top row*) From *left* to *right*: reference, dualISO 100–

400, dualISO 100–800, and dualISO 100–1600. (*Bottom row*) From *left* to *right*: dualISO 100–3200, dualISO 100–6400, dualISO 100–12800, and dualISO 100–25600

ACKNOWLEDGEMENTS

This project was funded by the Swedish Foundation for Strategic Research (SSF) through grant IIS11-0081, Linköping University Center for Industrial Information Technology (CENIIT), and the Swedish Research Council through the Linnaeus Environment CADICS.

REFERENCES

1. M Aggarwal, N Ahuja, Split aperture imaging for high dynamic range. Int. J. Comput. Vis. **58**(1), 7–17 (2004)

2. C Aguerrebere, A Almansa, Y Gousseau, J Delon, P Musé, Single shot high dynamic range imaging using piecewise linear estimators, in *ICCP*, 2014

3. AO Akyüz, E Reinhard, Noise reduction in high dynamic range imaging. J. Vis. Commun. Image Represent.**18**(5), 366–367 (2007)

4. Alex. Dynamic range improvement for Canon DSLR with 8-channel sensor read-out by alternating iso during sensor readout. Technical documentation, url: http://acoutts.com/a1ex/dual_iso.pdf, July 2013.

5. J Astola, V Katkovnik, K Egiazarian. *Local Approximation Techniques in Signal and Image Processing.*SPIE- International Society for Optical Engineering, 2006

6. B Bayer. Color imaging array. US Patent 3 971 065, 1976.

7. P Debevec, J Malik, Recovering high dynamic range radiance maps from photographs, in *SIGGRAPH*, 1997, pp. 369–378

8. J Froehlich, S Grandinetti, B Eberhardt, S Walter, A Schilling, H Brendel. Creating cinematic wide gamut HDR-video for evaluation of tone

mapping operators and HDR-displays. In *SPIE Electronic Imaging*, pages 90230X-90230X. International Society for Optics and Photonics, SPIE digital library, 2014.

9. M Granados, B Ajdin, M Wand, C Theobalt, H Seidel, H Lensch, Optimal hdr reconstruction with linear digital cameras, in *CVPR*, 2010

10. S Hajisharif, J Kronander, J Unger, HDR reconstruction for alternating gain (iso) sensor readout, in*Eurographics 2014 Short Papers*, ed. by MW Eric Galin, 2014

11. F Heide, M Steinberger, YT Tsai, M Rouf, D Pajak, D Reddy, O Gallo, J Liu, W Heidrich, K Egiazarian, J Kautz, L Pulli. FlexISP: a flexible camera image processing framework. *ACM Transactions on Graphics (Proceedings SIGGRAPH Asia 2014)*, 33(6), December 2014

12. S Kang, M Uyttendaele, S Winder, R Szeliski, High dynamic range video. ACM Transactions on Graphics (Proceedings of SIGGRAPH 2003) **22**(3), 319–325 (2003)

13. K Kirk, H Andersen, Noise characterization of weighting schemes for combination of multiple exposures, in*Proc. British Machine Vision Conference (BMVC)*, 2006, pp. 1129–1138

14. H Knutsson, CF Westin, Normalized and differential convolution, in *CVPR*, 1993

15. J Kronander, S Gustavson, G Bonnet, A Ynnerman, J Unger, A unified framework for multi-sensor HDR video reconstruction. Signal Processing: Image Communications **29**(2), 203–215 (2014)

16. J Kronander, S Gustavson, G Bonnet, J Unger, Unified HDR reconstruction from raw CFA data, in *IEEE International Conference on Computational Photography (ICCP)*, 2013

17. P Lancaster, K Salkauskasr, Surfaces generated by moving least squares methods. Math. Comput. **87**, 141–158 (1981)

18. C Loader, *Local regression and likelihood* (Springer, New York, 1999)

19. A Manakov, JF Restrepo, O Klehm, R Hegedüs, E Eisemann, HP Seidel, I Ihrke, A reconfigurable camera add-on for high dynamic range, multi-

spectral, polarization, and light-field imaging. ACM Transaction (Proc. SIGGRAPH 2013) **32**(4), 1–47 (2013)

20. S Mann, RW Picard, On being 'undigital' with digital cameras: extending dynamic range by combining differently exposed pictures, in *IS&T*, 1995

21. P Milanfar, A tour of modern image filtering: new insights and methods, both practical and theoretical. IEEE Signal Process. Mag. **30**(1), 106–128 (2013)

22. T Mitsunaga, SK Nayar, Radiometric self calibration, in *CVPR*, 1999, pp. 374–380

23. K Myszkowski, R Mantiuk, G Krawczyk. *High Dynamic Range Video.* Synthesis lectures on computer graphics and animation, a publication in Morgan and Claypool, 2008

24. SG Narasimhan, SK Nayar, Enhancing resolution along multiple imaging dimensions using assorted pixels. IEEE Transaction on Pattern Analysis and Machine Intelligence **27**(4), 518–530 (2005)

25. S Nayar, T Mitsunaga, High dynamic range imaging: spatially varying pixel exposures, in *CVPR*, 2000

26. E Reinhard, W Heidrich, S Pattanaik, P Debevec, G Ward, K Myszkowski. High dynamic range imaging: acquisition, display and image-based lighting (Morgan Kaufmann Publishers Inc., San Francisco, CA, USA, 2005)

27. M Schoberl, A Belz, J Seiler, S Foessel, A Kaup, High dynamic range video by spatially non-regular optical filtering, in *Image Processing (ICIP), 2012 19th IEEE International Conference*, 2012, pp. 2757–2760

28. L Stankovic, Performance analysis of the adaptive algorithm for bias-to-variance tradeoff. IEEE Transaction on Signal Processing **52**(5), 1228–1234 (2004)

29. H Takeda, S Farsiu, P Milanfar, Kernel regression for image processing and reconstruction. IEEE Trans. Image Process. **16**(2), 349–366 (2007)

30. R Tibshirani, T Hastie, Local likelihood estimation. J. Am. Stat. Assoc. **82**(398), 559–567 (1987)

31. MD Tocci, C Kiser, N Tocci, P Sen, A versatile HDR video production system. ACM Transactions on Graphics(Proceedings of SIGGRAPH 2011) **30**(4), 1–41 (2011)

32. C Tomasi, R Manduchi, Bilateral filtering for gray and color images, in *ICCV*, 1998, pp. 839–846

33. OT Tursun, AO Akyüz, A Erdem, E Erdem. The state-of-the-art in HDR deghosting: a survey and evaluation. *Computer Graphics Forum (Proceedings of Eurogprahics STARs)*, 2015

34. J Unger, S Gustavson, High-dynamic-range video for photometric measurement of illumination, in *SPIE Electronic Imaging*, 2007

35. J Unger, S Gustavson, M Ollila, M Johannesson, A real time light probe, in *Proceedings of the 25th Eurographics Annual Conference, volume Short Papers and Interactive Demos*, 2004, pp. 17–21

Chapter 6

Selecting scenes for 2D and 3D subjective video quality tests

Margaret H Pinson1*†, Marcus Barkowsky2† and Patrick Le Callet2

1 National Telecommunications and Information Administration (NTIA), Institute for Telecommunication Sciences (ITS), U.S. Department of Commerce (DOC), 325 Broadway St, Boulder, CO 80305, USA.

2 IRCCyN CNRS UMR 6597, Polytech Nantes, Université de Nantes, LUNAM Université, rue Christian Pauc, BP 50609, Nantes Cedex 3 44306, France.

ABSTRACT

This paper presents recommended techniques for choosing video sequences for subjective experiments. Subjective video quality assessment is a well-understood field, yet scene selection is often driven by convenience or content availability. Three-dimensional testing is a newer field that requires new considerations for scene selection. The impact of experiment design on best practices for scene selection will also be considered. A semi-automatic selection process for content sets for subjective experiments will be proposed.

KEYWORDS

Video quality, Subjective testing, Stereoscopic 3D, Content selection, Video quality assessment, Scene selection

1. INTRODUCTION

Advances in the consumer video market include higher resolution (Full-HD, 4K, 8K), additional dimensions and reconstruction precision (three-dimensional (3D), high dynamic range, wide color gamut), associated media (audio wavefield synthesis, emotive devices), and interaction methods (mobile phones, social networks, see-through glasses with augmented reality). These technologies have caused a renewed interest in the analysis of quality of experience through subjective and objective measurement methods. This rapid development in audiovisual technology creates new challenges in quality of experience assessment and analysis, and these new challenges require new subjective experiments to be conducted. In most cases, subjective experiments are necessary to establish ground truth data that helps in training, verification, and validation of objective measurement methods. In order for these subjective experiments to add value to the research community, testing conditions must be carefully considered.

Regardless of future audiovisual technology, scene selection will always be one important component of the testing conditions for video quality testing. Selection should be based on video characteristics and the purpose of the experiment, not on personal preference or convenience. For emerging video technologies, limited content choice may be a major factor. It is therefore important to provide guidelines that identify content that is suitable for testing the emerging technologies.

In this paper, we first describe guidelines for scene selection for traditional, entertainment-oriented tests that were developed using over two decades of experience in designing video quality subjective tests. Second, we explore new issues that are critical for selecting 3D scene content. Third, we review experimental design considerations common to both types of subjective testing.

2. BASIC SCENE SELECTION

Entertainment-oriented subjective video quality tests try to represent a wide range of entertainment content in a scene pool containing approximately eight to ten clips. It is impossible to include every genre and visual effect with only eight or ten clips, but approaching this ideal improves a test's accuracy.

3. AVOID OFFENSIVE CONTENT

It is important to avoid subject matter that may be offensive, controversial, polarizing, or distracting:

- Violence
- Indecent, revealing, or suggestive outfits
- Erotic situations
- Drugs and drug paraphernalia
- Politics
- Religion
- Horror films
- Medical operations

Offensive, controversial, polarizing, or distracting content may change how subjects rate the video sequences. Subjects may give the clip a lower mean opinion score (MOS) or fail to pay close attention to the rating task.

4. CONSIDER CONTENT EDITING AND CAMERAWORK

The impact of scene content editing and camerawork cannot be underestimated. Viewer instructions for subjective testing should include a statement such as: 'Please do not base your opinion on the content of the scene or the quality of the acting.' Yet ratings inevitably include both the clip's artistic and technical qualities.

To illustrate this issue, we will examine the scenes selected for the Video Quality Experts Group (VQEG) high-definition television test [1]. This international test produced six subjectively rated databases. The six scene pools were carefully selected by Margaret Pinson to have very similar objective characteristics. During the selection process, all original scenes were judged to have a quality of 'good' or better by an expert panel of video quality subjective testing researchers. Each dataset included 13 original video sequences, which were rated on the absolute category rating (ACR) 5-level scale of excellent = 5, good = 4, fair = 3, poor = 2, and bad = 1. The ratings from all subjects were averaged to compute a MOS. These MOS were rank-sorted to identify the original video sequences in each dataset that have the highest and lowest MOS. Figures 1 and 2 show sample frames from the original sequences with the highest and lowest MOS, respectively.

Figure 1. Original sequences with high MOS.

The average MOS drops from 4.7 in Figure 1 to 4.1 in Figure 2. So on average, the available range for subjects' ratings of the impaired video sequences shrank:

- On average by 16% (i.e., from (4.7 to 1) to (4.1 to 1))
- At most by 28% (i.e., dataset vqegHD6, from (4.9 to 1) to (3.8 to 1))

- Theoretically up to half of the scale (i.e., from (5.0 to 1) to (3.0 to 1)) if sequences with 'fair' quality had been allowed

Figure 2. Original video sequences with low MOS.

The precision of subjective ratings is more a trait of the subject than the scale, as demonstrated by Tominaga et al. [2]. The distribution of ratings will not narrow simply because subjects have a smaller portion of the scale to work with when rating all versions of some sequences. In practical terms, this means that the data analysis will be less able to distinguish between distortions for sequences with poor editing and camerawork.

The impact of editing and camerawork can be seen in these sequences. Figure 1 scenes contain more scene cuts, animation, vibrant colors, and good scene composition. These qualities add visual interest and improve the esthetic appeal. Figure 2 sequences contain a variety of minor problems that had a large cumulative impact on MOS, such as motion blur, analog noise, camera wobble, poor scene composition, long shot lengths (e.g., no scene cuts), a boring topic, or an uninteresting presentation (e.g., the action in vqegHD5 src2 would be more exciting if seen from a closer zoom). These minor problems have a large cumulative impact on quality. These differences can be best understood by watching the videos on the Consumer Digital Video Library (CDVL; http://www.cdvl.org). Sequence 'vqegHD6 src 14' from Figure 1 can be found by searching for the title 'Common SRC 14,' and 'vqegHD6 src 4' from Figure 2 can be found by searching for the title 'NTIA Green Bird.'

Niu and Liu [3] analyze the differences between professionally produced video and amateur video. They propose an algorithm that detects whether or not a video has professional production quality. Niu and Liu describe the quality impact of camera motion, shot length (e.g., duration between scene cuts), lighting, color palette, noise, focus, and depth of field.

5. CHOOSE SCENES THAT EVENLY SPAN A WIDE RANGE OF CODING DIFFICULTY

Video encoders, video decoders, error concealment software, and video quality metrics often adapt to the coding difficulty of the video. Thus, some algorithmic deficiencies appear only in hard-to-code scenes, while others appear only in easy-to-code scenes. If the scene pool for a subjective experiment considers only easy-to-code scenes (or only hard-to-code scenes), then the system under test will not be fully characterized. For example, when scenes are coded at a low bitrate, the motion caused by the *I*-frame update is typically difficult to detect in a hard-to-code scene yet becomes obvious in an easy-to-code sequence with very little motion, such as 'NTIA Snow Mountain' from CDVL. As another example, a sequence with a person running across the scene can be problematic for some error concealment algorithms because filling in the missing video with prior content causes the running person to disappear.

Easy-to-code scenes are widely available because they are easy to shoot. Finding hard-to-code content is more challenging. To simplify the task of judging scene complexity, we use an objective complexity metric such aswhere I_n is the luma plane of source sequence image number *n*, $\max_{time}$and mean_{time} are the maximum and mean values in the time series, respectively, and std_{space} and rms_{space} are the standard deviation and root mean square over all pixels in one image, respectively.

- Spatial perceptual information (SI) from ITU-T Rec. P.910 [4]

$$\text{SI} = \max_{time}\left\{\text{std}_{space}\left[\text{sobel}(I_n)\right]\right\} \tag{1}$$

- Temporal perceptual information (TI) from ITU-T Rec. P.910 [4]

$$\text{TI} = \max_{time}\left\{\text{std}_{space}\left[I_n - I_{n-1}\right]\right\} \tag{2}$$

- Criticality from Fenimore et al. [5]

$$\mathrm{SI}(I_n) = \mathrm{rms}_{\mathrm{space}}[\mathrm{sobel}(I_n)] \tag{3}$$

$$\mathrm{TI}(I_n) = \mathrm{rms}[I_n - I_{n-1}] \tag{4}$$

$$\mathrm{Criticality} = \log_{10}\{\mathrm{mean}_{\mathrm{time}}[\mathrm{SI}(I_n) \times \mathrm{TI}(I_n)]\}, \tag{5}$$

Alternatively, the scenes can be classified visually. To estimate coding difficulty, we encode all video content at a constant, low bitrate. The hard-to-code sequences will have a much lower resultant quality than the easy-to-code sequences.

At a minimum, we recommend the following:

- Two clips that are very difficult to code (e.g., criticality ≥ 3.5)
- Two clips that are very easy to code (e.g., criticality ≤ 2.5)
- One high spatial detail clip (e.g., many small objects, SI ≥ 200 [4])
- One high motion clip (e.g., an object that moves across the screen in 1 s, which corresponds to an angular speed of 33°/s on a Full-HD display at 3H distance)

6. CONSIDER FREQUENCY AND PLACEMENT OF SCENE CUTS

Scene cuts interact in interesting ways with quality perception and with video codecs. Winkler [6] analyzes prior research on spatial masking and temporal masking. Scene cuts mask impairments that occur temporally one frame to a few hundred milliseconds after a scene cut (i.e., 'forward masking'). 'Backward masking' can also occur, masking impairments before a scene cut.

Encoders can introduce a new group of pictures in response to a scene cut. This affects the bitrate allocation during encoding and the propagation of transmission errors during decoding. Scene cuts occur very frequently in movies and broadcast television [3]; they do not typically occur in other applications such as videoconferencing or surveillance.

Scene cuts complicate subjective testing. The concern is that the encoded quality may be dramatically different before and after the scene cut due to changes in properties of the video content. The task of judging quality, usability or experience thus becomes more difficult, because the perceived quality changes. Some researchers only select content that does not have scene cuts. This was the prevalent opinion expressed in VQEG and ATIS throughout the 1990s.

The problem is that these results may not fully represent user experiences. This is the prevalent opinion expressed in VQEG today. Our preference regarding scene cuts is to select the following:

- About half of the clips with scene cuts
- One clip with rapid scene cuts (e.g., every 1 to 2 s)
- About half of the clips without scene cuts

Note that the 'differing quality' phenomenon is not unique to scenes with scene cuts. This also occurs spatially or temporally in continuously filmed content. Different parts may be better focused or intentionally blurred, relatively still, or containing significant motion. Any of these variations will trigger quality differences that might make the subject's task more difficult.

7. SELECT SCENES WITH UNUSUAL PROPERTIES

We learn the most from unique scenes with extraordinary features that may stimulate anomalous behavior in the transmission chain. For example, consider a scene showing a closeup view of a person. Test subjects know how people should look, move, and sound. Their internal reference helps them notice the unnatural motion of a reduced frame rate. That reduced frame rate may be less obvious when watching a video of a machine. A frame rate or frame freeze will become imperceptible if it occurs during a still or nearly still segment of a video sequence, as would a frame freeze. By contrast, a frame freeze that occurs in the middle of a camera pan will be obvious.

The following scene traits can interact in unique ways with a codec or a person's perception. Our ideal scene pool includes all of these traits:

- Animation, graphic overlays, and scrolling text
- Repetitious or indistinguishable fine detail (e.g., gravel, grass, hair, rug, pinstripes)
- Sharp black/white edges
- Blurred background, with an in-focus foreground
- Night or dimly lit scene
- Ramped color (e.g., sunset)
- Water, fire, or smoke (for unusual shapes and shifting patterns)
- Jiggling or bouncing picture (e.g., handheld camera)
- Flashing lights or other extremely fast events
- Action in a small portion of the total picture
- Colorful scene
- Small amounts of analog noise (e.g., camera gain from dim lighting)
- Multiple objects moving in a random, unpredictable manner
- Visually simple imagery (e.g., black birds flying across a blue sky)
- Very saturated colors
- Rotational movement (e.g., a carousal or merry-go-round seen from above)
- Camera pans
- Camera zoom
- Tilted camera

8. CONSIDER INTERLACE ISSUES

Interlacing and deinterlacing artifacts can occur when a scene contains edges that move within the frame. Moving diagonal edges are particularly noticeable. These artifacts become particularly visible, and thus objectionable, on moving diagonal edges. The traditional deinterlacing detection sequence is a Silicon Optix test disc[a] sequence showing an American flag waving in the breeze. Deinterlacing artifacts are easily visible on the high-contrast edges of the red and white stripes. The pictures in the work of Jung et al. [7] and Koo et al. [8] show the impact of deinterlacing problems using this flag sequence. Although any content with moving diagonal edges may be used, interlacing problems are more easily seen on strong contrast edges, which may trigger additional impairments.

9. NEW ISSUES WHEN SELECTING 3D SEQUENCES

Content selection in 3D subjective assessment tests is made even more complicated due to the introduction of binocular disparity. To ensure viewing comfort for any given target display size, new restrictions must be applied when shooting or selecting 3D content [9].

Besides the comfortable viewing criterion for 3D content, the inclusion of the stereopsis in the content allows for particular content that is perceived differently from its two-dimensional (2D) counterpart. Win et al. [10] demonstrate that the 2D and 3D versions of the same sequence receive different subjective scores and that simply wearing 3D glasses has a negative impact upon the perceived quality. Jumisko-Pyykkö and Utriainen [11] found that 2D and 3D presentation modes on a small mobile device yielded very different response levels to questions about satisfaction, quality, and acceptability. When asked about their viewing experience, subjects selected very different qualitative terms. Therefore, 3D subjective experiments should include sequences that exercise stereopsis in a variety of ways.

10. CHOOSE CONTENT THAT AVOIDS VISUAL DISCOMFORT AND EYE FATIGUE

Because poorly produced 3D content may cause visual discomfort and eye fatigue, content editing and camerawork become a critical factor when selecting 3D content. Professional stereographers seek to maintain the 3D effect while minimizing discomfort. The conventional advice includes restricting the scene depth, positioning important objects in the plane of the monitor, and limiting crossed parallax (i.e., preventing objects from appearing too close to the viewer) [12]. Mendiburu [13] provides an in-depth primer on 3D camerawork from a stereographer's perspective. 3D@Home (http://www.3dathome.org) provides a variety of useful information, including a tutorial on adapting 3D content to different display technologies, recommendations for creating 3D content, and a list of training courses.

Several research studies have examined this issue from an engineer's perspective. Lee et al. [14] analyze the underlying properties of reconstruction of 3D content on stereoscopic screens and the allowable depth budget. Chen et al. [15] propose a detailed shooting rule for 3D content, based on the results of several subjective experiments.

11. INCLUDE A VARIETY OF MOTION DIRECTIONS

One commonly used advantage of 3D is the ability to portray motion in the depth plane (e.g., motion toward or away from the viewer). This effect is often used in production. However, fast depth motion can lead to visual discomfort [16, 17]. The non-translational motion behavior (i.e., motion in the depth plane) challenges video coding algorithms, causing the appearance of different artifacts in the two views, which often results in binocular rivalry.

Fast motion was already mentioned for 2D sequences (e.g., include one high motion clip). Fast planar motion (i.e., motion parallel to the screen) becomes an important feature for 3D, because it can introduce visual discomfort in 3D viewing [18, 19]. The magnitude of visual discomfort caused by objects moving in the depth plane depends on the position and size of the object, as well as its motion amplitude and speed [20].

The pop-out effect occurs when an object with a large positive disparity is shown in front of the screen for a limited duration. The pop-out effect stresses the 3D effect and is therefore often used as a short-term attractor for 3D visualization.

A 3D scene pool should include at least two sequences with slow motion in depth, sequences with different amounts of planar motion (e.g., slow to fast), and one pop-out effect. The goal is to maximize motion diversity while avoiding motion that causes visual discomfort. The professional stereographer filming guidelines mentioned above can help the experimenter make this assessment, but, in the end, the experimenter is responsible for conducting an ethical experiment that will not cause subjects undue discomfort. The level of visual discomfort caused by candidate 3D sequence should be subjectively assessed by a panel of experimenters during 3D sequence selection.

12. VARY THE DEPTH BUDGET AND DISPARITY

Depth budget is a term that combines the positive and negative parallax into a single measurement [12]. The depth budget determines the nearest and furthest objects that the viewer perceives using stereopsis. As the depth budget increases, the differences between what the left eye and right eye see increase.

A large depth budget is caused by shooting 3D sequences at short distances (e.g., filming objects less than 5 m away) or using hyper-stereoscopic shooting (usually resulting from separating the two cameras at a large distance compared to their zoom factor). Sequences with a large depth budget are susceptible to transmission degradations. For example, their coding gain due to redundancy reduction between the views may be limited by the large disparity and the number of occlusion regions. A large depth budget can also cause crosstalk artifacts to become more pronounced.

A small depth budget is caused by shooting 3D sequences at greater distances with a higher zoom factor but without increasing the interocular distance (e.g., filming objects more than 6 m away) or limiting the depth information (i.e., distance between objects from the camera's point of view). This reduces the perceived depth effect, with the limiting case being 2D. A small depth budget decreases the added value of 3D but generally also reduces visual degradations due to transmission and display properties. A small depth budget minimizes viewer discomfort.

Another interesting disparity effect occurs when the object of interest is not the closest object to the camera. Such sequences can cause unexpected perception issues, because visual attention is attracted by close objects [21]. Our ideal 3D scene pool includes a variety of depth budgets and focal objects at differing disparities.

13. LOOK FOR SCENES THAT INTERACT IN UNIQUE WAYS WITH 3D

The stereoscopic appearance of graphical animations or cartoons differs significantly from natural content. First, optimal camera positions for reconstruction of virtual 3D scenes may be guaranteed. Second, cartoon-type content often contains high image contrasts between flat textured regions; this does not occur in natural content. Likewise, coding algorithms respond differently to mixed content sequences with pronounced contours such as vector graphics.

We vary the distribution of small structures and large structures, fine details, and uniform areas. This is known as frequency distribution, and it influences the perception of 3D [22].

Subtitles or other graphical overlays have large occlusion areas and a high contrast between the foreground text and the video background. Subtitles and other graphical overlays may be particularly impacted by coding and transmission algorithms when contours get smoothed. The depth position of the foreground text may become less obvious, and depth cue conflicts may occur with the background.

14. EXPERIMENTAL DESIGN AND IMPLEMENTATION ISSUES

The goal of experimental design is to objectively answer a question about an opinion and reach statistically significant conclusions. The nature of human perception inherently confounds all of the variables involved, which adds difficulty.

The critical issue here is that scene choices do not bias the results - either by indicating differences where none exist or by missing significant differences in the response of a variable. When these errors stem from the choice of scenes, the error likely cannot be detected unless an additional subjective test is conducted.

15. CHOOSE A RATING METHOD THAT SOLVES EDITING AND CAMERAWORK PROBLEMS

Some subjective scales may reduce the impact of editing and camerawork on the ratings. We recommend the following subjective scales for experiments where there is a need to minimize the impact of editing and camerawork:

1) Double stimulus impairment scale (DSIS), also known as degradation category rating, ITU-T Rec. P.910

2) Pair comparison (PC), also known as double stimulus comparison scale and comparison category rating, ITU-R Rec. BT.500

3) Double stimulus continuous quality scale (DSCQS), ITU-R Rec. BT.500

4) Subjective assessment of multimedia video quality (SAMVIQ), ITU-R Rec. BT.1788

5) Simultaneous double stimulus for continuous evaluation (SDSCE), ITU-R Rec. BT.500

These subjective rating scales reduce the impact of editing and camerawork by exposing subjects to both the impaired and the source video, using the source video as a point of reference. The differences between rating methods can be best understood by examining the treatment of the reference video and the comparison task performed by the subject:

- *Labeled reference*. Subjects are told that they are observing the source video.

- *Unlabeled reference*. Subjects are unaware that they are observing the source video.

- *Direct comparison*. Subjects watch two versions of the same sequence and then rate the perceptual difference.

- *Implied comparison*. Subjects watch two or more versions of the same sequence and then rate the quality of each sequence on the same scale. The subjects do not explicitly rate the perceptual difference themselves, yet it is assumed when looking at the rating interface that this comparison will be made by the experimenter.

- *Indirect comparison*. Subjects watch and rate each sequence separately. The unlabeled reference sequence is hidden among the sequences to be rated. The source and impaired sequence ratings are subtracted to compute a difference rating, but the subjects would typically not know that this will occur.

For implied and indirect comparisons, the ratings from the source and impaired sequences are subtracted to compute a difference rating. We expect the standard deviation of these difference ratings to be slightly larger than the standard deviation of the ratings of the individual sequences. The actual impact on the standard deviation will depend upon how much correlation exists between the ratings of the source sequence and the ratings of the impaired sequence. If uncorrelated, we would expect an increase of 41% (i.e., a square root of two increases in the standard deviation). If perfectly correlated, the standard deviation of the difference will be 0. Data from the VQEG reduced reference and no reference (RRNR-TV) test show an 18.1% increase for the 525-line experiment and a 9.6% for the 625-line experiment. These tests were conducted using the ACR with hidden reference (ACR-HR) method from ITU-T Rec. P.910.

We do not recommend the use of indirect comparisons when trying to minimize the impact of editing and camerawork on ratings. An indirect comparison is used by the ACR-HR method. The same technique can be used with single stimulus continuous quality evaluation from ITU-T Rec. BT.500; however, that technique has not been standardized.

Table 1 identifies the approach used by each of the recommended subjective methods. As of this paper's publication, no studies have been published demonstrating an in-depth analysis of how effective these methods are at eliminating the impact of production quality on subjective ratings.

Table 1. Strategies for reducing the impact of editing and camerawork on subjective ratings

	Direct comparison	Implied comparison
Labeled reference	DSIS	SAMVIQ, SDSCE
Unlabeled reference	PC	DSCQS

16. DO NOT SKIMP ON YOUR SCENE TOTAL

Experimental design is always a compromise between the number of impairments, the number of scenes, and each subject's participation time. It is tempting to reduce the number of scenes (or subjects) so that the number of impairments can be increased. The problem is that only limited conclusions can be drawn when the degradations are analyzed over a narrow range of contents, and those conclusions may not generalize. This makes it impossible to accurately characterize a system under test. The following guidelines optimize the ratio of content variety for the number of degradations.

An entertainment-oriented subjective video quality test of 2D content should use a scene pool containing approximately eight to ten clips. A robust 3D subjective test requires 10 to 14 sequences, because of the additional factors introduced (e.g., motion direction, depth of field, disparity, and unique 3D content interactions).

The impact of the number of scenes on an experiment can be seen in Pinson et al. [23]. This article analyzes 13 subjective experiments. Each explored the relationship between the following:

- Audio subjective quality (***a***)
- Video subjective quality (***v***)

- The overall audiovisual subjective quality (***av***)

One way to measure this is the Pearson correlation between ***av*** and the cross term (***a*** × ***v***). Figure 3shows a histogram of these correlations, split by the number of scenes in the experiment:

- Limited (one or two)
- Normal (five to ten)

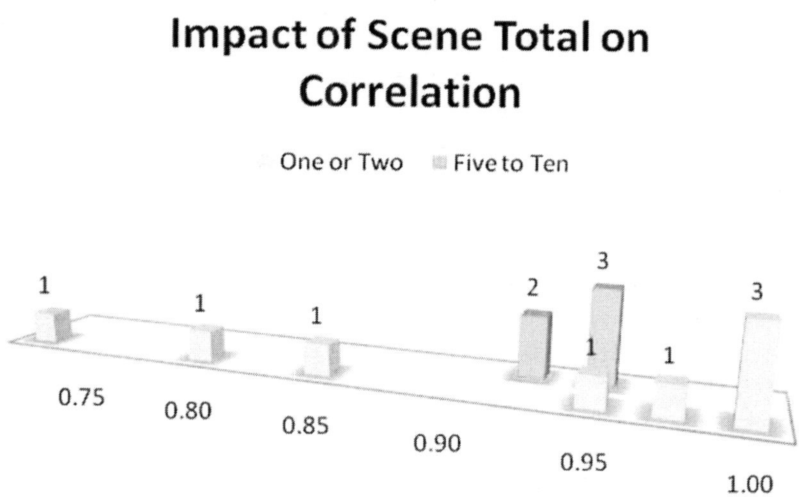

Figure 3. An analysis of 13 subjective tests shows that experiment accuracy depends upon the scene total.

The former spans a range of Pearson correlation from 0.72 to 0.99, indicating that chance played a large role. The latter are tightly clustered, indicating a high degree of repeatability.

17. AVOID OVERTRAINING BY MAXIMIZING DIVERSITY

A common problem is selecting scenes from one small pool of video content. This biases research results toward characteristics of those video sequences. Overtraining is a likely by-product of small scene pools or reusing the same sequences in multiple experiments. For example, an objective model might yield very poor quality estimates when exposed to new content or an encoder might yield very poor quality for some content types (e.g., fire, smoke, confetti, a wood parquet floor, fireworks, saturated red, long dissolves, a pinstripe shirt). Instead, we encourage you to find new sequences for each experiment.

Poor scene selection can invisibly bias experimental results. This is easier to see by examining an experiment with good scene selection. For example, Barkowsky et al. [24] analyze a subjective test that investigated the quantization parameter (QP) parameter on the quality of H.264 encodings. Quantization is the primary algorithmic cause of lost information in the MPEG-2 and H.264 video encoders, so QP is directly linked to image degradation. This experiment's nine scenes were chosen using the criteria described in the section 'Basic scene selection.' Six scenes show similar QP/quality response curves, while the other three show unique behaviors. Without those three scenes, the reported ability of QP to predict quality would have been inflated.

A small number of websites host professionally produced source video content. CDVL [25] is a repository of broadcast quality video content and provides free video clip downloads of video clips for research and development purposes. CDVL's goal is to foster research and development into consumer video processing and quality measurement. Winkler [26] identifies two other websites that provide uncompressed source video, plus 27 subjective quality image and video databases.

Freely available 3D content is rare. Some 3D sequences are provided by Urvoy et al. [27], Goldmann et al. [28], and Cheng et al. [22].

18. BE AWARE OF TEST FORMAT IMPLICATIONS

The format of a subjective video quality experiment is intentionally artificial. Aural clues that are normally provided by the accompanying audio are missing. Consider these real-world examples:

- The video freezes at the beginning of a movie when a character is introduced, and the character's name is overlaid. The viewer knows that this is intentional because the music and voiceover continue.

- The video flickers quickly between the picture and black to signify that we are seeing past events. A sound effect indicates that this is a flashback.

- For artistic reasons, the video has a digital effect overlay of another color (see Figure 4, left). The edge pattern is similar to what might occur with a transmission error.

- The picture intentionally contains impairments typical of old film, to imply that events occurred long ago (see Figure 4, right).

- Very rapid scene cuts (e.g., 0.25 s apart) can make it appear that the video is fast-forwarding or skipping content in response to network problems.

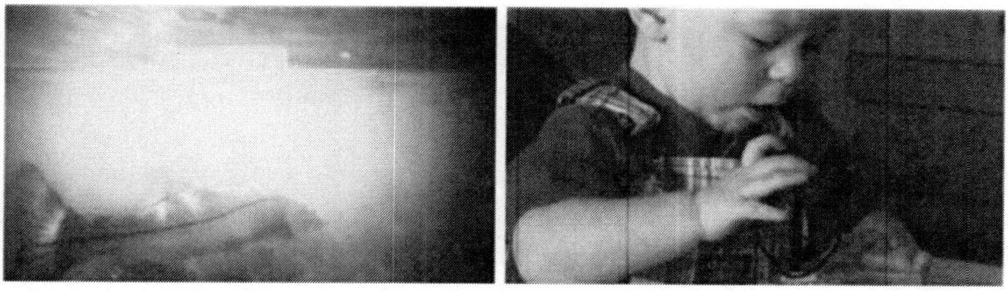

Figure 4. Artistic video effects that may look like impairments: color overlay (left) and old film (right).

Without the extra information from the audio track, these artistic effects are indistinguishable from network transmission errors, channel switches, display issues, or other sources of degradation.

19. PERFORM SCENE SELECTION ON THE DEVICE TO BE TESTED

Video quality subjective testing has traditionally involved uncompressed video played to broadcast quality monitors. This controlled for the effect of the video playback and monitor from the data and helped us focus on video encoding, network transmission, and video decoding.

Subjective testing on mobile devices must use compressed playback and lower quality monitors - and account for their confounding impact on the subjective data. The computer that used to view, select, edit, and impair the video is probably a more powerful computer - perhaps a high-end PC with a large monitor. Switching to the device under test will impact the appearance of your sequence [29]. We recommend that you always perform final scene selection on the device under test.

20. SEMI-AUTOMATIC SELECTION OF SOURCE SCENE POOLS

Selecting a non-biased, well-balanced source sequence set for a subjective experiment may prove difficult for a single researcher. The following suggests an approach to achieve semi-automatic scene selection.

Begin by enumerating attributes for the available video sequences. This often requires a subjective judgment that should ideally be deferred to a group of observers. Possible attributes include whether or not the scene contains rapid scene cuts, the amount of saturated color presence, and how professional is the editing. Some attributes are concrete and thus Booleans (e.g., whether or not the scene contains flashing lights), but most of the properties are measured along a subjective scale (e.g., to what extent is this a night scene). To reduce selection bias, the definition of each attribute should be established and then a panel of observers asked to rate the attributes of each available video sequence (e.g., 100 videos from the CDVL database).

This approach does not necessarily require standardized environments, and thus, using crowd-sourcing technologies may be appropriate [30]. After obtaining a vector of attributes for each video sequence, data mining algorithms may be applied. Consider the following semi-automatic algorithm:

A. An expert in subjective experiment preparation picks an initial video sequence.

B. The semi-automatic algorithm then suggests a set of video sequences which correlate least to the selected video sequence over all scale value dimensions (see Figure 5).

C. The researcher then picks a second video sequence.

D. The algorithm takes into consideration the properties of both sequences to recommend options for the third scene (see Figure 6).

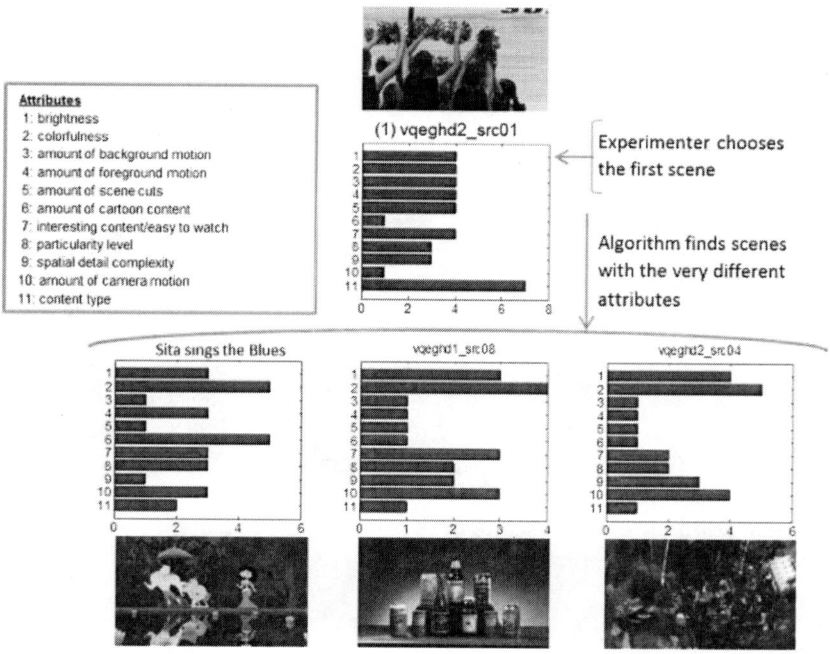

Figure 5. Semi-automated scene pool selection steps A and B.

This selection and search process continues iteratively (i.e., steps C and D). This allows the selection of video sequences to be more objective and avoids bias while still allowing for interaction when particular video properties are not taken into consideration by the automation.

Figures 5 and 6 illustrate the semi-automatic scene pool selection algorithm using a database of about 200 video sequences and the 11 attributes displayed in Figure 5. In a preliminary experiment, three observers rated each attribute on a scale of one to ten.

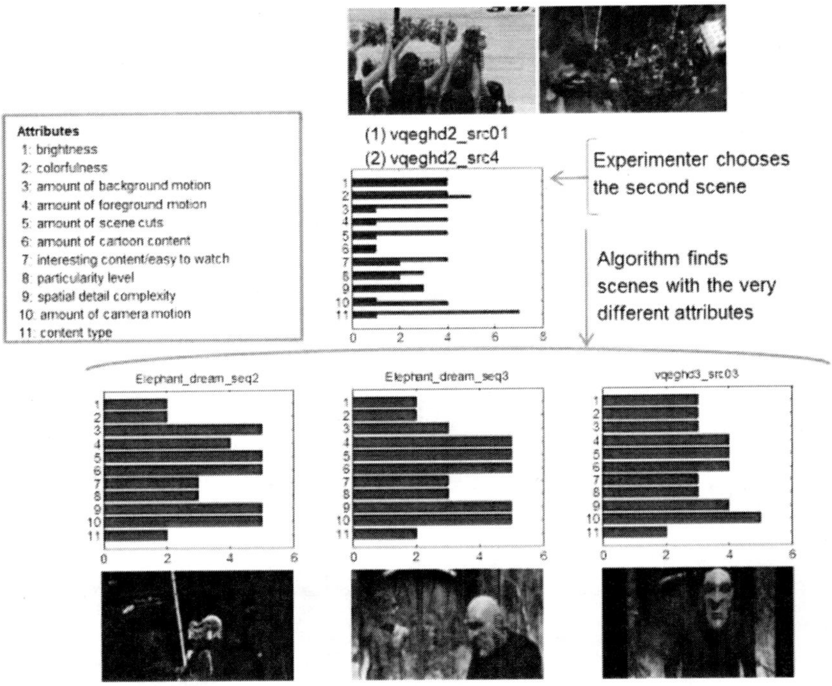

Figure 6. Semi-automated scene pool selection steps C and D.

The criterion for selecting the most diverging video sequences was calculated as follows. The distance metric was Pearson linear correlation coefficient, calculated over all 11 attributes. The distance was measured between each of the selected sequences and each of the remaining candidate sequences. The distance metric was averaged over the selected sequences (e.g., one sequence for Figure 5 and two sequences for Figure 6). The three sequences with the maximum average distance (i.e., minimum correlation) are shown in Figures 5 and 6. Notice that the algorithm proposed three very different options for the second sequence in Figure 5. However, all three proposals for the third sequence were cartoon sequences with mostly dark features, as may be found in the open-source movie 'Elephants Dream' [31].

21. CONCLUSIONS

The correct selection of scene pools for subjective experiments has been previously mostly limited by content availability. Limited research has been performed on the influence of source variety selection in subjective experiments with respect to reproducibility of assessment results. In most cases, only the influence on degradations, such as coding performance, has been studied.

This paper proposed guidelines for the selection of scene pools with a large variety of content, including a semi-automatic selection process. Mostly 2D video content has been addressed, as it is widely available. For the newly available stereoscopic content dimension, guidelines have been proposed which are meant to facilitate the collection of meaningful source video content or to provide hints for producing or shooting missing content types. Similar guidelines for scene pool selection should be developed for other types of subjective assessments, for example, audiovisual quality assessment.

ENDNOTES

[a]Certain commercial equipment, materials, and/or programs are identified in this report to specify adequately the experimental procedure. In no case does such identification imply recommendation or endorsement by the National Telecommunications and Information Administration nor does it imply that the program or equipment identified is necessarily the best available for this application.

NOTES

Margaret H Pinson, Marcus Barkowsky contributed equally to this work.

ACKNOWLEDGEMENTS

The authors would like to thank technical copy editor Lilli Segre, technical reviewer Wade Allen, technical reviewer Andrew Catellier and editorial sponsor John Vanderau.

Margaret H. Pinson's work was funded by the US government through the NTIA. Patrick Le Callet's and Marcus Barkowsky's work is financed by the French ministry for higher education and research. It was partly conducted within the scope of the PERSEE project which is financed by ANR (project reference: ANR-09-BLAN-0170), and the JEDI (Just Explore DImensions) ITEA2 project which was supported by the French industry ministry through DGCIS.

REFERENCES

1. VQEG: *Report on the validation of video quality models for high definition video content, (Video Quality Experts Group, June 2010).* . Accessed August 2013

2. Tominaga T, Hayashi T, Okamoto J, Takahashi A: *Performance comparisons of subjective quality assessment methods for mobile video. Paper presented at the 2nd Quality of Multimedia Experience (QoMEX).* Trondheim; 2010.

3. Niu Y, Liu F: What makes a professional video? A computational aesthetics approach. *IEEE Trans Circ Syst Video Tech* 2012., 22(7):

4. ITU: *ITU-T Recommendation P.910. Two Criteria for Video Test Scene Selection. Section 6.3*. ITU, Geneva; 1994.

5. Fenimore C, Libert J, Wolf S: *Perceptual effects of noise in digital video compression. Paper presented at the 140th SMPTE technical conference*. Pasadena; 1998.

6. Winkler S: Issues in vision modeling for perceptual video quality assessment. *IEEE Signal Process Mag*1999., 78(2):

7. Jung Y, Yang S, Yu P: An effective de-interlacing technique using two types of motion information. *IEEE Trans. Consum. Electron* 2003., 49(3):

8. Koo HI, Lee SH, Cho NI: A new EDI-based deinterlacing algorithm. *IEEE Trans. Consum. Electron* 2007., 53(4):

9. Chen W, Fournier J, Barkowsky M, Le Callet P: *New requirements of subjective video quality assessment methodologies for 3DTV. Paper presented at the 5th international workshop on video processing and quality metrics (VPQM)*. Scottsdale; 2010.

10. Win SL, Caviedes J, Heynderickx I: *2D vs. 3D visual quality evaluation: the depth factor. Paper presented at the 7th international workshop on video processing and quality metrics (VPQM)*. Scottsdale; 2013.

11. Jumisko-Pyykkö S, Utriainen T: *User-centered quality of experience: is mobile 3D video good enough in the actual context of use? Paper presented at the 5th international workshop on video processing and quality metrics (VPQM)*. Scottsdale; 2010.

12. Minoli D: *3D Television (3DTV) Technology, Systems, and Deployment*. CRC Press, Florida; 2011.

13. Mendiburu B: *3D Movie Making: Stereoscopic Digital Cinema from Script to Screen*. Focal Press, Oxford; 2009.

14. Lee S, Jung YJ, Hosik S, Ro YM: *Subjective assessment of visual discomfort induced by binocular disparity and stimulus width in stereoscopic image. Paper presented at SPIE electronic imaging, stereoscopic displays and applications*. Burlingame; 2013.

15. Chen W, Fournier J, Barkowsky M, Le Callet P: *New stereoscopic video shooting rule based on stereoscopic distortion parameters and comfortable viewing zone. Paper presented at SPIE electronic imaging, stereoscopic displays and applications XXII*. San Francisco; 2011.

16. Li J, Barkowsky M, Wang J, Le Callet P: *Study on visual discomfort induced by stimulus movement at fixed depth on stereoscopic displays using shutter glasses. Paper presented at the 17th international conference on digital signal processing (DSP)*. Corfu; 2011.

17. Speranza F, Tam WJ, Renaud R, Hur N: *Effect of disparity and motion on visual comfort of stereoscopic images, in Proceedings of SPIE stereoscopic displays and virtual reality systems XIII, 6055*. San Jose; 2006.

18. Li J, Barkowsky M, Le Callet P: *The influence of relative disparity and planar motion velocity on visual discomfort of stereoscopic videos. Paper presented at the 3rd international workshop on quality of multimedia experience (QoMEX)*. Mechelen; 2011.

19. Lambooij M, Fortuin M, IJsselsteijn WA, Heynderickx I: *Measuring visual discomfort associated with 3D displays. Paper presented at stereoscopic displays and applications XX*. San Jose; 2009.

20. Speranza F, Tam WJ, Renaud R, Hur N: *Effect of disparity and motion on visual comfort of stereoscopic images. Paper presented at stereoscopic displays and virtual reality systems XIII*. San Jose; 2006.

21. Wang J, Le Callet P, Tourancheau S, Ricordel V, Da Silva MP: Study of depth bias of observers in free viewing of still stereoscopic synthetic stimuli. *J Eye Mov Res* 2012., 5(5):

22. Cheng E, Burton P, Burton J, Joseski A, Burnett I: *RMIT3DV: pre-announcement of a creative commons uncompressed HD 3D video database. Paper presented at the 4th international workshop on quality of multimedia experience (QoMEX)*. Yarra Valley; 2012.

23. Pinson M, Ingram W, Webster A: Audiovisual quality components. *IEEE Signal Process. Mag* 2011., 28(6):

24. Barkowsky M, Pinson M, Pèpion R, Le Callet P: *Analysis of freely available subjective dataset for HDTV including coding and transmission distortions. Paper presented at the 5th international workshop on video processing and quality metrics for consumer electronics (VPQM)*. 2010.

25. Pinson M, Wolf S, Tripathi N, Koh C: *The consumer digital video library. Paper presented at the 5th international workshop on video processing and quality metrics for consumer electronics (VPQM)*. Scottsdale; 2010.

26. Winkler S: Analysis of public image and video databases for quality assessment. *IEEE J Sel Top Signal Process* 2012., 6(6):

27. Urvoy M, Barkowsky M, Cousseau R, Koudota Y, Ricordel V, Le Callet P, Gutiérrez J, Garcia N:*NAMA3DS1-COSPAD1: subjective video quality assessment database on coding conditions introducing freely available high quality 3D stereoscopic sequences. Paper presented at the 4th international workshop on quality of multimedia experience (QoMEX)*. Yarra Valley; 2012.

28. Goldmann L, De Simone F, Ebrahimi T: *A comprehensive database and subjective evaluation methodology for quality of experience in stereoscopic video. Paper presented at the electronic imaging (EI), 3D image processing (3DIP) and applications*. San Jose; 2010.

29. Catellier A, Pinson M, Ingram W: *A Webster, Impact of mobile devices and usage location on perceived multimedia quality. Paper presented at the 4th international workshop on quality of multimedia experience (QoMEX)*. Yarra Valley; 2012.

30. Keimel C, Habigt J, Horch C, Diepold CK: *Video quality evaluation in the cloud. Paper presented at the 19th international packet video workshop (PV)*. Munich; 2012.

31. Blender Foundation, The Orange Project: *Elephants Dream in stereoscopic 3D.* . Accessed March 2013

Chapter 7

Adaptive multiple description video coding and transmission for scene change

Mengmeng Zhang and Huihui BaiEmail author

1 College of Information Engineering, North China University of Technology, Beijing, China.

2 Institute of Information Science, Beijing Jiaotong University, Beijing, China.

ABSTRACT

In view of perfect compatibility with the standard source and channel codec, temporal sampling-based multiple description coding (MDC) has become a better choice for practical applications. However, for the frames change from one scene to another temporal correlation may be destroyed by temporal sampling extremely, which results in the false estimation when the related frames are lost at the side decoder. Therefore, in this article the frames containing scene change are detected and duplicated before temporal sampling, which maintains better temporal correlation in each description. Furthermore, for better rate distortion performance temporal sampling is employed adaptively, that is, frame skipping or up-sampling according to the motion characteristics in original video. The experimental results exhibit better performance of the proposed scheme than other schemes whether in the on–off MDC environment or packet lossy network, especially about 15 dB improvements for the frames with scene change. Therefore, it may be a promising choice for video transmission over error-prone channels, especially over wireless networks.

KEYWORDS

Video coding, Multiple description coding, Temporal sampling

1. INTRODUCTION

In the recent years, the increasing demands for multimedia communication have generated a lot of research interests in developing novel image or video compression technologies. Due to network congestion and delay sensibility, it is always a great challenge for video transmission over lossy network. Multiple description coding (MDC) is an attractive approach to solve this problem. It can efficiently combat packet loss without any retransmission thus satisfying the demand of real-time services and relieving the network congestion [1].

MDC encodes the source message into several bit streams (descriptions) carrying different information which then can be transmitted over multiple channels. In its simplest form, two parallel channels are assumed to connect the source with the destination. If only one channel works, the descriptions can individually be decoded to sufficiently guarantee a minimum fidelity in the reconstruction at the receiver. However, when both channels work, the descriptions from the channels can be combined to yield a higher fidelity reconstruction.

In the past years, many approaches for realizing MDC have been proposed, such as those using interleaved scalar quantizer [2], lattice vector quantizer [3, 4], pairwise correlating transforms [5], FEC [6], and so on. Although these methods have shown good performance, they are incompatible with widely used standard codecs, such as H.26x and MPEG-x.

To overcome the limitation, pre- and post-processing-based MDC may be a good choice. In pre-processing, the original source is split into multiple sub-sources before encoding and then these sub-sources can be encoded separately by the standard codec to generate multiple descriptions. The study of [7] is a typical example, which employs hierarchical B pictures in the H.264/AVC scalable extension [8] for a pre-processing-based MDC. Furthermore, sub-sampling technique can also be applied in pre-processing to realize multiple sub-sources, such as the MD video coder based on spatial sampling [9] and the MD video coder based on temporal sampling [10]. In the method of spatial sampling, through zero padding inside each individual frame, only the correlation of intra-frame is considered to improve side distortion and the temporal correlation of inter-frame is neglected completely. In [10], the method of temporal sampling is proposed to make motion compensation interpolation (MCI) more efficient for lost frames, which turns to better rate distortion performance. However, considering the video sequences containing different scenes, simple MCI method may lead to false interpolated reconstruction at the decoder. Recently, for robust transmission over wireless network, in [11, 12] some new MD methods like distributed MDC have been proposed to achieve better rate distortion performance by optimized redundancy allocation for the splitting video sub-sequences.

To address this problem from scene change, a preliminary scheme is presented in [13]. Here, in this article an improved MD coding based on adaptive temporal sampling is proposed to make sure the decoder can work correctly when scene changes. According to the temporal correlation in the original video, the frames containing scene change can be detected before temporal sampling. Then, these frames are duplicated and transmitted over both channels for better side reconstruction. Furthermore, adaptive temporal sampling is applied, that is, frame skipping and up-sampling in terms of motion characteristics between the frames, which can achieve better rate distortion performance.

The rest of this article is organized as follows. In the following section, the proposed MD video coding scheme is presented including pre- and post-processing stages and improvement for scene change. The performance of the proposed scheme is examined against some other relevant MD coders in Section "Experimental results". We conclude the article in Section "Conclusions".

2. PROPOSED MDC SCHEME FOR SCENE CHANGE

Figure 1 illustrates the proposed MDC scheme for scene change. In the pre-processing stage, scene change is first detected, and then considering the different motion information between frames, if the inter-frame motion is enough smooth some frames are skipped to obtain high compression efficiency. On the other hand, if the abrupt motion occurs, the original video sequence is up-sampled to generate a new-length video with adaptively redundant frames. In the post-processing, the corresponding decoders should be designed with two main functions. One is down-sampling the decoded video stream to erase the redundant frames. The other is using error concealment methods to estimate lost frames. The details of adaptive temporal sampling and the improvement for scene change are shown in the following subsections.

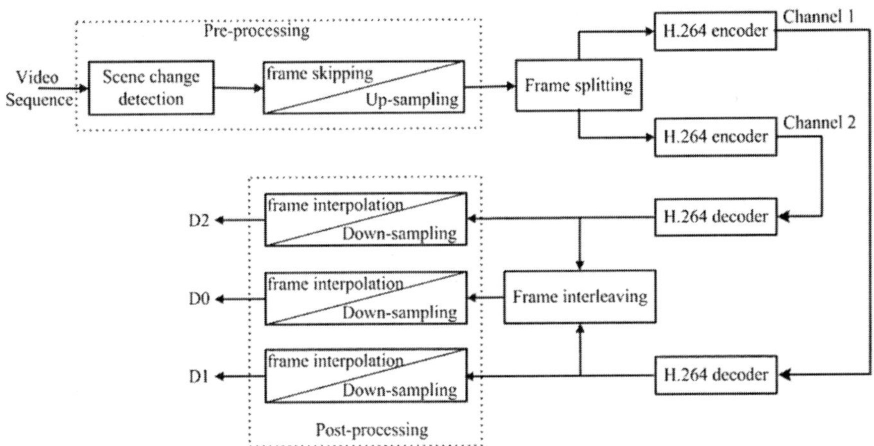

Figure 1. Block diagram of proposed scheme.

3. ADAPTIVE TEMPORAL SAMPLING IN PRE-PROCESSING

In terms of the principle of MDC, higher quality of side decoded video will result from more correlations in descriptions because better error concealment is available, but more redundancy introduced will also bring about lower efficiency to the central decoder. Obviously, it is a better solution that the redundancy added should make a tradeoff between the reconstructed quality and compression efficiency. As a result, in the pre-processing stage, the sampling with flexible frame rate is employed to introduce the adaptive redundancy. Since unstable motion appearance of inter-frames will affect the performance of error concealment at the side decoder, the rate of sampling should be various according to the motion information between any two neighboring frames. More interpolated frames or higher rate of up-sampling will be utilized to smooth the abrupt motion between the frames. On the other hand, if no abrupt motion happens, no redundant frames are needed. Furthermore, if the motion information between continuous frames is enough stable, some middle frames can be skipped to guarantee the high compression efficiency. Such method of pre-processing mainly aims to generate descriptions with regular motion which can make better estimation of lost frames available at the side decoder.

For any two neighboring frames denoted by F_k and F_{k+1}, all the motion vectors for each macroblock are computed and their maximum value can be obtained. Here, it is denoted by $\|MV\|_{(k,k+1)}$ and $\|MV\|_{(k,k+1)} = \sqrt{x^2+y^2}$ ((*x*, *y*) is the coordinates of the maximal motion vector). Then, the module $\|MV\|_{(k,k+1)}$ is compared with the threshold T_1. If $\|MV\|_{(k,k+1)} <= T_1$, some frames may be skipped. But, the number of skipped frames depends on the module of maximal motion vectors between F_k and the following frames of F_{k+1}. At the same time, considering the balance of two channels and better evaluation at side decoder, even frames in the middle are skipped. For example, if $\|MV\|_{(k,k+2)} <= T_1$, $\|MV\|_{(k,k+3)} <= T_1$, and $\|MV\|_{(k,k+4)} >= T_1$, then two frames F_{k+1} and F_{k+2} are skipped and F_k and F_{k+3} are retained for better side reconstruction. Furthermore, if $\|MV\|_{(k,k+1)} >= T_2$, the motion between the two frames is considered unstable so redundant frames are interpolated to smooth such motion information. In view of the balance of two channels, even frames are interpolated to maintain equal frame number of two descriptions. Consequently, the number of interpolated frames is computed by $2 \times \lceil(\|MV\|/T_2 - 1)/2\rceil$ and the redundant frames can be generated using the general algorithm of motion compensated interpolation, such as [10]. It is noted that for an original video with *N* frames if the mean value of all $\|MV\|_{(k,k+1)}$ can be computed as follows.

$$T = \frac{1}{N-1}\sum_{k=1}^{N-1}\|MV\|_{(k,k+1)} \tag{1}$$

Then the thresholds T_1 and T_2 are set empirically as $T_1 = T$ and $T_2 = 2T$.

In the pre-processing, new interpolated frames and skip some other frames may increase the encoding computational complexity to some extent. However, the increasing complexity mainly comes from the decision of interpolated or skipped frames. After the simple decision using motion vector, only a few frames need to be interpolated or skipped. Therefore, it cannot lead to higher complexity.

Additionally, the labels ('O', 'I', or 'S') are set for each frame to distinguish the original frame, interpolated one, or skipped one, then indexed with odd or even numbers and transmitted over two channels, respectively. Here, the labels are coded by entropy encoder, which nearly can be neglected compared with the total bit rate.

4. IMPROVEMENT FOR SCENE CHANGE

It is noted that the above temporal sampling method is proposed assuming any two neighboring frames are correlative in the video. However, considering the video comprised by different scenes, there is no correlation between the last frame in previous scene and the first frame in subsequent scene even if the two frames are neighboring. Here, we design the video sequence "merged" with three scenes, that is, the first 30 frames of "coastguard.qcif", "bridge close.qcif", and "highway.qcif" as an example, which is shown in Figure 2a–c. If using the simple comparison between $\|MV\|_{(k,k+1)}$and the threshold T_2, the interpolated frames will be inserted between two neighboring frames where scene change happens. Obviously, this will lead to substantial quality degradation, as shown in Figure 2d–e.

To address this problem, we must find out where scene change occurs in the video first. Here, we utilize the sum of compensated absolution difference (SCAD) as the criterion. The value of SCAD can be calculated as follows. Let $p_k(x,y)$ denote the pixel at the coordinates (x,y) in the current frame F_{k-1}. And its previous frame F_{k-1} can be considered as the reference frame. Then, the best match block for each block in frame F_k can be searched in its reference frame F_{k-1} and all the searched block from frame F_{k-1} can be produced as the motion compensated frame F_k'. Therefore, the SCAD can be calculated by $\sum_{x=1}^{M}\sum_{y=1}^{N} p_k(x,y) - p_k'(x,y)$, where $p_k'(x,y)$ is the pixel at the coordinates (x,y) in the motion compensated frame F_k' and the resolution of the video is $M \times N$pixels. Figure 3 shows the statistics of SCAD values for the video "merged". From Figure 3, the obvious scene changes can be found out at the sharp changes of the curve.

Figure 2. Three different scenes in the test video sequence "merged". (**a**) Scene 1, (**b**) Scene 2, (**c**) Scene 3, (**d**) Frame interpolated between Scenes 1 and 2, (**e**) Frame interpolated between Scenes 2 and 3.

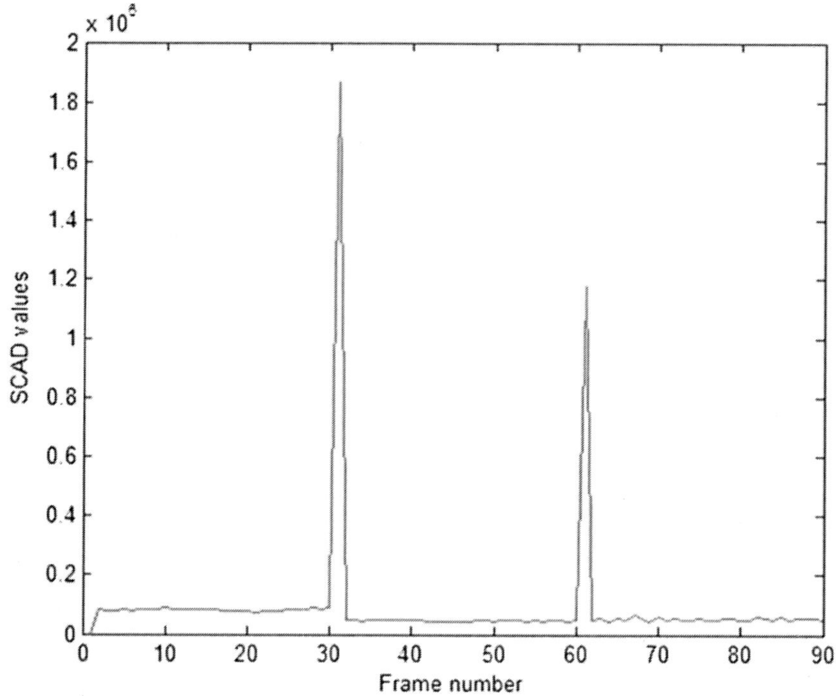

Figure 3. The SCAD values in the test video sequence "merged".

To distinguish the scenes in the video, new marks are needed, that is, 'A' represents the first frame of a scene and 'Z' represents the last frame. When scene change appears, both the first and the last frames of the current scene will be transmitted over all channels to ensure the intact rebuilding of frames. Here, take two channels as example. At the encoder frame F_{k-1} and F_k with scene change will be duplicated and the 'ZZAA' will be labeled at the same time. Then adaptive temporal sampling will be applied, which is introduced in Section "Adaptive temporal sampling in pre-processing". At the decoder, if two channels can work the duplicated frames will be deleted to obtain the central reconstruction. If only one channel works, side reconstruction can be accepted according to the labels.

5. ADAPTIVE TEMPORAL SAMPLING IN POST-PROCESSING

5.1 Decoder design for the on–off environment

In the post-processing stage, two situations for decoding should be taken into account, that is, the design of central or side decoder. Since the two descriptions are generated by odd and even splitting, at the central decoder the video streams from the standard decoder can be interleaved and realigned in the same way firstly. According to the labels, the interpolated frames can be down-sampled and the skipped frames can be interpolated to obtain the central reconstruction. If only one channel works, that is, the side decoder is employed, all the skipped frames with label 'S' should be interpolated first and reset their labels with 'O'. Then, four possibilities exist at the side decoder.

1) If the current label is 'O' but its following label is 'I', the represented frame is just the reconstructed one.

2) If the current label is 'I' but its following label is 'O', the represented frame is the interpolated frame and it can be regarded as the reconstructed one.

3) If the current label is 'I' and its following label is also 'I', the continuous frames represented by 'I' should be merged to a reconstructed frame.

4) If the current label is 'O', and its following label is also 'O', a new frame should be interpolated between the two frames denoted by 'O'.

In Figure 4, a simple example illustrates the pre- and post-processing. The original video sequence has ten frames denoted by F_1 to F_{10}. After pre-processing, the motion-modified video has 16 frames. From the figure, we can see even frames are interpolated adaptively, such as two frames interpolated between F_1 and F_2, four frames interpolated between F_4 and F_5. At the same time, even frames are skipped adaptively, such as two frames F_6 and F_7 skipped. After splitting by odd and even frames, the generated descriptions are denoted by video on channel 1 and video on channel 2 and the labels are 'OIOIIOSIO' and 'IOOIISOIO', respectively. At the receiver, the skipped frames with label 'S' are reconstructed first and reset the labels with 'O', so the labels can be updated as 'OIOIIOOIO' on channel 1 or 'IOOIIOOIO' on channel 2, respectively. When only channel 1 works, the reconstruction from side decoder 1 is achieved like the figure. The two interpolated frames between frames 3 and 5 will be merged into a new reconstructed one while a new frame is interpolated between frames 5 and 7 to estimate the lost frame 6. On the other hand, if two channels work, the lossless frames except two skipped frames F_6 and F_7 can be achieved without the processing by H.264 codec.

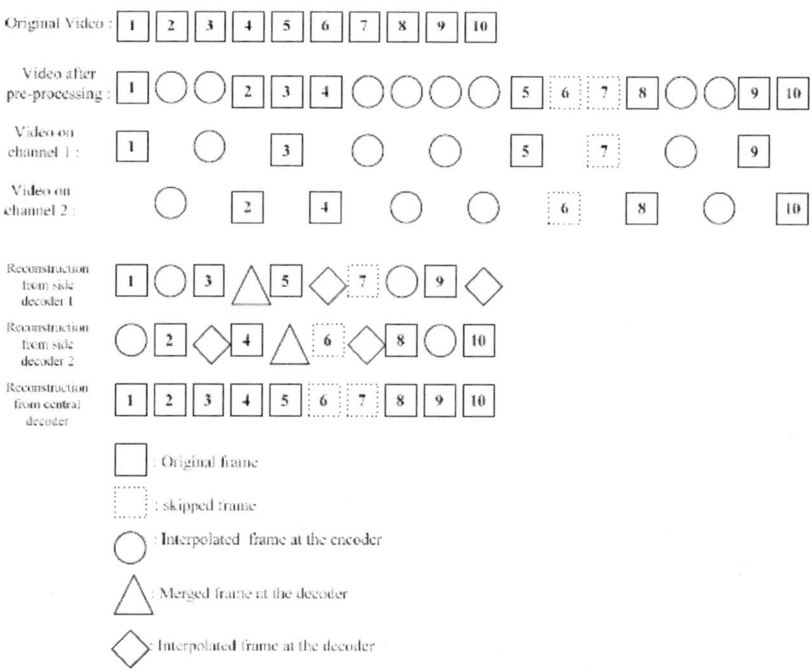

Figure 4. A simple example for the pre- and post-processing stages.

5.2 Decoder design for packet lossy network

In packet lossy network, due to both descriptions received with packet losses, only central decoder should be designed in post-processing stage and it is different from the approach in on–off MDC environment.

Figure 5 shows the block diagram of central decoder in packet lossy network. After H.264 decoding, the two generated video sequences are interleaved by odd and even frames to produce a new video data. Then, such video data are processed to obtain central reconstruction.

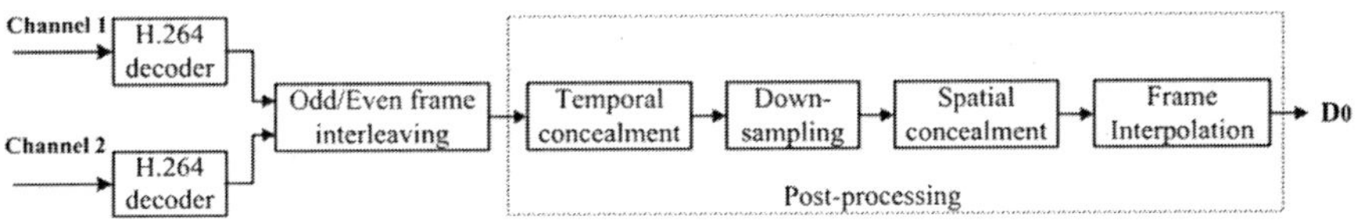

Figure 5. Block diagram of central decoder for packet lossy network.

In post-processing stage, temporal error concealment is first used to reconstruct those lost packets. Since the redundant frames exist, more motion information can be preserved than the conventional scheme, which turns to better reconstruction quality. After temporal concealment, those redundant frames are down-sampled. However, with the increasing of packet loss rate, there are still errors which are difficult to be concealed only by motion compensation, such as Figure 6a. Furthermore, error propagation will happen when such frames are up-sampled to interpolate skipped ones. As a result, before frame interpolation, spatial error concealment is employed to improve the performance from temporal error concealment. Figure 6b shows obvious visual improvement to substantiate the performance of spatial concealment. Here, the standard test video "coastguard.qcif" is coded at 80 kbps per channel with packet loss rate 15% per channel.

Figure 6. Error concealment in post-processing. (**a**) without spatial concealment: 26.742 dB; (**b**) with spatial concealment: 27.868 dB.

6. EXPERIMENTAL RESULTS

6.1 Performance in on–off MDC channels

Here, there are mainly two experiments taken into account to present the efficiency of adaptive sampling in temporal domain. The first one is shown the better performance of the proposed scheme than the conventional scheme without pre-processing stage. In the second experiment, the advantage of the proposed scheme is illuminated compared with the scheme using spatial sampling [9].

In the first experiment, the standard test video "coastguard.qcif" is used with 30 frames per second. For a fair comparison, the same mode and parameters are chosen in H.264 encoder and decoder [14].

Figure 7 shows the central and side distortion of the proposed scheme against the conventional scheme at the bit rate from 50 to 300 kbps per channel. From the figures, we can clearly see that our proposed scheme can still consistently improve around 0.8–1.5 dB in central distortion and 0.5–1.7 dB in side distortion. Obviously, this is just a global comparison for the whole video. In fact, some individual frames may achieve more advantages over the conventional schemes. From Figure 8, the side reconstructed frames by the two compared schemes are presented to illustrate the visual improvements of the proposed scheme at the bit rate 140 kbps.

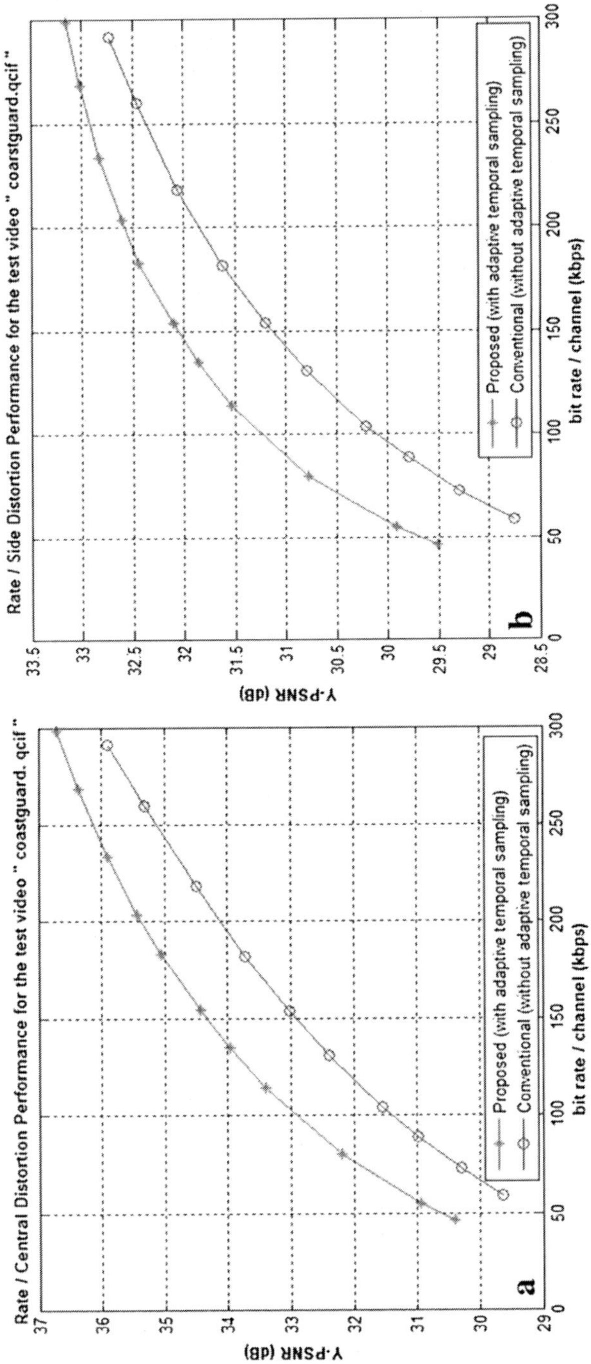

Figure 7. Comparison between the proposed and conventional scheme. (**a**) Rate/central distortion performance; (**b**) Rate/side distortion performance.

Figure 8. Comparison of side reconstruction for 72nd frame. (**a**) The conventional scheme: 22.999 dB, (**b**) the proposed scheme: 32.014 dB.

Figure 9 shows an example of the pre-processing for the standard video sequence "Coastguard.qcif". From Figure 9, it is shown the maximum values of motion vectors, that is, $\|MV\|$s. Here, the threshold T = 1.6003. In the original video "Coastguard.qcif", according to the pre-processing mentioned in Section "Adaptive temporal sampling in pre-processing", only 30 frames need to be interpolated and 18 frames need to be skipped, which can also be found in Figure 9.

Furthermore, Figure 10 shows the performance comparison between the proposed scheme and other schemes, such as the scheme in [9] using spatial sampling and the schemes in [11, 12] using distributed MDC. From Figure 10, we can see that compared with the scheme in [9] better rate and central/side distortion performance achieved by the proposed scheme, that is, at the same bit rate, 1–2 dB improvement in central distortion and 1–3 dB in side distortion. Additionally, compared with the schemes [11, 12] the proposed scheme has obtained 0.5–1.5 dB improvement in central distortion and 1–2 dB in side distortion.

6.2 Performance in packet lossy network

Here, the standard test video "coastguard.qcif" is chosen to examine our proposed scheme with 30 frames per second. For a fair comparison, the same mode and parameters are chosen in H.264 encoder and decoder.

Furthermore, the organization of packets is a checkerboard type for all the cases.

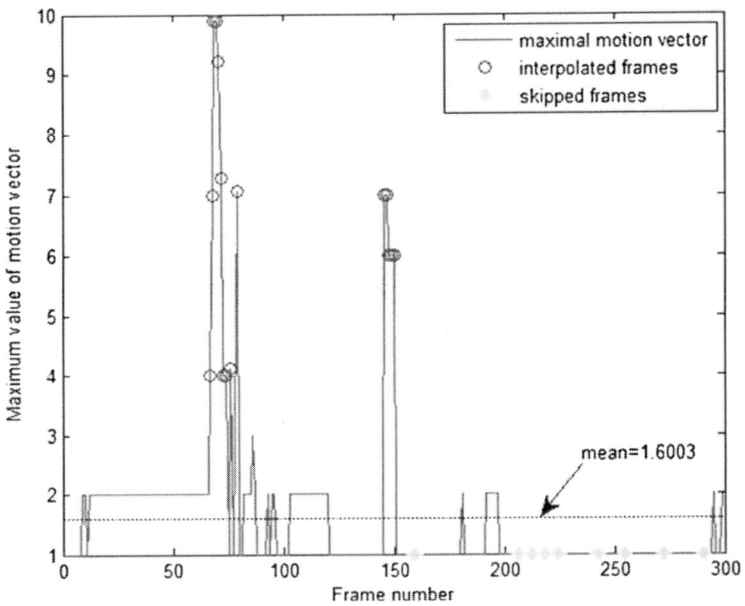

Figure 9. An example of pre-processing for the test video "coastguard.qcif": maximal motion vector between frames and the number of interpolated or skipped frames.

First, we validate the effectiveness of the proposed decoder with temporal-spatial concealment. In Figure 11, at the different bit rate 30, 80, and 180 kbps, the decoder with temporal-spatial concealment has better performance than the decoder only with temporal concealment. Especially at the larger packet loss rate, the proposed scheme has improved around 0.8–1 dB.

In Figure 12, at the same bit rate 180 kbps, the proposed scheme has achieved better performance than the conventional ones. The improvements are brought from 0.6 to 1.1 dB. Note that for low packet loss rate, the improvement is greater. With high packet loss rate, both the proposed scheme and the conventional one cannot do well in error concealment with so many packets lost.

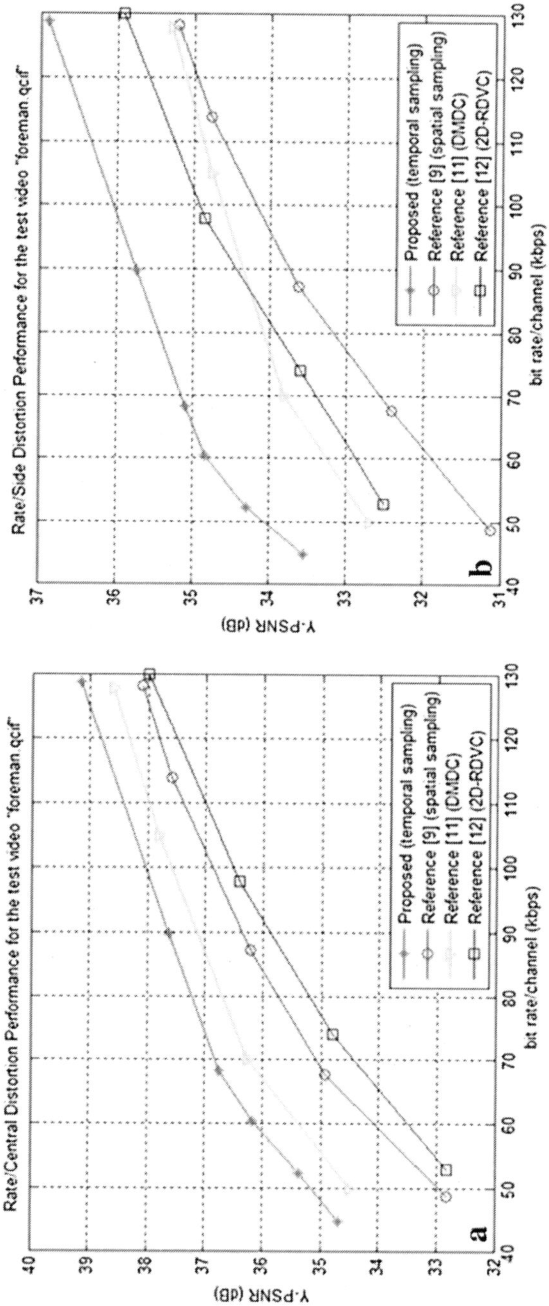

Figure 10. Comparison between the proposed and reference scheme [[9]]. **(a)** Rate/central distortion performance, **(b)** rate/side distortion performance.

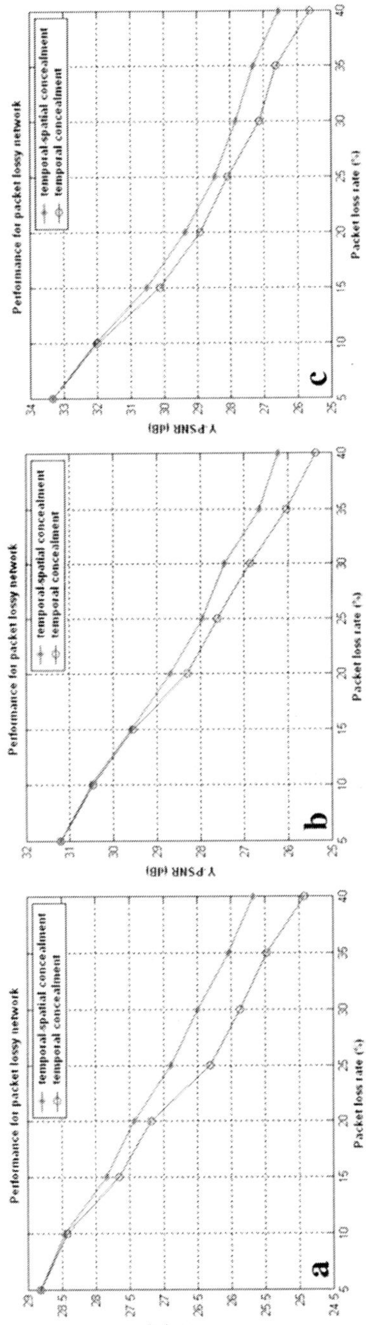

Figure 11. Comparison between the temporal-spatial concealment and temporal concealment. (a) 30 kbps, (b) 80 kbps, (c) 180 kbps.

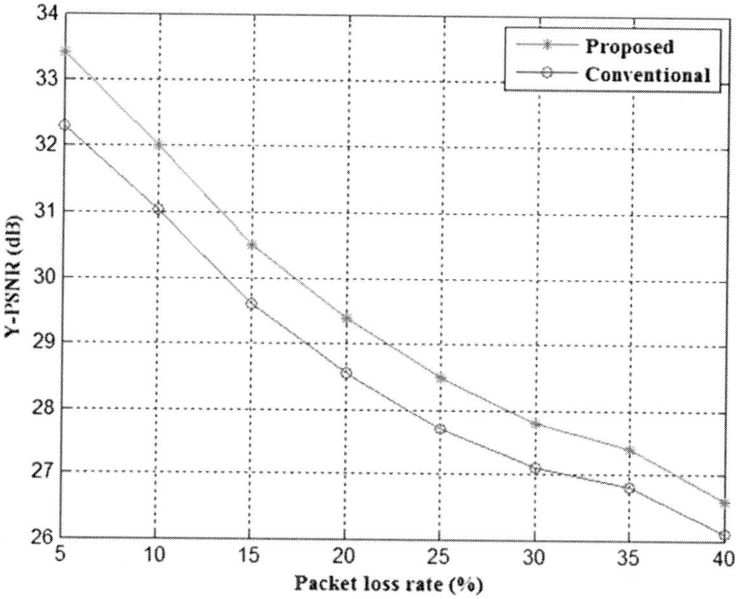

Figure 12. Comparison between the proposed scheme and the conventional one.

6.3 Performance for scene change

Here, the test video "merged" in Section "Proposed MDC scheme for scene change" is used to exhibit the better performance of the proposed scheme for scene change. In the proposed one the three scene changes have been taken into account when using adaptive temporal sampling while in the compared one scene changes have also been processed only through adaptive temporal sampling. For fair comparison, the same method of adaptive temporal sampling has been adopted for the above two schemes.

Figure 13 shows the central and side distortion of the proposed scheme against the compared scheme at the bit rate from 50 to 450 kbps per channel. Here, the bit rate means the total bit rate from both channels, the central quality denotes the reconstruction from both channels and the side quality is the average PSNR values from two side decoders. From the figures, we can clearly see that our proposed scheme can still consistently improve around 2–5.5 dB in side distortion although it has a slight decline in the central distortion. Obviously, this is just a global comparison for the whole video. In fact, some individual frames with scene change may achieve more advantages over the compared scheme. In Figure 14, the proposed scheme has achieved 15 dB improvement performance at 240 kbps for the frames with scene change.

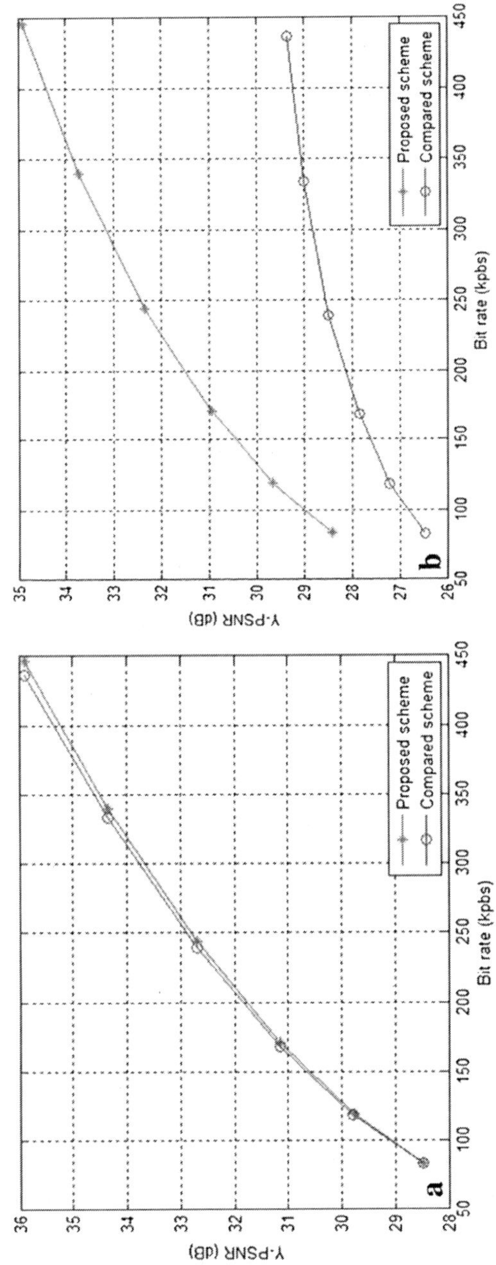

Figure 13. Rate-distortion performance. (**a**) Central quality; (**b**) side quality.

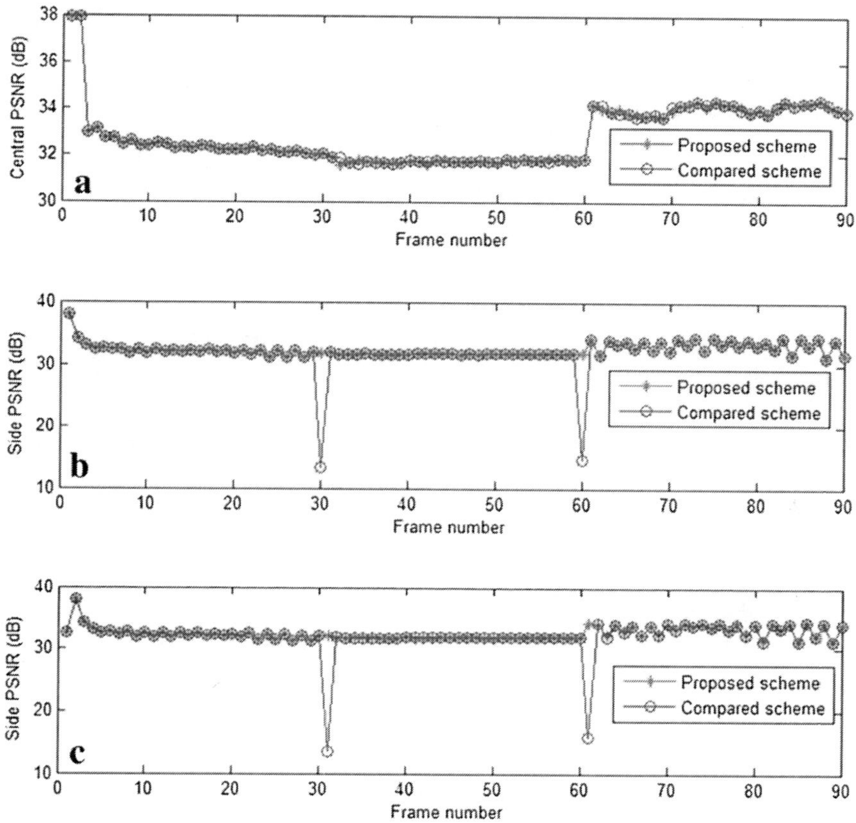

Figure 14. PSNR values of each frame. (**a**) Central decoder; (**b**) side decoder 1; (**c**) side decoder 2.

7. CONCLUSIONS

In view of perfect compatibility with the standard codec, the MD video coding based on pre- and post-processing may be a better choice in the practical applications. In this article, adaptive frame skipping or up-sampling is employed in the pre-processing to obtain better tradeoff between the compression efficiency and reconstructed quality. Furthermore, when scene change happens in the original video, the pre-processing are improved to avoid error frame interpolation, even severe quality degradation. As a result, the proposed MD video coding scheme has demonstrated superior rate-distortion performance to the conventional MD video coder and spatial sampling-based scheme, which may be a promising choice for video transmission over error-prone channels, especially over wireless networks.

ACKNOWLEDGMENT

This study was supported in part by the 973 program (2012CB316400), the National Natural Science Foundation of China (Nos. 61103113, 60903066), the Beijing Natural Science Foundation (No. 4102049), the Specialized Research Fund for the Doctoral Program of Higher Education (No. 20090009120006), the Fundamental Research Funds for the Central Universities (No. 2011JBM214), the Jiangsu Provincial Natural Science Foundation (BK2011455) and PHR (IHLB) (PHR201008187).

REFERENCES

1. Goyal VK: Multiple description coding: compression meets the network. *IEEE Signal Process. Mag.* 2001, 18(5):74-93.

2. Vaishampayan V, John S: *Balanced interframe multiple description video compression*. 3rd edition. International Conference on Image Processing (ICIP), Kobe, Japan; 1999:812-816.

3. Bai H, Zhu C, Zhao Y: Optimized multiple description lattice vector quantization for wavelet image coding.*IEEE Trans. Circuits Syst. Video Technol.* 2007, 17(7):912-917.

4. Liu M, Zhu C: M-description lattice vector quantization: index assignment and analysis. *IEEE Trans. Signal Process.* 2009, 57(6):2258-2274.

5. Reibman AR, Jafarkhani H, Yao Wang MT, Reibman AR, Jafarkhani H, Yao W, Orchard MT, Puri R: Multiple-description video coding using motion-compensated temporal prediction. *IEEE Trans. Circuits Syst. Video Technol* 2002, 12(3):193-204.

6. Chang S, Cosman PC, Milstein LB: Performance analysis of channel symmetric FEC-based multiple description coding for OFDM networks. *IEEE Trans. Image Process.* 2011, 20(4):1061-1076.

7. Zhu C, Liu M: Multiple description video coding based on hierarchical B pictures. *IEEE Trans. Circuits Syst. Video Technol.* 2009, 19(4):511-521.

8. ITU-T and ISO/IEC JTC 1: *Advanced Video Coding for Generic Audiovisual Services*. ITU-T Rec. H.264 & ISO/IEC 14496-10; 2005. Version 4, July

9. Wang D, Canagarajah N, Redmill D, Bull D: *Multiple description video coding based on zero padding*. International Symposium on Circuits and Systems (ISCAS), Vancouver, CA; 2004:205-208.

10. Bai H, Zhao Y, Zhu C: *Multiple description video coding using adaptive temporal sub-sampling*. International Conference on Multimedia and Expo (ICME), Beijing China; 2007:1331-1334.

11. Crave C, Guillemot B, Crave O, Guillemot C, Pesquet-Popescu B, Tillier C: Distributed temporal multiple description coding for robust video transmission. *EURASIP J. Wirel. Commun. Netw.* 2008. Article ID 183536 (2008)

12. Wang A, Li Z, Zhao Y, Wang W, Bai H: Two-description distributed video coding for robust transmission.*EURASIP J. Adv. Signal Process.* 2011, 76: 2011.

13. Zhang M, Bai H: *Temporal sampling based multiple description video coding for scenes switching*. Data Compression Conference (DCC), Snowbird Utah, USA; 2012:413-413.

14. ITU-T Rec. H.264 ISO/IEC 14496-10 AVC: *Draft ITU-T Recommendation and Final Draft International Standard of Joint Video Specification*. JVT Doc JVT-G050, Joint Video Team (JVT) of ISO/IEC MPEG & ITU-T VCEG(ISO/IEC JTC1/SC29/WG11 and ITU-T SG16 Q.6) 7th Meeting, Pattaya, Thailand; 2033. 7-14 March

Chapter 8

Facial expression recognition and histograms of oriented gradients: a comprehensive study

Pierluigi Carcagnì*†, Marco Del Coco† , Marco Leo† and Cosimo Distante†

National Research Council of Italy, Institute of Applied Sciences and Intelligent Systems, Via della Libertà, 3, 73010 Arnesano , LE, Italy

ABSTRACT

Automatic facial expression recognition (FER) is a topic of growing interest mainly due to the rapid spread of assistive technology applications, as human–robot interaction, where a robust emotional awareness is a key point to best accomplish the assistive task. This paper proposes a comprehensive study on the application of histogram of oriented gradients (HOG) descriptor in the FER problem, highlighting as this powerful technique could be effectively exploited for this purpose. In particular, this paper highlights that a proper set of the HOG parameters can make this descriptor one of the most suitable to characterize facial expression peculiarities. A large experimental session, that can be divided into three different phases, was carried out exploiting a consolidated algorithmic pipeline. The first experimental phase was aimed at proving the suitability of the HOG descriptor to characterize facial expression traits and, to do this, a successful comparison with most commonly used FER frameworks was carried out. In the second experimental phase, different publicly available facial datasets were used to test the system on images acquired in different conditions (e.g. image resolution, lighting conditions, etc.). As a final phase, a test on continuous data streams was carried out on-line in order to validate the system in real-world operating conditions that simulated a real-time human–machine interaction.

KEYWORDS

Facial expression recognition HOG SVM

1. BACKGROUND

Facial expression is one of the most common non-verbal way that humans use to convey internal emotional states and, consequentially, plays a fundamental role in interpersonal interactions. Although there exists a wide range of possible facial expressions, psychologists have identified the six basic ones (happiness, sadness, fear, disgust, surprise, and anger) that are universally recognized (Izard 1971). It is straightforward that a system capable to perform an automatic recognition of the human emotions is a desirable task for a set of emerging applications related to assistive technologies, digital signage, audience measurement and so on. More specifically, the capability to automatically recognize the emotional state of a human being is a key factor to the challenging field of the human–robot interaction since on the one hand it allows to introduce behavioral metrics and on the other hand it could increase the level of technology acceptance. Unfortunately, the design of a system with a high recognition rate is a non trivial task due to a wide set of problems. Some of the involved issues, such as scene illumination conditions (Song et al.2010) and camera viewpoint (Lucey et al. 2010), can be addressed by selecting a proper acquisition set-up or by preprocessing operations. On the other hand, the variability in appearance of different subjects, and even of the same subject, performing the same expression introduces a bias factor that stresses the decision block of the FER system and that requires further investigation to be properly handled. Moreover, a robust FER system should deal with the intrinsic variations in performing the same expression for subjects of different ethnic and cultural backgrounds. For these reasons, in the last years, the interest of the computer vision community in FER has exponentially grown-up and a wide range of solutions can be found in literature. Proposed solutions can be divided into two main categories: the first category includes the solutions that classify human emotions by processing a set of consecutive images while, the second one, includes the approaches which perform FER on each single image. By working on image sequences much more information is available for the analysis. Usually, the neutral expression is used as a reference and some characteristics of facial traits are tracked over time in order to recognize the evolving expression (Dornaika et al. 2011). To this end, the use of key points and texture information (Song et al. 2010), a modified version of the well known Local Binary Patterns (LBP) combined with moments (Ji and Idrissi 2012), a pyramid of LBP (Khan et al. 2013), a combination of Independent Component Analysis (ICA), Fisher Local Discriminant Analysis (FLDA) and Hidden Markow Models (HMM) (Uddin et al. 2009), optical flow and non-linear features (Siddiqi et al. 2014), are some of the most effective approaches used to represent facial traits to be tracked over time. The major drawback of these approaches is the inherent assumption that the sequence content evolves from the neutral expression to another one that has to be recognized. This constrain strongly limits their use in real world applications where the evolution of facial expressions is completely unpredictable. For this reason, the most attractive solutions are those performing facial expression recognition on a single image. The approaches in literature that work on a single image can be conveniently categorized depending on the strategies they use to lead towards the recognition of emotions. In this way, two main categories arise:

- Component based approaches
- Global approaches

Component based approaches preliminary extract some facial components and then try to classify expressions on the basis of the matching among corresponding components or by comparing the geometrical configuration among different components. An example is given by Pantic and Rothkrantz (2000) where an automatic facial expression system based on geometrical features is presented. The same authors in Pantic and Rothkrantz (2004) introduce a recognition system for facial expression analysis from static face images by exploiting ten profile-contour fiducial points and 19 fiducial points of the contours of the facial components. A comparison between geometric positions of a set of fiducial points and a set of multi-scale and multi-orientation Gabor wavelet coefficients is investigated in Zhang et al. (1998). Loconsole et al. (2014) propose the use of linear and eccentricity geometrical features in association with a machine learning classifier in order to maximize the discriminative capability and test their approaches with the recent Radboud Faces Database Langner et al. (2010). Poursaberi et al. investigate the use of Gauss–Laguerre wavelets in association with geometrical position of fiducial points in order to provide valuable information for the upper/lower face zone Poursaberi et al. (2012).

The work in Zhang and Tjondronegoro (2011) proposes the use of "salient" distance features, which are obtained by extracting patch-based 3D Gabor features, selecting the most discriminative patches and performing patch matching operations. More recently, Happy and Routray (2015) propose a novel framework for expression recognition by using appearance based features of selected facial patches depending on the position of facial landmarks that are active during emotion elicitation. Then patches are further processed to obtain the salient ones containing the most discriminative features for classification.

Unfortunately, although the idea of making use of a preliminary selection of salient facial components and a subsequent emotion recognition phase based on geometrical or textural matching has been widely investigated, the achieved classification performances do not fulfill the demanding requirements of the technologies that a FER system has to serve. The main unresolved issues concern the alignment of components in different facial images, especially in case of extreme expressions. Moreover, they experienced high computational time due to the load for the fine extraction of the facial components (especially when iterative strategies are used) and then they appear to be not suitable for real world applications especially if low-power systems are involved (e.g. assistive robot, consumer analysis devices) (Sadeghi et al. 2013).

The above mentioned problems can be overcome by using "Global Approaches" i.e. approaches that directly try to extract a representation of the expressions from the appearance of the global face. This research area has been deeply investigated, but there is still much effort to do since it is very challenging to find a global set of descriptors able to robustly characterize human expression traits. Some of the most recent related works, that have arisen as a consequence of the theoretical improvements in the definition of more reliable local descriptors, are listed below. In Shan et al. (2009) authors use Local Binary Pattern (LBP) even in low resolution and compressed input images whereas, in Zhao and Zhang (2011), the same descriptors are combined with a kernel-based manifold learning method called Kernel Discriminant Isometric map (KDIsomap). Ramirez Rivera et al. (2013) propose in a new descriptor, named local directional number pattern (LDN), that extracts directional information by using compass masks and encodes such information using the prominent direction indices. The sparse representation-based classification (SRC) is used with a principal component analysis (PCA)-based dictionary in Mohammadi et al. (2014), in combination with the local phase quantization (LPQ) in Zhen and Zilu (2012) and Gabor filters in Liu et al. (2012). An algorithm for facial expression recognition, by integrating curvelet transform and online sequential extreme learning machine (OSELM) with radial basis function (RBF) hidden node, is proposed in Uçar et al. (2014).

As revealed in the previous discussion, FER problem is clearly related to the facial deformation. Different persons could express the same emotion with some differences, but the majority of the involved muscles work in such a way to give a coherent characterization of that emotions among different people of different ethnicity and gender.

This paper proposes an comprehensive study of the application of histogram of oriented gradients descriptor (HOG) in the FER problem highlighting as this powerful technique could be effectively exploited for this purposes. HOG is a shape descriptor that counts occurrences of gradient orientations in localized portions of an image and that is mainly used for the purpose of object detection but that is also intuitively useful to model the shape of the facial muscles by means of an edge analysis. To the best of our knowledge, HOG descriptor has been used as a tool for FER purposes in a few works. The use of a log-likelihood map in association with a hierarchical decision tree, in order to select the most discriminative HOG features in the HOG grid, is presented in Orrite et al. (2009) whereas the use of HOG and SVM is proposed in the context of a specific challenge in Dahmane and Meunier (2011) and successively in Chen et al. (2014); the first one uses an adaptive grid size whereas the second one focuses its novelty on the selection of sub-regions of interest. Anyway, in both cases, the descriptor is exploited with its standard parameters and the results are not completely satisfactory. HOG, jointly to sparse coding, is analyzed by OuYang and Sang (2013) in order to make the FER problem more robust respect to occlusions. The HOG descriptor is also used in conjunction with other descriptors. For instance it is associated to the Weber's Local Descriptor (WLD) one in Wang et al. (2013). In Barroso et al. (2013) it is concatenated to LBP and SIFT (Scale-invariant feature transform) and a good analysis of the influence of the knowledge of the subject is done. The only work that performs a more accurate investigation of importance of parameters is Gritti et al. (2008) where authors, anyway, focus their attention on the alignment perturbations for different descriptors [HOG, Local Ternary Pattern (LTP), LBP and Gabor filters] and demonstrate that the best FER performances are obtained using LBP. Anyway, all the above mentioned works do not perform any investigation about how the parameters of the HOG descriptor can affect the FER process and therefore it is not proved that HOG descriptor has been exploited at its best.

The study, carried out in this paper, highlights that a proper set of the HOG parameters can make this descriptor one of the most suitable to characterize facial expression peculiarities. This has been demonstrated by a large experimental session where, exploiting a consolidated algorithmic pipeline, results showed that, using HOG to characterize facial expression peculiarities, the experienced FER outcomes can outperform the most commonly used FER frameworks. The algorithmic pipeline takes as input a single frontal facial image and it performs a preliminary face detection and registration (Castrillón et al. 2007) (allowing the following procedural phase to be performed in a more effective way). HOG descriptor is then applied on the registered face and finally the classification is performed by means of a set of SVMs. Additional experimental sessions, carried out on different publicly available datasets, give evidence that the emerged HOG parameter configuration is not dependent on the input data since it can be left unchanged when the FER pipeline is applied on different sets of data assuring anyway very encouraging FER performances outcomes. As a final step, a test on continuous data streams has been carried out on-line in order to validate the findings of the study in real-world operating conditions that simulated a real human–machine interaction. In this experimental phase, a temporal window and a consistency rule have been introduced to handle the incoming video streams in real time.

The rest of the paper is organized as follows: in "Methodology overview" the proposed pipeline is detailed with an in-depth description of each operating step. "Experimental data setup" is aimed at the datasets description whereas in "Experimental results: phase 1" the optimization of the HOG parameters and the comparison of the optimized pipeline with alternative appearance descriptors and leading state of the art approaches are supplied and discussed. "Experimental results: phase 2" reports the FER performances on additional publicly available datasets and, finally, "Experimental results: phase 3" reports the evaluation of the proposed approach on video sequences. "Conclusions" concludes the paper.

2. METHODOLOGY OVERVIEW

Facial expression recognition, from generic images, requires an algorithmic pipeline that involves different operating blocks. The scheme in Fig. 1 has been used in this work: the first step detects human faces in the image under investigation and then detected faces are registered (Castrillón et al.2007). This preliminary operations allow the system to get the quite similar position for the eyes and in this way the subsequent HOG descriptor may be applied using a coherent spatial reference. The vector of features extracted by HOG is finally used for the classification of the facial emotions by means of SVM strategies. Finally, the managing of the temporal images stream is demanded to an ad-hoc decision rule. Each operating step is detailed in the following subsections.

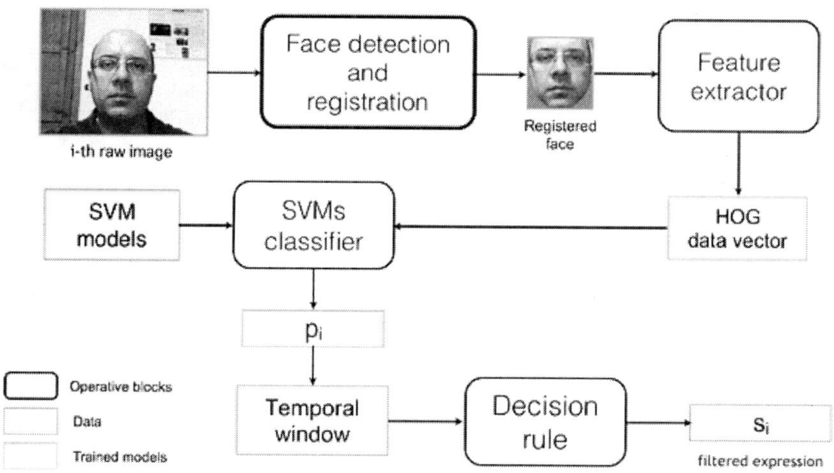

Figure 1. Proposed system pipeline: faces are cropped and registered and then HOG descriptor is applied to build a data vector that is provided as input to a SVM bank that gives the estimation of the observed facial expression. Finally, the prediction is queued in the temporal window exploited by the decision rule in order to filter possible misclassifications

3. FACE DETECTION AND REGISTRATION

In this step, human faces are detected in the input images and then a registration operation is done. The registration is a fundamental preprocessing step since the subsequent algorithms work better if they can evaluate input faces with predefined size and pose. The face detection is performed by means of the general frontal face detector proposed by Viola and Jones (2004) which combines increasingly more complex classifiers in a cascade. Whenever a face is detected, the face registration is carried out as follows: the system, at first, fits an ellipse to the face blob (exploiting facial features color models) in order to rotate it to a vertical position and hence a Viola-Jones based eye detector searches the eyes. Finally, eye positions, if detected, provide a measure to crop and scale the frontal face candidate to a standard size of 65×59 pixels. The above face registration procedure is schematized in Fig. 2.

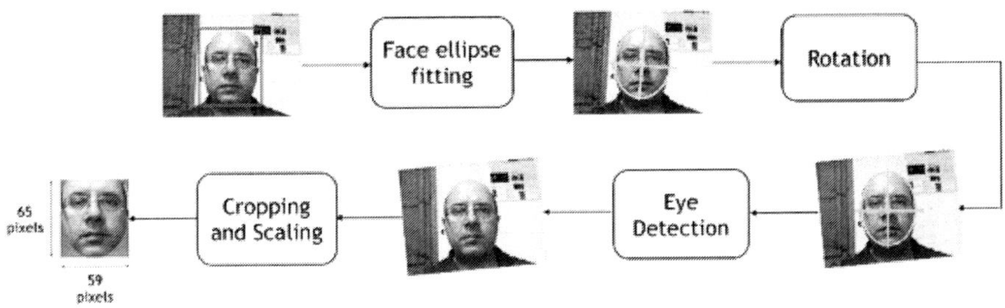

Figure 2. Face registration: the detected face is fitted in an ellipse used to rotate the face in a perfectly vertical position; successively eyes are detected and used to scale the image and to crop the area of interest

The registered face is then modeled using different features (average color using red-green normalized color space and considering just the center of the estimated face container; eyes patterns; whole face pattern) in order to re-detect it, for tracking purposes, in the subsequent frames (Castrillón et al. 2007). Finally, it is given as input to the features extractor based on the HOG descriptor.

4. HOG DESCRIPTOR

Local object appearance and shape can often be characterized rather well by the distribution of local intensity gradients or edge directions, even without precise knowledge of the corresponding gradient or edge positions.

This statement leads to the definition of the HOG technique that has been used in its mature form in Scale Invariant Features Transformation (Lowe 2004) and it has been widely exploited in human detection (Dalal and Triggs 2005). HOG descriptor is based on the accumulation of gradient directions over the pixel of a small spatial region referred as "cell" and in the subsequent construction of a 1D histogram whose concatenation supplies the features vector to be considered for further purposes. Let L be an intensity (grayscale) function describing the image to be analysed. The image is divided into cells of size $N \times N$ pixels (as in Fig. 3a) and the orientation $\vartheta x,y$ of the gradient in each pixel is computed (Fig. 3b, c) by means of the following rule:

$$\theta_{x,y} = \tan^{-1} \frac{L(x, y+1) - L(x, y-1)}{L(x+1, y) - L(x-1, y)} \tag{1}$$

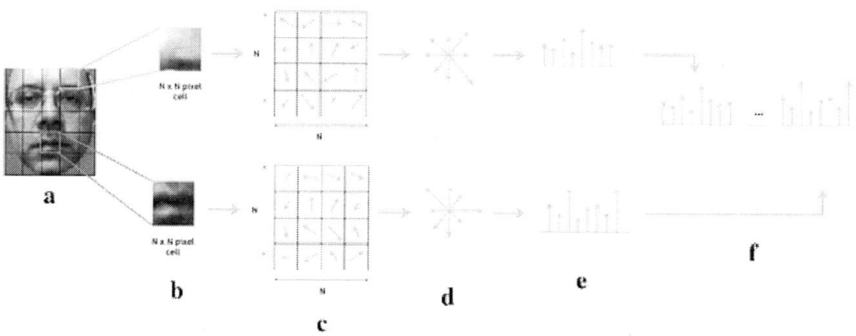

Figure 3. HOG features extraction process: image is divided in cells of size $N \times N$ pixels. The orientation of all pixels is computed and accumulated in an M-bins histogram of orientations. Finally, all cell histograms are concatenated in order to construct the final features vector. The example reports a cell size of 4 pixels and 8 orientation bins for the cell histograms

Successively, the orientations ϑji i=1...N2, i.e. belonging to the same cell j are quantized and accumulated into a M-bins histogram (Fig. 3d, e). Finally, all the achieved histograms are ordered and concatenated into a unique HOG histogram (Fig. 3f) that is the final outcome of this algorithmic step, i.e. the features vector to be considered for the subsequent processing.

5. SVM PREDICTION

The HOG features vectors are then given as input to a group of Support Vector Machines (SVMs). SVM is a discriminative classifier defined by a separating hyperplane. Given a set of labelled training data (supervised learning), the algorithm computes an optimal hyperplane (the trained model) which categorizes new examples in the right class. Given the training vectors *xxi*∈R*n*,*i*=1,...,*l* and the corresponding set of *l* labels *yi*∈{1,−1}, the following primal optimization problem is solved:

$$\min_{w,b,\xi} \quad \frac{1}{2}w^T w + C\sum_{i=1}^{l} \xi_i$$

$$\text{subject to} \quad y_i(w^T \phi(x_i) + b) \geq 1 - \xi_i,$$

$$\xi_i \geq 0, i = 1, \ldots, l,$$

where *ξi* is the misclassification error for the *i*th training vector; *ξ* is the total misclassification error; *ww*is the normal vector to the hyperplane; *b*/‖*ww*‖ determines the offset of the hyperplane from the origin along the normal vector *ww* (with ‖·‖ the norm operator); *ϕ*(*xxi*) maps *xxi* into a higher-dimensional space and *C*>0 is the regularization parameter.

Further theoretical notions about SVM, together with related implementation issues, can be found in Cortes and Vapnik (1995). The classical SVM approach is suitable only for a two classes problem but, unfortunately, FER involves multi-class handling. Multi-class problems can be addressed by the “one-against-one” method proposed in Knerr et al. (1990), an approach based on the construction of an SVM classifier for each pairwise of classes and a voting system aided to elect the predicted class when an unseen item is tested. More specifically, let *k* be the number of classes, then *k*(*k*−1)/2classifiers *Kij* are trained from the available data of the *i*th and *j*th classes. The final prediction is returned by a voting system: the unseen example is analysed by each classifier *Kij* that gives a vote to one or to the other class. Finally, the class with the largest number of votes is chosen. Although many other methods are available for multi-class SVM classification, in Hsu and Lin (2002) a detailed comparison is given with the conclusion that “one-against-one” is a competitive approach. In particular, the multi *C*-support vector classification (multi *C*-SVC) learning task implemented in the LIBSVM library (Chang and Lin 2011) was used in the experiments reported in "Experimental results: phase 1, Experimental results: phase 2 and Experimental results: phase 3". Radial Basis Function

(RBF) was used as kernel as suggested in Hsu et al. (2003) for non-linearly separable problems with penalty parameter C=1000 and γ=0.05 .

6. TEMPORAL ANALYSIS

To make the system suitable for video sequence analysis, a decision making strategy based on the temporal consistency of FER outcomes has been introduced. The decision, about the expression in a video, is taken by analyzing a temporal window of size m and verifying if at least n (n<m) frames in the window are classified as containing the same facial expression. More specifically, the system performs a frame by frame analysis in the time window w of size m and for each frame an expression classification outcome is given as pi where p is the predicted expression and i is the current frame index.

The expression in the window is classified as the expression s if

$$\sum_{j=i-m+1}^{i} \left(\Lambda(p_j, s)\right) \geq n \tag{2}$$

where $\Lambda(pj,s)$=1 if pj=s and 0 otherwise.

This procedure allows the system to manage a temporal stream for a subject avoiding wrong expression predictions due to sporadic misclassifications.

7. EXPERIMENTAL DATA SETUP

All the experimental sessions have been carried out on two publicly available datasets of image sequences specifically acquired for FER issues. The first dataset is the Chon-Kanade (CK+) Lucey et al. (2010): it is made up by image sequences of people performing 6 facial expressions. Each sequence starts with a neutral face expression and ends with the expressive face. The variety of subjects in terms of gender, as well as ethnicity and age, makes the dataset one of the most used to test the performance of FER solutions.

In order to extract, from the available sequences, a balanced (i.e. quite the same number of instances for each considered expression) subset of images containing expressive faces, the following images were selected: the last image for the sequences related to the expression of anger, disgust and happiness; the last image for the first 68 sequences related to expression of surprise; the last and the fourth from the last images for the sequences related to the expressions of fear and sadness. At the end, a subset of 347 images was obtained with the following distribution among the considered classes of expressions: anger (45), disgust (59), fear (50), happiness (69), sadness (56) and surprise (68). An additional configuration of the previous subset was also introduced in order to test the performance with 7 classes and in this case 60 facial images, with neutral expression, were added to the aforementioned ones. In the last years a new dataset for FER analysis, named as Radboud Faces Database (RFD) Langner et al. (2010), has been introduced. The dataset contains images of 67 subjects performing 8 facial expressions (anger, disgust, fear, happiness, contemptuous, sadness, surprise and neutral) with 3 gaze directions and 5 different face orientations. The frontal facial image, with frontal gaze direction, was selected for each subject. In this way 2 subsets were obtained: the first one with 7 expressions (anger, contemptuous, disgusted, fearful, happy, sad, surprised) for a total of 469 images and the second one where 67 instances of the neutral expression were added to the previous ones (for a total of 536 images). In Figs. 4 and 5 some examples in the considered subsets of images are reported.

8. EXPERIMENTAL RESULTS: PHASE 1

This section reports, in the first subsection, the procedure by which the parameters of the HOG descriptor were optimized to get the best FER performance on the Chon-Kanade (CK+) dataset with 6-expressions. In the successive subsection, the comparison of the optimized pipeline with alternative appearance features descriptors is then detailed and, in the last subsection, the comparison with related techniques in the state of the art is finally reported. All the results in this section are referred to single images and consequentially have been carried out by neglecting the time window analysis.

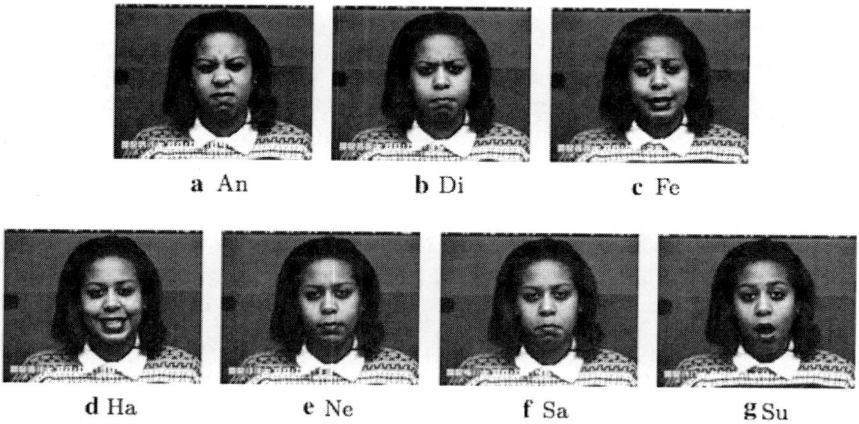

Figure 4. Examples of expressions for the CK+ dataset. *An* Anger, *Di* Disgusted, *Fe* Fearful, *Ha* Happy, *Ne*Neutral, *Sa* Sad, *Su* Surprised

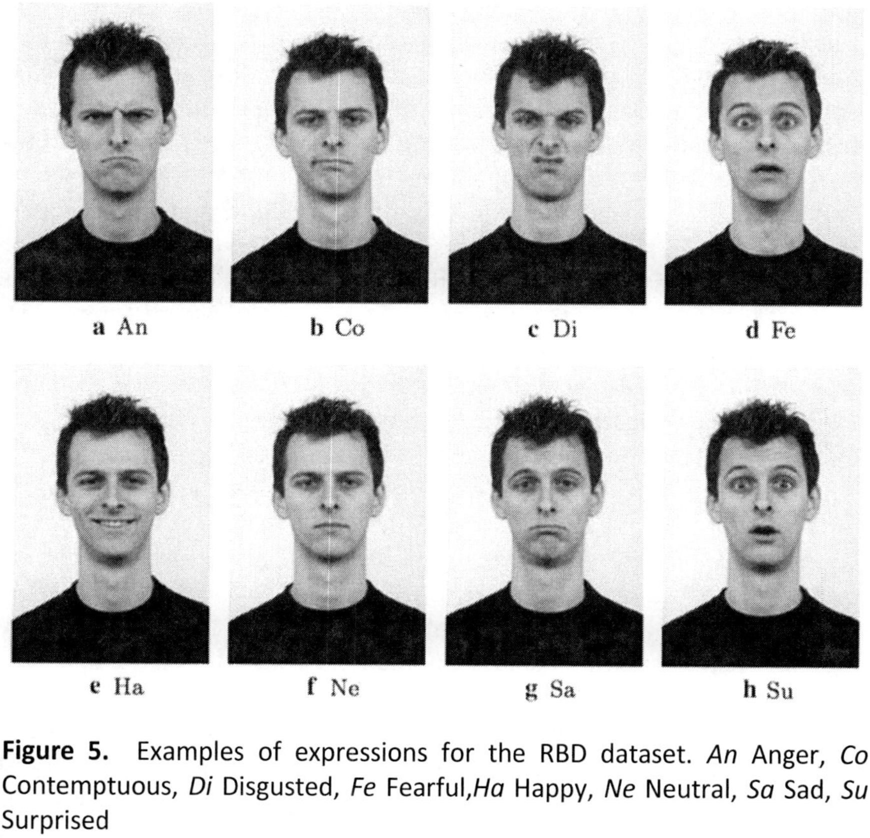

Figure 5. Examples of expressions for the RBD dataset. *An* Anger, *Co* Contemptuous, *Di* Disgusted, *Fe* Fearful,*Ha* Happy, *Ne* Neutral, *Sa* Sad, *Su* Surprised

8.1 HOG parameters optimization

This subsection is aimed at selecting the optimal values for the internal HOG parameters, i.e. the best configuration to capture the most discriminative information for the FER problem. More specifically, the average recall value has been employed for performance evaluation. This choice had been driven looking at the most recent works (as Happy and Routray 2015) where average recall is employed as the main performance value for comparison among different methods. HOG descriptor is characterized by two main parameters, the cell size and the number of orientation bins. Cell size represents the dimension of the patch involved in the single histogram computation. The importance of this parameter has been highlighted in Déniz et al. (2011) where the same grid like HOG extraction was exploited and the fusion of HOG descriptors at different scales has been used to effectively address the face recognition issue. Using a large cell size, the appearance information of a significant region of the facial image is squeezed into a single cell histogram and then some details, useful for subsequent classification, can be lost. On the other hand, with a small cell size, high resolution analysis can be carried out but, in this way, the discrimination between useful and useless extracted details is demanded to the classifier that could be unable to perform this additional task in the best way. The number of orientation bins refers instead to the quantization levels of the gradient information. A low number of orientations could lead to some loss of information and a consequent reduction in FER performance. Vice versa, a high number of quantization levels could spread-out the information along the bins, decreasing the FER performance as well. For these reasons, the choice of these parameters has to be carefully carried out by taking into consideration the goal to be reached in a particular application context. How this choice was made for FER purposes is described below. First, with regard to the cell size, a qualitative assessment can be made: in Fig. 6 the registered versions of a neutral and a surprised face expression are shown with the related processing outcomes obtained by HOG descriptor with a fixed number of 8 orientations and different values of cell size (3, 8 and 15 pixels). It is quite evident that the case with cell size of 15 pixels led to a loss of information: no correspondences between facial traits and HOG histogram can be accomplished since the accumulation of orientations was related to a large image region. On the contrary, the use of a small cell size (3 pixel) produced a very crowded distribution of the bins and then the information cannot be adequately encoded. So far, from Fig. 6, could be deduced that the most discriminative representation is given, instead, by the use of a middle cell size (in the examples 8 pixels).

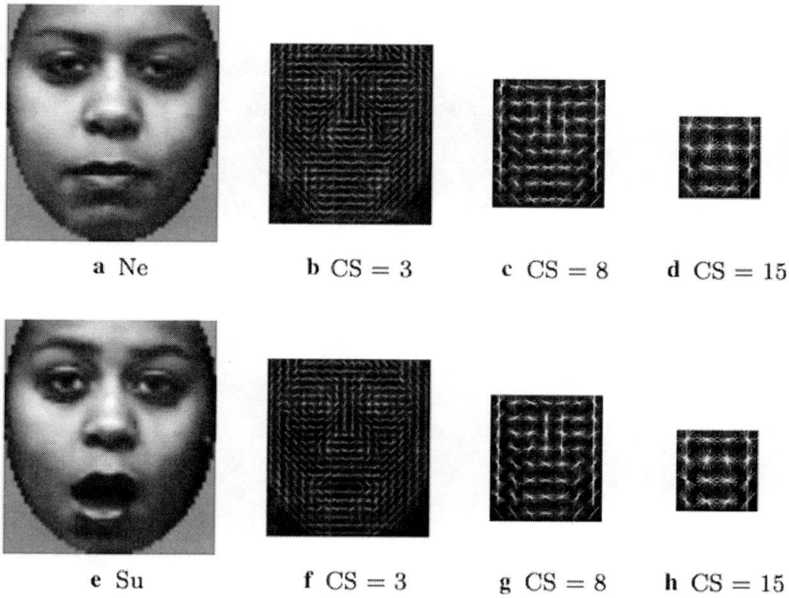

Figure 6. Examples of HOG (9 orientations) processing on registered face images (*Ne* Neutral, *Su* Surprised.). CS is the cell size of the processed images

The above qualitative evaluation can be also strengthened by a quantitative analysis of the FER performance sensitivity to both cell size and number of orientation bins. To perform this evaluation, the proposed algorithmic pipeline was tested using a 10-fold cross validation with 12 possible values of the cell size (from 4 to 15 pixels) and different number of orientation bins (3, 5, 7, 9, 12, 15 and 55).

FER results, for different numbers of orientation bins, are graphically reported onto the y-axis in Fig. 7 where the x-axis reports the cell size. From Fig. 7 it is possible to infer that a cell size of 7 pixels led to the best FER performance. Concerning the choice of the number of orientations, the best results were obtained with value set to 7 even if also with 9 or 12 orientations the FER performance did not change significantly.

Choosing the optimal parameters configuration (cell size of 7 pixels and 7 orientation bins), the proposed pipeline is able to correctly classify the images, supplied as input during the 10-fold cross validation process, with average performance that can been numerically expressed with a recall of 95.9 %, a precision of 95.8 %, an accuracy of 98.9 % and a F-score of 95.8 %.

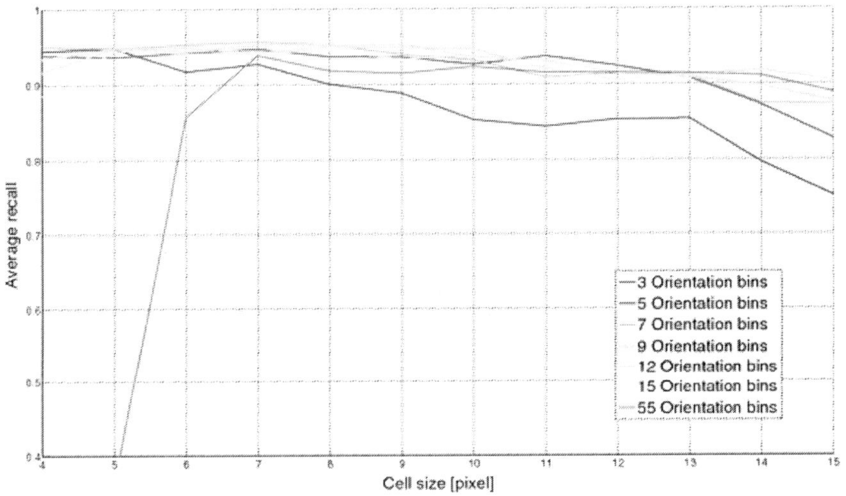

Figure 7. FER results using different cell sizes and number of orientation bins for the HOG descriptor: the x-axis reports the cell size in pixel and the y-axis refers to the average recall percentage

8.2 Is HOG descriptor the best choice?

Given the used pipeline, this subsection tries to give experimental evidence of the superiority of HOG descriptor compared to three commonly used descriptors of local appearance: Local Binary Pattern (LBP) Da and Sang (2009), Spatial Weber's Local Descriptor (SWLD) Chen et al. (2010); Ullah et al.2012) and Compound Local Binary Pattern (CLBP) Ahmed et al. (2011). Moreover, a computational cost analysis is presented in order to have an overview also from this prospective.

More specifically, LBP is a local feature descriptor widely utilized to describe texture appearance in pattern recognition problems. The original LBP assigns a label to each pixel. Each pixel is used as a threshold and compared with its neighbors. If the neighbor is higher it takes value 1 otherwise it takes value 0. Finally, the thresholded neighbor pixel values are concatenated and considered as a binary number that becomes the label for the central pixel. To account for the spatial information, the image is then divided into sub-regions. LBP is applied to each sub-region and a histogram of L bins is generated from the pixel labels.

SWLD is the spatial version of WLD, a robust descriptor inspired by the psychological Weber's law (Jain 1989). It is based on the fact that the human perception of a pattern depends on the amount of change in intensity of the stimulus as well as on the original stimulus intensity. The WLD descriptor consist of two components: differential excitation (to detect the local salient patterns) and gradient orientations.

Finally, the CLBP is an extension of the LBP descriptor. Compared to LBP, CLBP encodes the sign of the differences between the center pixel and its P neighbors as well as the magnitude of the differences.

For all the aforementioned descriptors, a preliminary parameters optimization procedure was done. After that, the LBP and CLBP with a radius of 1 pixel and 8 neighbours over a 5 × 5 grid and the SWLD with values of parameters T, M, S set to 8, 4 and 4 over a 4 × 4 grid were used.

Table 1 reports the average FER performance along the 10-fold cross validation on the Chon-Kanade (CK+) dataset with 6-expressions: it is possible to observe that none of the comparing techniques (LBP 91.7 %, CLBP 92.3 %, SWLD 86.5 %) reached the FER performance of the HOG descriptor (95.8 %) and these results confirmed that the edges and shapes modeling performed by HOG is more suitable to describe the facial expression if compared with the texture oriented descriptors that are unable to describe the facial deformation among different expressions.

Table 1. Performance comparison of HOG descriptor respect to LBP, CLBP and SWLD descriptors

LBP	CLBP	SWLD	HOG
91.7	92.3	86.5	*95.8*

Italic value indicates the best result

The computational cost prospective has to be discussed too. The values (processing time for the descriptor computation and the SVM prediction), reported in Table 2 and illustrated in the bar diagram of Fig. 8, have been computed considering an average of 500 frames employing an Intel i7 processor class based Linux machine. The analysis of these results shows as the LBP descriptor allows to save about 0.4 ms with respect to the HOG one. Nevertheless, the processing time for the face detection and registration step (41, 9 ms) is 2 magnitude greater than the discussed times making this advantage quite negligible.

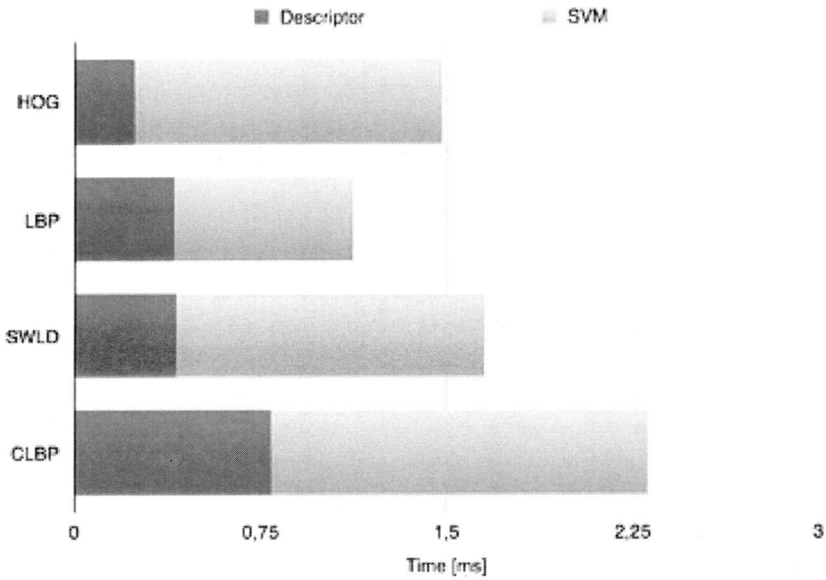

Figure 8. *Bar* diagram of processing time for descriptor computation and SVM prediction stages respect to LBP, CLBP and SWLD descriptors

Table 2. Processing time for the detection, descriptor computation and SVM prediction stages

	Detection	Descriptor	SVM	Total time
HOG	41.9	0.24	1.24	43.38
LBP	41.9	0.40	0.72	43.02
SWLD	41.9	0.41	1.24	43.55
CLBP	41.9	0.79	1.52	44.21

All the values are expressed in ms

8.3 Comparison with the state of the art

In this section the achieved results are compared with those of the leading State-of-the-Art FER solutions. Differently from other research fields, in the FER one there is not a shared dataset to be used as benchmark for a fair evaluation of different algorithms. In order to avoid errors introduced by the re-implementation of each method, most of the works in the literature refer to CK+ dataset that, unfortunately, is dramatically unbalanced and, for this reason, it requires a selection of a subset of available expression occurrences before to be used. How this selection has to be performed is not well stated and then the reported comparisons are always biased by this important drawback. In addition, there is not a standardised evaluation procedure even if most of the works make use of a cross-validation procedure and then represent the recognition performance by means of confusion matrices. In order to accomplish this crucial task, in this paper, the approach implemented in the most up-to-date works for FER recognition is then used (Happy and Routray 2015), i.e. a CK+ subset of observations was selected and then a k-fold cross validation was used to fill the confusion matrix. In this way, the performance of the comparing approaches can be extracted from the relative papers avoiding to affect them by implementation issues. To be fairest as possible, for most of the sequences in the dataset, we retained only one image (we experimentally proved that choosing more than one image the overall performance increase). For balancing reasons, for a few sequences also the fourth image from the last one was retained and, in this way, the largest possible subset of images (in respecting a reasonable balancing among categories) was build. Choosing the fourth from the last image introduces less correlation then the third from the last or the second from the last.

Table 3 reports the comparison results demonstrating that the proposed approach gave the best average recognition rate. In particular, it is worth noting that the performance achieved by the approach under investigation exceed also those of the recent work in Happy and Routray (2015) that represents the reference point for the FER problem. A deeper analysis of the Table 3 evidences that the proposed method suffers more than competitors to recognize the expression of disgust. This drawback could be due to the fact that, while performing this expression, the facial muscles shape is quite similar to that of the expression of anger (see Figs. 4, 5) hence the edge analysis performed by HOG, sometimes, cannot be able to bring to light differences as other approaches based on texture analysis can instead highlight. However, this is a limitation only for the recognition of the expression of disgust since for all the remaining expressions the FER performance of the proposed method largely exceed those of the comparing methods highlighting that the analysis of the edges is the best method to recognize facial expressions as it throws away all possible ambiguity introduced by non-edge based features.

Table 3. Performance comparison of our approach versus different State-of-the-Art approaches (CK+ 6 expressions)

	Uddin et al. (2009)	Poursaberi et al. (2012)	Zhong et al. (2012)	Zhang and Tjondronegoro (2011)	Happy and Routray (2015)	Proposed
An	82.5	87.1	71.4	87.1	87.8	88.6
Di	97.5	91.6	95.3	90.2	93.3	89.0
Fe	95.0	91.0	81.1	92.0	94.3	100
Ha	100	96.9	95.4	98.1	94.2	100
Sa	92.5	84.6	88.0	91.5	96.4	100
Su	92.5	91.2	98.3	100	98.5	97.4
AV	93.3	90.4	88.3	93.1	94.1	*95.8*

Italic value indicates the best result

An Anger, *Di* Disgusted, *Fe* Fearful, *Ha* Happy, *Sa* Sad, *Su* Surprised

9. EXPERIMENTAL RESULTS: PHASE 2

This section extends the experimental evaluation of the proposed solution to other datasets of facial expressions. In particular, the next subsection reports the analysis of the HOG parameters repeated using alternatively as benchmark one of the remaining 3 datasets described in "Experimental data setup". During this experimental evaluation it was demonstrated that, given the preliminary registration of the facial images, the configuration process converged to the same values, i.e. it was independent from the considered dataset. After that, in the last subsection, the detailed FER accuracies of the proposed approach, for all the datasets, are reported using confusion matrices that are then deeply discussed.

9.1 Generalization of the optimization of HOG parameters

In this subsection, the optimization of the HOG parameters (already carried out for the 6-expressions CK+ dataset and reported in "Experimental results: phase 1") is extended to the remaining 3 datasets described in "Experimental data setup": the CK+ with 7 expressions and the RFD with 7 and 8 expressions. This experimental step was carried out in order to verify that the best configuration of HOG parameters revealed in "Experimental results: phase 1" keeps still valid also for a different testing set. The plots relative to the 3 related additional experiments are shown in Figs. 9, 10 and 11and they demonstrate that a cell size of 7 pixels and 7 orientation bins is again the best HOG parameters configuration to obtain the highest FER performance. This is a very important result, since it allows the proposed pipeline to be used without any initial parameter setting, even in the presence of different operative contexts. In other words, given the preliminary image registration, the FER proposed solution becomes parameter independent and then suitable to be used as a black-box.

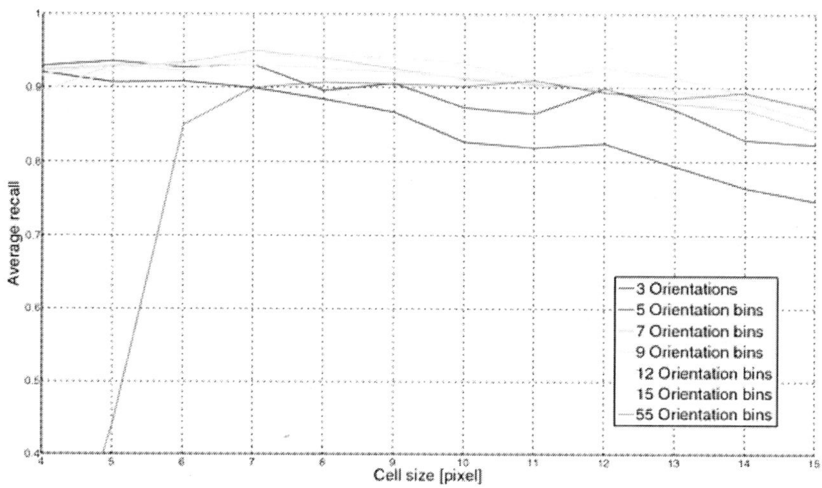

Figure 9. HOG optimization results (CK+ with 7 expressions): the x-axis reports the cell size in pixel and the y-axis refers to the average recall percentage

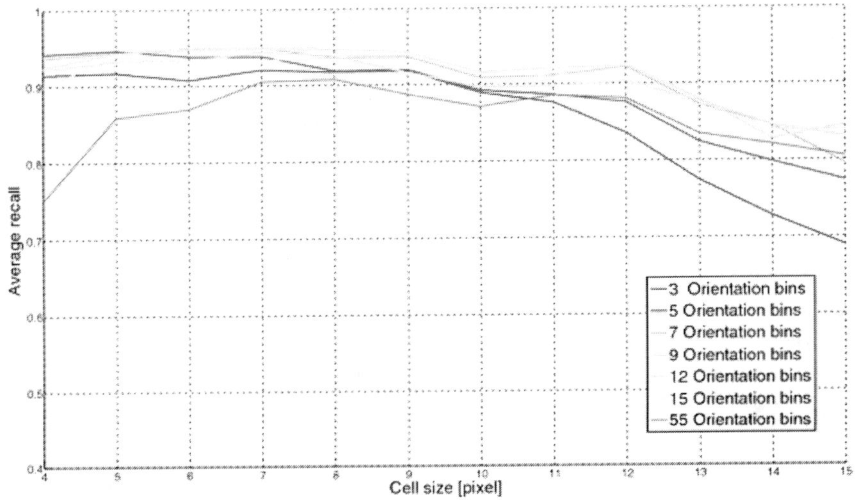

Figure 10. HOG optimization results (RFD with 7 expressions): the x-axis reports the cell size in pixel and the y-axis refers to the average recall percentage

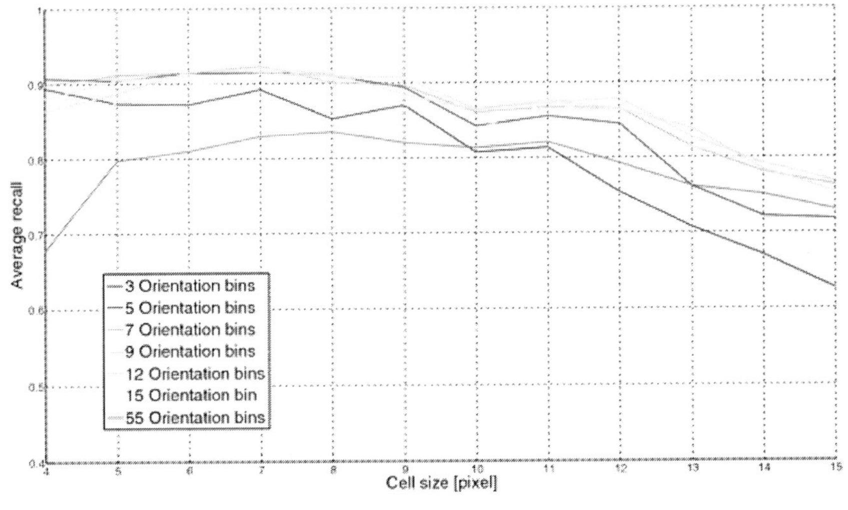

Figure 11. HOG optimization results (RFD with 8 expressions): the x-axis reports the cell size in pixel and the y-axis refers to the average recall percentage

9.2 Confusion matrices for all the datasets

Once established, in previous subsection, that there is a unique best configuration of the HOG parameters, the performance of the proposed approach were better analyzed. In particular, in a multi-class recognition problem, as the FER one, the use of an average performance value among all the classes could be not exhaustive since there is no possibility to inspect what is the separation level, in terms of correct classifications, among classes. To overcome this limitation, for each dataset the confusion matrices [expressed in terms of recall in order to keep coherence with other works (Happy and Routray 2015)] are then reported in Tables 4, 5, 6 and 7. This makes possible a more detailed analysis of the results that can point out the misclassification cases and the interpretation of their possible causes. Additional information is given in the bar diagram of Fig. 12 and in Table 8 where the average precision, recall, accuracy and F-score are provided for all the datasets. First of all, from the confusion tables it is possible to observe that the proposed pipeline achieved an average performance value rate over 90 % for all the tested datasets and that, as expected, its FER performance decreased when the number of classes, and consequently the problem complexity, increased. In fact, in the case of the CK+ dataset with 6 expressions, the recall was of 95.9 % whereas after the addition of the neutral expression it decreased to 94.1 %. For the RFD, with 7 expressions, the FER recall was of 94.9 % whereas the addition of the neutral class led to a value of recall of 92.9 %. These are very encouraging results considering the challenging benchmark used for testing.

Looking at the bar diagram in Fig. 12 and at the values in Table 8 it is possible to observe also the other considered metrics, as precision, accuracy and F-score, had the quite same behavior of the recall one among the different datasets.

Going into a more detailed analysis, Tables 4 and 5 highlight an ambiguity between anger, disgusted and sad expressions. This becomes quite reasonable if the examples in Figs. 4 and 5 are observed: for all the aforementioned expressions, strict lips and low position of eyebrows are in fact very similar, in both location and appearance. For the same reasons, the neutral expressions introduced some misclassifications in Tables 5 and 7 whereas the contemptuous expression was sometimes classified as neutral or sad one. Similarly, the sad expression experimented some erroneous classification in the anger face expression due to the strict lips and low position of eyebrows that are very similar for the two expressions. Finally, the happy expression is the most insensitive to ambiguities and reached the 100 % of classification in all the tests (except for the RFD with 6 expressions).

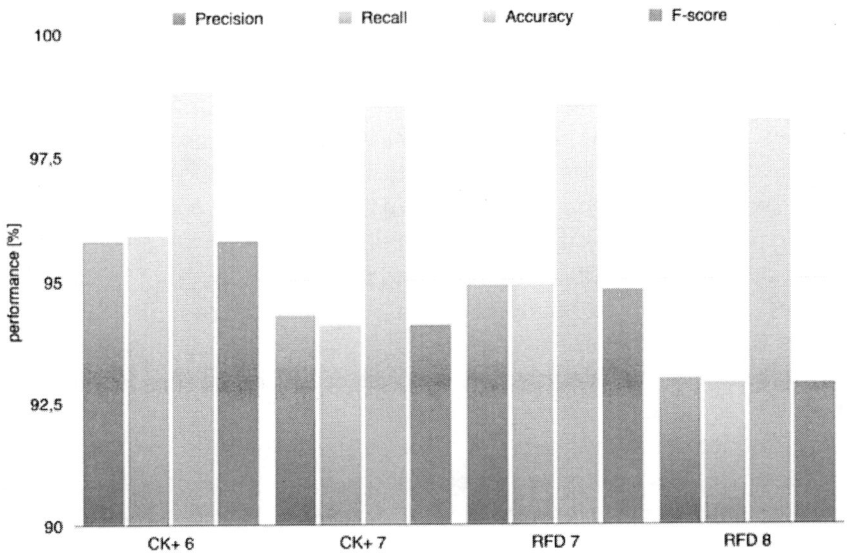

Figure 12. Bar diagram of average precision, recall, accuracy and F-score for the 4 tested datasets

Table 4. Performance of proposed approach (CK+ 6 expressions)

	An	Di	Fe	Ha	Sa	Su
An	88.6	4.5	2.4	0	4.5	0
Di	5.6	89.0	1.8	1.8	0	1.8
Fe	0	0	100	0	0	0
Ha	0	0	0	100	0	0
Sa	0	0	0	0	100	0
Su	1.3	0	1.3	0	0	97.4

Average performances: recall = 95.9 %, precision = 95.8 %, accuracy = 98.8 %, F-score = 95.8 %. (orientation bins = 7, cell size = 7)

An Anger, *Di* Disgusted, *Fe* Fearful, *Ha* Happy, *Sa* Sad, *Su* Surprised

Table 5. Performance of proposed approach (CK+ 7 expressions)

	Ne	An	Di	Fe	Ha	Sa	Su
Ne	89.6	1.8	0	0	0	8.6	0
An	4.4	86.8	4.4	0	0	4.4	0
Di	0	5.4	92.9	1.7	0	0	0
Fe	0	0	0	93.9	4.1	0	2.0
Ha	0	0	0	0	100	0	0
Sa	0	0	1.8	0	0	98.2	0
Su	1.3	0	0	1.3	0	0	97.4

Average performances: recall = 94.1 %, precision = 94.3 %, accuracy = 98.5 %, F-score = 94.1 %. (orientation bins = 7, cell size = 7)

Ne Neutral, *An* Anger, *Di* Disgusted, *Fe* Fearful, *Ha* Happy, *Sa* Sad, *Su* Surprised

Table 6. Performance of proposed approach (RFD 7 expressions)

	An	Co	Di	Fe	Ha	Sa	Su
An	98.4	0	0	0	0	1.6	0
Co	3.0	92.5	0	1.5	0	3.0	0
Di	0	0	97.0	0	0	1.5	1.5
Fe	0	1.5	0	94.0	0	1.5	3.0
Ha	0	0	0	0	100	0	0
Sa	6.0	1.5	1.5	7.4	0	83.6	0
Su	0	1.5	0	0	0	0	98.5

Average performances: recall = 94.9 %, precision = 94.9 %, accuracy = 98.5 %, F-score = 94.8 %. (orientation bins = 7, cell size = 7)

An Anger, *Co* Contemptous, *Di* Disgusted, *Fe* Fearful, *Ha* Happy, *Sa* Sad, *Su* Surprised

Table 7. Performance of proposed approach (RFD 8 expressions)

	An	Co	Di	Fe	Ha	Ne	Sa	Su
An	97.0	0	0	0	0	1.5	1.5	0
Co	1.5	88.1	0	0	0	7.5	2.9	0
Di	0	1.5	98.5	0	0	0	0	0
Fe	0	0	0	92.5	0	3.0	0	4.5
Ha	0	1.5	0	0	98.5	0	0	0
Ne	0	10.4	0	0	0	86.6	3.0	0
Sa	7.4	3.0	0	3.0	0	1.5	85.1	0
Su	0	1.5	0	0	0	1.5	0	97.0

Average performances: recall = 92.9 %, precision = 93.0 %, accuracy = 98.2 %, F-score = 92.9 %. (orientation bins = 7, cell size = 7)

An Anger, *Co* Contemptous, *Di* Disgusted, *Fe* Fearful, *Ha* Happy, *Ne* Neutral, *Sa* Sad, *Su* Surprised

Table 8. Performance of proposed approach among different datasets (CK+ 6 expressions, CK+ 7 expressions, RFD 7 expressions, RFD 8 expressions)

	Pecision	Recall	Accuracy	F-score
CK+ 6	95.8	95.9	98.8	95.8
CK+ 7	94.3	94.1	98.5	94.1
RFD 7	94.9	94.9	98.5	94.8
RFD 8	93.0	92.9	98.2	92.9

10. EXPERIMENTAL RESULTS: PHASE 3

The experiments reported in previous sections were relative to the recognition of facial expressions in a single image containing a clearly defined expression. In common application contexts, the automatic systems have to perform FER by analyzing image sequences in which not all the images contain a clear expression, or where there are transitions between expressions. This section aims, thus, at analyzing the behavior of the proposed pipeline, in its whole proposed form, when applied to video sequences. To this end the experiments of this phase were conducted in two steps: a quantitative accuracy evaluation using video sequences of the CK+ dataset in the first step; a qualitative accuracy evaluation using on-line continuous video streaming in the second step. In both steps the system has been equipped with the model trained on the CK+ dataset with 7 expressions employed in the previous experiments.

In the first step, the quantitative performance evaluation of the capability to recognize the expressions embedded into the video sequences of the CK+ dataset is reported. CK+ sequences start with a neutral face expression that evolves to the expressive one; the number of frames, for a particular expression, changes for every subject. In this case the time window has been customized to manage this specific expression change. More specifically, a sequence i was considered correctly recognized if in the first $m1$ frames there exist at least $n1$ images classified as containing the neutral expression and, at the same time, in the last $m2$ frames there exist at least $n2$ images classified as containing the expression with which the sequence is labeled. In the experiments, the following setting was used: $n1=1$, $m1=3$, $n2=4$, $m2=5$ and, over the 327 labeled sequences, the percentage of correct classification was of 72.2 %.

In Fig . 13 two examples of correct classification of CK+ image sequences are reported. In the first one, both the first 3 frames and the last 5 frames were correctly classified whereas in the second one an error occurred in the second frame but that was filtered by the overall decision rule.

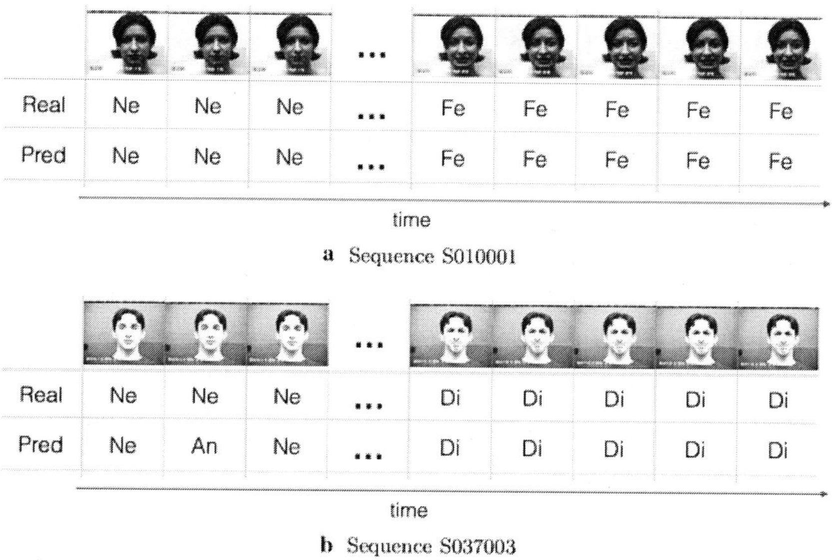

Figure 13. Examples of expression recognition in CK+ sequences: **a** from Neutral to Fearful and **b** from Neutral to Disgusted. For each sequence the first 3 and the last 5 frames are reported i.e. the frames containing the labelled expressions. The *first row* reports the facial images, the *second row* shows the ground-truth labels and finally, in the *third row*, the predicted expressions are pointed out

In order to get evidence of how the system works on the whole image sequences, in Fig. 14 the system outcomes on 6 sequences of the CK+ dataset are plotted along time. It can be observed that in the most of cases a sharp prediction change occurred along the expression mutation whereas sometimes the prediction is unstable due to the uncertainty of the system over the transition frames.

Finally, in the second experimental step, an on-line test, exploiting the whole process proposed in "Methodology overview", was performed using an ARM Cortex A-15 class processor (2.3 Ghz) embedded system equipped with a 640 × 480 pixels webcam. Subjects of different gender and age have been involved in the experiments. More specifically, to all subjects were asked to sit in front of the camera and to randomly perform some of the aforementioned expressions. It is worth noting that no constraints, about the transition from the neutral expression to the expressive one, have been introduced leaving the user free to perform every possible transition among different expressions.

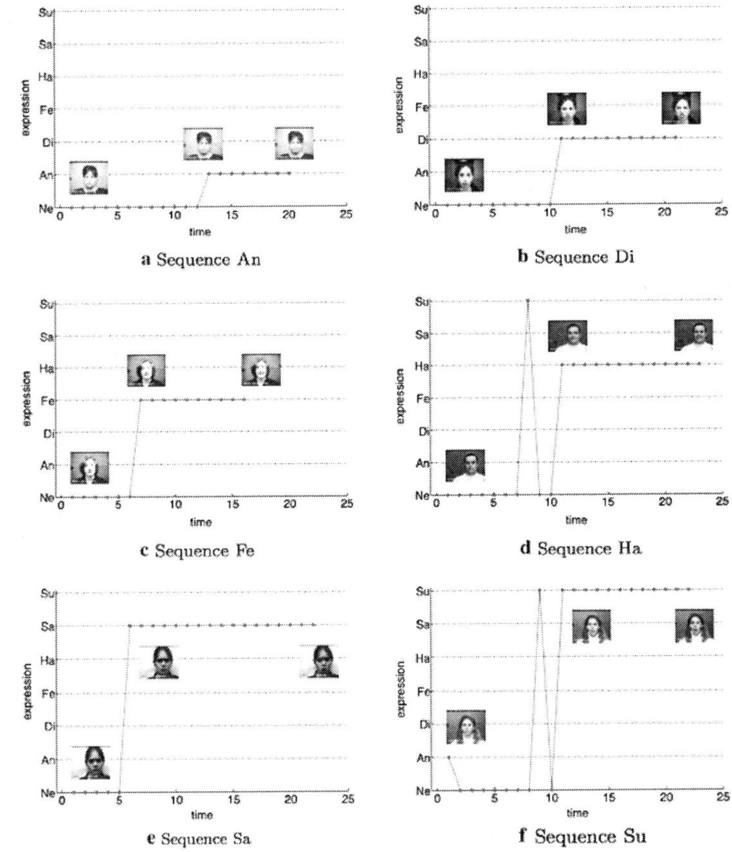

a Sequence An
b Sequence Di
c Sequence Fe
d Sequence Ha
e Sequence Sa
f Sequence Su

Figure. 14 Plot of detected emotions on 6 examples of CK+ sequences: **a** from Neutral to Angry, **b** from Neutral to Disgusted, **c** from Neutral to Fearful, **d** from Neutral to Happy, **e** from Neutral to Sad, **f** from Neutral to Surprised. The *x* axis is representative of the temporal variations of the expression (from neutral to expressive); the *y* axis shows the predicted expression (*Ne* Neutral, *An* Anger, *Di* Disgusted, *Fe*Fearful, *Ha* Happy, *Sa* Sad, *Su* Surprised.). For each plot the starting image, the image after the expression prediction change and the final expression are reported

The system evaluated in this step, from a qualitative point of view, exhibited a good capacity to recognize all the emotions performed by the users with a quite low presence of false positives, thanks to the filtering performed by the temporal windows approach. Some examples of the system output are reported in Fig. 15.

Finally, it is worth noting as the proposed approach is able to reach a processing rate of 7 fps that is a notable value taking into account the limited computational resources of the employed embedded system. By our experience, such a frame processing rate is sufficient for considering the proposed system as suitable for real time applications oriented to implement a natural human–machine interaction.

As an additional experiment the robustness to non-frontal face poses was tested. As expected, the detector was able to work in a range of [-30,30] degrees of variation with respect to the frontal view. All the expressions in the detected faces were correctly classified by the system demonstrating its capability to hold very good FER performance (comparable with those obtained in case of frontal faces) even in case of non-frontal facial views. Figure 16 shows some examples of classification of expressions when different degrees of facial orientation were experienced.

11. CONCLUSIONS

In this paper a comprehensive study of how the HOG descriptor could be effectively exploited for facial expression recognition purposes has been carried out. In order to perform the above mentioned investigation, a pipeline, commonly used in FER analysis and equipped with an HOG descriptor, has been used as baseline. Then, the classification performance, on a well known FER dataset, has been analyzed as a function of the HOG parameters setting (cell size and number of orientation bins). Results highlighted a configuration of HOG parameters able to fit the specific aspects of facial expressions that allows a high classification performance capable to overcome the performances of the leading state of the art approaches. In order to prove that the achieved HOG configuration is general, i.e. it does not depend on the input data, the pipeline was tested on three additional datasets. As a final step, experiments on video sequences gave evidence that the proposed approach is also suitable to be used in real-world application contexts.

Figure. 15. Examples of expression detection performed by the proposed system: the expression evolves over time (from the *top to the bottom*); once the decision making rule is satisfied, the out-coming prediction is printed out. From *left to right* the neutral, sad and surprised expressions are shown

Figure. 16. Examples of expression detection with non-frontal faces. The qualitative tests show that, for an angle between −30 and 30 degrees, the detector is able to correctly register the face and the classifier is enough robust to guarantee classification performance comparable with the frontal face case

Future works will deal with two main aspects. On the one hand the system will be tested in the field of assistive technologies. In particular, a humanoid social robot will be equipped with the proposed FER solution in order to acquire awareness about the emotional state of the interacting user and consequently to react with a specific behavior. On the other hand a more wide analysis of the influence of non frontal face effect will be done and the effectiveness of face frontalization algorithm Hassner et al. (2014) will be tested.

NOTES

Pierluigi Carcagnì, Marco Del Coco, Marco Leo and Cosimo Distante contributed equally to this work

AUTHORS' CONTRIBUTIONS

PC implemented the algorithms for face detection, normalization and features extraction; he set up the imaging system for data acquisition and he wrote down the relative paragraphs in the paper. MDC implemented the involved algorithmic procedures for SVM and k-fold classification, collected and analysed the experimental data and he wrote down the relative paragraphs in the paper. ML designed the experimental proofs, analysed experimental outcomes and conceived their representations. Moreover he was involved in drafting the manuscript and in revising it critically. CD conceived the proposed approach, supervised the experimental phase and corrected the paper. All the authors read and approved the final manuscript.

REFERENCES

1. Ahmed F, Hossain E, Bari ASMH, Shihavuddin A (2011) Compound local binary pattern (clbp) for robust facial expression recognition. In: IEEE 12th International Symposium On Computational Intelligence and Informatics (CINTI), pp 391–395

2. Barroso E, Santos G, Proença H (2013) Facial expressions: Discriminability of facial regions and relationship to biometrics recognition. In: IEEE Workshop On Computational Intelligence in Biometrics and Identity Management (CIBIM), pp 77–80

3. Castrillón M, Déniz O, Guerra C, Hernández M (2007) Encara2: Real-time detection of multiple faces at different resolutions in video streams. J Vis Commun Image Represent 18(2):130–140

4. Chang C-C, Lin C-J (2011) Libsvm: a library for support vector machines. ACM Trans Intell Syst Technol (TIST) 2(3):27

5. Chen J, Shan S, He C, Zhao G, Pietikainen M, Chen X, Gao W (2010) Wld: a robust local image descriptor. IEEE Trans Pattern Anal Mach Intell 32(9):1705–1720

6. Chen J, Chen Z, Chi Z, Fu H (2014) Facial expression recognition based on facial components detection and hog features. In: International

Workshops on Electrical and Computer Engineering Subfields, pp 884–888

7. Cortes C, Vapnik V (1995) Support-vector networks. Mach Learn 20(3):273–297

8. Dahmane M, Meunier J (2011) Emotion recognition using dynamic grid-based hog features. In: IEEE International Conference On Automatic Face Gesture Recognition and Workshops (FG 2011), pp 884–888

9. Dalal N, Triggs B (2005) Histograms of oriented gradients for human detection. In: IEEE Computer Society Conference On Computer Vision and Pattern Recognition (CVPR), vol 1, pp 886–8931

10. Da B, Sang N (2009) Local binary pattern based face recognition by estimation of facial distinctive information distribution. Opt Eng 48(11):117203–1172037

11. Déniz O, Bueno G, Salido J, De la Torre F (2011) Face recognition using histograms of oriented gradients. Pattern Recognit Lett 32(12):1598–1603

12. Dornaika F, Lazkano E, Sierra B (2011) Improving dynamic facial expression recognition with feature subset selection. Pattern Recognit Lett 32(5):740–748

13. Gritti T, Shan C, Jeanne V, Braspenning R (2008) Local features based facial expression recognition with face registration errors. In: 8th IEEE International Conference On Automatic Face Gesture Recognition, FG 08, pp 1–8

14. Happy SL, Routray A (2015) Automatic facial expression recognition using features of salient facial patches. IEEE Trans Affect Comput 6(1):1–12

15. Hassner T, Harel S, Paz E, Enbar R (2014) Effective face frontalization in unconstrained images. arXiv preprint

16. Hsu C-W, Lin C-J (2002) A comparison of methods for multiclass support vector machines. IEEE Trans Neural Netw 13(2):415–425

17. Hsu C-W, Chang C-C, Lin C-J et al (2003) A practical guide to support vector classification. http://www.csie.ntu.edu.tw/~cjlin/papers/guide/guide.pdf

18. Izard CE (1971) The Face of Emotion. Century psychology series. Appleton-Century-Crofts, United States

19. Jain AK (1989) Fundamentals of digital image processing. Prentice-Hall Inc, Upper Saddle River

20. Ji Y, Idrissi K (2012) Automatic facial expression recognition based on spatiotemporal descriptors. Pattern Recognit Lett 33(10):1373–1380

21. Khan RA, Meyer A, Konik H, Bouakaz S (2013) Framework for reliable, real-time facial expression recognition for low resolution images. Pattern Recognit Lett 34(10):1159–1168

22. Knerr S, Personnaz L, Dreyfus G (1990) Single-layer learning revisited: a stepwise procedure for building and training a neural network. Neurocomputing, vol 68. NATO ASI SeriesSpringer, Berlin Heidelberg, pp 41–50

23. Langner O, Dotsch R, Bijlstra G, Wigboldus DHJ, Hawk ST, van Knippenberg A (2010) Presentation and validation of the radboud faces database. Cognit Emot 24(8):1377–1388

24. Liu W, Song C, Wang Y, Jia L (2012) Facial expression recognition based on gabor features and sparse representation. In: 12th International Conference On Control Automation Robotics Vision (ICARCV), pp 1402–1406

25. Loconsole CL, Miranda CR, Orvalho V (2014) Real-time emotion recognition: a novel method for geometrical facial features extraction. In: Proceedimgs of International Conference on Computer Vision Theory and Applications, VISAPP

26. Lowe DG (2004) Distinctive image features from scale-invariant keypoints. Int J Comput Vis 60(2):91–110

27. Lucey P, Cohn JF, Kanade T, Saragih J, Ambadar Z, Matthews I (2010) The extended cohn-kanade dataset (ck+): A complete dataset for action unit and emotion-specified expression. In: IEEE Computer Society

Conference On Computer Vision and Pattern Recognition Workshops (CVPRW), pp 94–101

28. Lucey P, Lucey S, Cohn JF (2010) Registration invariant representations for expression detection. In: International Conference On Digital Image Computing: Techniques and Applications (DICTA), pp 255–261

29. Mohammadi MR, Fatemizadeh E, Mahoor MH (2014) Pca-based dictionary building for accurate facial expression recognition via sparse representation. J Vis Commun Image Represent 25(5):1082–1092

30. Orrite C, Gañán A, Rogez G (2009) Hog-based decision tree for facial expression classification. In: Araujo H, Mendonça A, Pinho A, Torres M (eds) Pattern Recognition and Image Analysis, vol 5524., Lecture Notes in Computer ScienceSpringer, Berlin Heidelberg, pp 176–183

31. OuYang Y, Sang N (2013) Robust automatic facial expression detection method. J Softw 8(7):1759–1764

32. Pantic M, Rothkrantz LJ (2000) Expert system for automatic analysis of facial expressions. Image Vis Comput 18(11):881–905

33. Pantic M, Rothkrantz LJM (2004) Facial action recognition for facial expression analysis from static face images. IEEE Trans Syst Man Cybern Part B Cybern 34(3):1449–1461

34. Poursaberi A, Noubari HA, Gavrilova M, Yanushkevich SN (2012) Gauss–Laguerre wavelet textural feature fusion with geometrical information for facial expression identification. EURASIP J Image Video Process 2012(1):1–13.

35. Ramirez-Rivera A, Castillo R, Chae O (2013) Local directional number pattern for face analysis: Face and expression recognition. IEEE Trans Image Process 22(5):1740–1752

36. Sadeghi H, Raie A-A, Mohammadi M-R (2013) Facial expression recognition using geometric normalization and appearance representation. In: 2013 8th Iranian Conference On Machine Vision and Image Processing (MVIP), pp 159–163

37. Shan C, Gong S, McOwan PW (2009) Facial expression recognition based on local binary patterns: a comprehensive study. Image Vis Comput 27(6):803–816

38. Siddiqi M, Ali R, Khan A, Kim E, Kim G, Lee S (2014) Facial expression recognition using active contour-based face detection, facial movement-based feature extraction, and non-linear feature selection. Multimedia Syst 1–15.

39. Song M, Tao D, Liu Z, Li X, Zhou M (2010) Image ratio features for facial expression recognition application. IEEE Trans Syst Man Cybern Part B Cybern 40(3):779–788

40. Uçar A, Demir Y, Güzeliş C (2014) A new facial expression recognition based on curvelet transform and online sequential extreme learning machine initialized with spherical clustering. Neural Comput Appl 1–12.

41. Uddin MZ, Lee JJ, Kim T-S (2009) An enhanced independent component-based human facial expression recognition from video. IEEE Trans Consum Electron 55(4):2216–2224

42. Ullah I, Hussain M, Muhammad G, Aboalsamh H, Bebis G, Mirza AM (2012) Gender recognition from face images with local wld descriptor. In: 19th International Conference On Systems, Signals and Image Processing (IWSSIP), pp 417–420

43. Viola P, Jones M (2004) Robust real-time face detection. Int J Comput Vis 57(2):137–154

44. Wang X, Jin C, Liu W, Hu M, Xu L, Ren F (2013) Feature fusion of hog and wld for facial expression recognition. In: IEEE/SICE International Symposium On System Integration (SII), pp 227–232

45. Zhang Z, Lyons M, Schuster M, Akamatsu S (1998) Comparison between geometry-based and gabor-wavelets-based facial expression recognition using multi-layer perceptron. In: Proceedings Third IEEE International Conference On Automatic Face and Gesture Recognition, pp 454–459

46. Zhang L, Tjondronegoro D (2011) Facial expression recognition using facial movement features. IEEE Trans Affect Comput 2(4):219–229

47. Zhao X, Zhang S (2011) Facial expression recognition based on local binary patterns and kernel discriminant isomap. Sensors 11(10):9573–9588

48. Zhen W, Zilu Y (2012) Facial expression recognition based on local phase quantization and sparse representation. In: Eighth International Conference On Natural Computation (ICNC), pp 222–225

49. Zhong L, Liu Q, Yang P, Liu B, Huang J, Metaxas DN (2012) Learning active facial patches for expression analysis. In: IEEE Conference On Computer Vision and Pattern Recognition (CVPR), pp 2562–2569

Chapter 9

A survey on automatic techniques for enhancement and analysis of digital photography

Claudio S. V. C. Cavalcanti, Herman Martins Gomes and José Eustáquio Rangel De Queiroz

Universidade Federal de Campina Grande, Rua Aprigio Veloso, 882 Bodocongo, Campina Grande, PB 58429-140, Brazil

ABSTRACT

The fast growth in the consumer digital photography industry during the past decade has led to the acquisition and storage of large personal and public digital collections containing photos with different quality levels and redundancy, among other aspects. This naturally increased the difficulty in selecting or modifying those photos. Within the above context, this survey focuses on systematically reviewing the state-of-art on techniques for the enhancement and analysis of digital photos. Nevertheless, it is not within the scope of this survey to review image quality metrics for evaluating degradation due to compression, digital sensor noise, and affine issues. Assuming the photos have good quality in those aspects, this review is centered on techniques that might be useful to automate the task of selecting photos from large collections or to enhance the visual aspect of imperfect photos by using some perceptual measure.

KEYWORDS

Image enhancement, Photographic analysis, Computational aesthetics, Survey

1. INTRODUCTION

In the late 1990s, there was an immense growth in the digital photography industry. Manufacturers began to produce digital cameras on a large scale and at decreasing prices [119]. Great changes have been noticed in photographic technology and practice since then. When using consumer analog film, the number of photos was limited by the roll size (which usually allowed at most 36 photos). Nowadays, with large capacity re-writable memory cards (e.g., 256 GB), the number of photos that can be acquired/stored has increased by approximately three orders of magnitude (if considering digital images, captured with a resolution of 8 MP). Digital photography also changed the way photos were printed. With film, photos had to be developed first, in order to be seen, whereas when shooting with a digital camera, printing is no longer a requirement, once it is possible to preview images in the camera viewer or on a monitor screen, and then to decide which ones to print.

One consequence of those changes is that taking photos has become an almost costless task. Thus, the judgment of what could be a good shot and the care for adjusting camera settings for a specific scene becomes less usual for most consumers and even for some professional photographers. As a result, large amounts of photos are taken and stored daily. This causes difficulties in selecting which ones to print or to publish, e.g., in digital albums. In summary, this results in a scenario involving a large amount of stored photos from which just a small part will be printed. In this survey, consumer photos are considered the ones obtained (1) with minor adjustments in camera settings, (2) aiming at portraying daily events, and (3) barely exploring art basic techniques. On the other hand, professional photos differ from consumer ones by the use of more elaborate techniques and better equipment utilization, which might improve the photo quality. In this survey, professional photos are not necessarily obtained by a professional photographer, and do not encompass other connotations of professional photos (e.g., artistic or journalistic).

There are several recent applications for which photo processing is an essential intermediate task, e.g., photo collage [149], slide showing [44], browsing [68, 85, 112, 150], storytelling [53], and photo summarization [28, 110, 117, 141].

The algorithms reviewed in this survey are organized into two categories: enhancement and analysis. Each category is divided in other sub-categories. An illustration for the division that is used in this work is shown in Fig. 1.

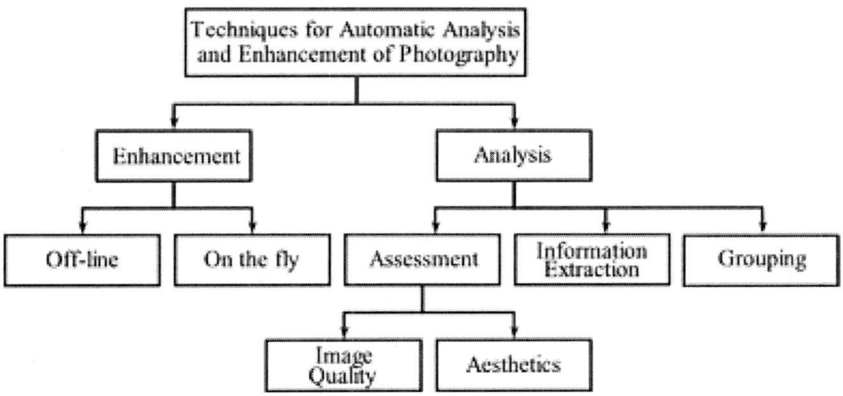

Figure 1. Block diagram illustrating the sub-areas in which this work is subdivided

While enhancement algorithms are intended to modify the image in such a way that it might become better-looking or appealing, analysis algorithms are designed to assess photos according to some criteria, such as composition, aesthetics, or overall quality.

A number of papers have been written on both image enhancement and analysis in the past years. This survey focuses in work on image processing techniques that were already tested or may be directly used in specific problems of photo enhancement and analysis. In order to avoid ambiguities, in this survey the words photo and photography are strictly related to consumer and professional photography.

Image enhancement algorithms can be classified as *on the fly* and *off-line*. While *on the fly*algorithms modify the photo conditions before the photo is taken, *off-line* algorithms perform changes after the acquisition took place. Although the *on the fly* algorithms might lead to better results than*off-line* algorithms, they must run faster since it might be necessary to do this in a real-time operation.*Off-line* algorithms are limited in the sense that they do not allow scene changes, e.g., it is not possible to zoom out from a photo or ask someone to open his/her eyes. However, there is no *a priori*time frame to produce the enhancement result.

Image analysis algorithms can be classified as *assessment*, *information extraction*, and grouping algorithms. Assessment algorithms analyze the visual aspect of a photo in two main facets: aesthetics and with respect to the *image quality assessment* (IQA). Formally, the main goal of IQA algorithms is to predict ratings in a human-like manner [21]. Although this definition is very broad, the term IQA is typically used to denote the evaluation of the image degradation (e.g., due to lossy compression or noise) [21, 62, 63, 118, 167, 178]. Therefore, in this survey, IQA is used with this latter meaning. There is also some ambiguity regarding the use of the expression *aesthetics quality assessment*. In this survey, aesthetics quality assessment algorithms are defined as the ones whose goal is to assign a score (or a class of scores, such as professional and amateur) to a photo based in the analyzed feature, e.g., photographic composition rules or number of faces found, as used by other authors [7, 74, 126, 145]. Moreover, information extraction algorithms search for elements of interest, such as the place a photo was taken, the existence of faces, and the presence of specific people in the environment, among others. Finally, grouping algorithms are defined in this survey as the ones which analyze images in order to find similarities between them.

It is not within the scope of this survey to review image quality assessment for evaluating degradation due to compression, digital sensor noise, and affine issues. Assuming the photos have good quality in those aspects, this review focuses on techniques that might be useful to automate the task of photo selection from large collections or to enhance the visual aspect of imperfect photos by using a perceptual measure.

This survey is organized as follows: in Sect. 2, the methodology employed for finding related work is presented. In Sect. 3, the work on image enhancement is reviewed, in particular, enhancement that could be performed to increase the quality of a photo in a printing or selection scenario. In Sect. 4, work on image (and photo) analysis are reviewed. In

Sect. 5, the main issues found in the reviewed approaches are discussed and summarized. Finally, in Sect. 6, some conclusions are given.

Table 1. Literature search results

Publication	C/J	Publisher	No. of papers
CVPR	C	IEEE	18
ICME	C	IEEE	15
CVIU	J	Elsevier	12
ICIP	C	IEEE	9
IJCV	J	Springer	8
Pattern recognition	J	Elsevier	8
MM	C	ACM	6
TIP	J	IEEE	6
IET-CV	J	IET	4
CIVR	C	ACM	3
Expert systems with applications	J	Elsevier	3
ECCV	C	Springer	2
Eurographics	C	Wiley-Blackwell	2
ICASSP	C	IEEE	2
IJPRAI	J	World Scientific	2
Transactions on consumer electronics	J	IEEE	2
Transactions on Graphics	J	ACM	2
Transactions on multimedia	J	IEEE	2
Visual communication and image representation	J	Elsevier	2
Other	J/C	-	42
Total			150

The first column corresponds to the publication name, the second column indicates if the publication is a conference or a journal, the third column shows the publisher name, and the fourth column shows the number of papers related to this survey

2. METHODOLOGY OF THE RESEARCH

This section is devoted to presenting the methodology adopted for searching the related work in the area. More specifically, information on search engines, digital libraries, and keywords used in the searching process is provided.

Two search strategies were employed, inspired by the traversing order of breadth-first and depth-first search strategies, respectively. Breadth-first search was performed within a set of predefined published conference proceedings and journals in a specified time period, but only the first level of the search tree was considered for reviewing. Depth-first search was performed by using a search engine to find papers given a set of keywords. A subsequent search was then performed by using the references of those papers as a starting point. This process was repeated until a maximum depth of 3 was reached.

In the following two subsections, more details on each type of performed search are given.

2.1 Breadth-first search

This strategy aimed at finding related papers in a set of recent technical publications, such as journals and conference proceedings, given a specified time frame. The search was performed in the database of conferences and journals of IEEE, ACM, Springer, and Elsevier. Besides, by using the search results, there was also performed a search for all papers published in a given conference or journal by using its table of contents.

The keywords used for the automatic search were *(consumer OR personal OR digital) AND (image(s) OR photo(s) or photograph(s) OR photographic archive) AND (value OR quality OR aesthetics OR visual quality) AND (evaluation OR assessment OR analysis OR estimation)*. A publication period between 2006 and 2012 was defined.

2.2 Depth-first search

In this strategy, the relevant papers were found by using the following methodology: (1) based on a set of keywords, for every result returned by a given search engine, (2) the bibliography was analyzed, and (3) relevant cited work was reviewed, including the root paper itself. This is a practical and useful method for reviewing the literature, once the search is seeded using papers already considered relevant by other researchers. The great advantage is that this method dramatically reduces the searching time for finding relevant papers. On the other hand, there are some drawbacks. First, some stop criteria have to be defined, otherwise this becomes an almost endless process. Second, not every citation is directly related to the research area, since it is common to find papers from correlated areas such as Artificial Intelligence and Neurobiology.

In order to perform this search, some constraints have to be defined. The search is performed in a single level. Another level is considered if and only if a cited paper is strictly related to the area.

2.3 Search results

Table 1 contains the conferences and journals returned from the above mentioned search method. It is also noted if it is a conference or a journal, the publisher name, and the number of papers selected for this survey.

In Table 1, *Other* refers to conferences or journals with only one related publication. Figure 2illustrates the balance between conference and journal papers that are reviewed in this survey.

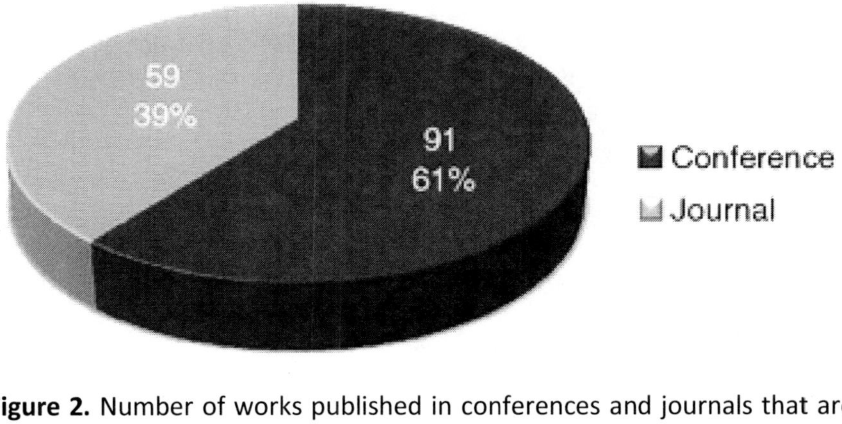

Figure 2. Number of works published in conferences and journals that are studied in this survey.

2.4 Considerations on the methodology

The methodology previously presented was defined in order to cover relevant papers in the research taxonomy defined in the previous section. Of course, work published prior to 2006, published in low impact conferences/journals or indexed with inadequate keywords might not have been included in this survey. Nonetheless, the number of relevant papers that were included in this survey (150) indicates that a good sample of the relevant work was considered.

3. ENHANCEMENT

This section focuses on the research on enhancement techniques applied to digital photography. Usually, the areas of enhancement and analysis work side-by-side, e.g., enhancement is often performed in order to obtain more precise analysis, and a good analysis may help identify which aspects of a digital photo should be enhanced. In spite of that, and for didactic purposes, these areas are discussed separately in this survey.

As mentioned in the previous section, enhancement work may be divided in *on the fly* and *off-line*.*On the fly* approaches are the ones for which it is possible to modify the environment during image acquisition, while in *off-line* approaches that is not possible, thus, usually the photos are modified or enhanced after acquisition. Nonetheless, both expressions, *off-line* and *on the fly*, are also used with other connotations. Chartier and Renaud employed *off-line* in a noise filtering context [22], while Ercegovac and Lang used the same term in a digital arithmetic context [46].

In the following two sections, more details on photo enhancement approaches are given.

3.1 On the fly enhancement

Although it is generally possible to improve photos by means of a wide range of enhancement algorithms (e.g., red eye correction, histogram processing, among others), there are some particular scenarios from which some information is completely lost during acquisition thus making useless a post-processing operation. Photograph acquisition is naturally a lossy process, which disregards factors such as color, temperature, environment, time and space of the environment, depth of the scene, among several others. For instance, a photo may be considered inadequate due to the zoom choice, e.g., a close-up should not be used when the goal is to show that the subject is in a given location. After the photo is shot, zooming out is not possible, and a good photo might be lost. In some specific situations, it is possible to perform some correction. However, the results are usually far inferior to a scenario in which a new photo could be obtained. For example, image brightness can be adjusted after acquisition in order to improve image aesthetics, but this may result in intensity clipping.

On the fly (or dynamic, live, real-time) enhancement algorithms are proposed to automatically perform or advise adjustments to the camera settings, before the photo is taken. The performed adjustments are intended to improve the photo quality or to avoid undesired conditions, such as inadequate focus and lighting.

Most modern digital cameras have embedded *on the fly* enhancement mechanisms, such as an exposure meter, an automatic focus adjustment, and a white-balance adjustment. Since those mechanisms are mostly based on low level information, high level information about scene contents is usually input by the user by means of an appropriate *scene* switch selection. For example, one may adjust the camera *scene* switch to *motion* when using camera to shoot a sports scene.

A fully automated system may require that high-level information, such as the location of people in the scene, should be used in order to increase the overall understanding of the scene, as well as to help algorithms to decide where and how to perform changes.

A first example of a fully-automatic approach is the face-priority auto-focus [125], which has been commercially used by several camera manufacturers. The goal is to set the focus of the camera to regions where there are faces, in order to avoid incorrect focus priority. For example, the Nikon D90 camera uses face position to correctly adjust focus on people present in the scene [107].

Another example, which recently became very popular, is the smile shutter function, which shots the photo only when every detected face in the image is smiling. Several cameras and prototypes incorporating the above features have been developed by camera manufacturers, such as Sony and Canon [47].

Photographic composition rules are also considered as important features for the dynamic adjustment of an image. The conformity with photographic composition rules can be achieved with slight movements of the camera. The production of an autonomous robot photographer is a possible direction to take to address this aspect. The robot developed by Byers et al. [13, 14] was designed to be placed in an event, moving towards possible subjects, proceeding the composition, and, finally, obtaining the photo. The subject of a photo may be identified by several approaches, such as considering the output of a skin detection algorithm and a laser range-finder sensor [13, 14]. This information may also be used for finding the path that a robot must follow to reach the subjects. After getting to the desired place, once again the scene is analyzed for achieving a good composition for the photo. Four composition rules (rule of thirds, empty space, no middle, and edge rule) were used to guide their system to obtain a good composition. The system performance was assessed in some real-world events such as a wedding reception and during the SIGGRAPH 2003 conference.

Another example of a robot photographer (but less independent than the one previously presented) is the Sony Party Shot [143]. The Sony Party Shot apparatus can be plugged into the camera for locating and photographing people by moving in three degrees of freedom (pan, tilt, and zoom). The limitation of this approach is the need to put the robot in a fixed position with the aim of locating people of that point of view, and taking photos.

Some approaches may consider acquiring multiple images with different camera settings in order to detect and/or correct issues after image acquisition. For example, two subsequent photos may be obtained with different camera apertures [4]. The acquired images are then combined for finding the subject and analyzing photo composition. Besides improving photographic composition of the image, it is also possible to locate the mergers (which occur due to the projection of a 3D world scene into a 2D representation, in which background objects appear to be connected to the objects in the foreground) [4].

Despite the obvious advantage of *on the fly* approaches to digital photography, there are a number of limitations. Since most algorithms demand high processing times and some level of scene understanding, *on the fly* processing might be impractical due to battery consumption. A high processing time can be understood as a period of time that exceeds the time between two scenes setups (e.g., people position and lighting conditions).

In order to improve scene understanding, stereo vision might be employed to find interesting objects, to provide depth estimates, and to improve image segmentation as well, which may help with the acquisition of better photos. In a dynamic environment, stereo vision may be obtained by the use of Pan–Tilt–Zoom (PTZ) cameras through simple-region SSD (sum of square difference) matching [158].

Finally, *on the fly* composition might be used for automatic and semi-automatic panorama creation [23].

3.2 *Off-line* enhancement

This section is devoted to discuss existing methods for the enhancement of photos that have already been acquired. The goal is to enhance a photo using only the existing information in the image file (i.e., pixels, Exchangeable Image File format—EXIF information, faces detected, etc.). Changes typically occur at pixel level, and are required when it is not possible to obtain another photo and the resulting photo has room for improvements. For *off-line* enhancement, the image representation might be in any color space, however Benoit et al. [5] have shown some advantages when using models based on the human visual system for low-level photo enhancement.

Generally, enhancement changes can be used for making more attractive a photo that presents some type of imperfection. For instance, after removing the imperfection that lens dust may cause, a photo may look more attractive [188]. It is also possible to improve photos by smoothing the subject's skin [77], by adjusting some general aspect, such as contrast and brightness for both generic [183] and specific type of photos (e.g., improving contours in nature photos [128]) or by removing an undesired object (e.g., an unknown person or a light pole [6, 170]). This last type of enhancement may be achieved by image inpainting, as discussed next.

Image inpainting has been largely used for enhancing photos [170]. Through inpainting, one might remove an element which harms the composition of a photo [170]. Inpainting algorithms remove elements from photos by evaluating the surrounding indicated area with statistical analysis and filling this area with a surrounding-like texture. Inpainting may be obtained by combining texture synthesis, geometric partial differential equations (PDEs), and coherence among neighbor pixels [6]. Patch sparsity algorithms are used for improving image inpainting [170].

Enhancement by example has also been employed [72]. When a user classifies a photo, he/she indirectly classifies the features he/she considers important. Processes such as sharpening, super-resolution, inpainting, white-balance, and deblurring are performed in photos so that they reflect the features present in example images. Other types of enhancement are the photo composite, in which a face can be replaced by another [86], and collage algorithms, in which groups selected images in a new one [149].

Cropping algorithms are designed for obtaining an image which has smaller dimensions than the original one. There are several methods for automatic [1, 3, 24, 138, 147, 179, 186] and semi-automatic [133] photo cropping. Cropping is performed by extracting an area of interest from an original photo [82, 147, 179], to improve the quality of the photographic composition [18, 133, 186], to retarget a photo to smaller displays [1, 3, 24, 138, 179], and to recompose the photo [87].

Most cropping methods have in common the use of content-aware strategies. Content detection may vary from face detection [18, 24, 138, 147, 186], saliency detection [1, 3, 24, 87, 147, 186], and user-interaction with tracking of the user's gaze [133].

Region of interest (ROI) cropping methods intend to remove a fraction of the original image which contains or includes some element of interest. The dimensions of the resulting image are dependent on the original image contents. Some restrictions may apply, such as maintaining the image original proportion or leaving some room from the element of interest to the photo edges [82, 147]. Common applications for such methods are thumbnail cropping and image summarization. A ROI cropping may be improved with face detection for images containing people. However, other elements of interest (e.g., animals) may be detected by using specific detectors [165] or a generic detector such as saliency maps. Saliency and spatial priors have been also used for content-aware thumbnail cropping [82].

Cropping for improving composition may help the photographer to achieve better results by modifying the image dimensions or image proportions. As it is going to be further discussed in Sect. 4.1, there are rules for analyzing the composition quality of a photo, such as the rule of thirds, which may be used in conjunction with small changes in the image dimensions, aiming at better composition by just removing a few pixel rows (or columns) of the photo. On the other hand, there are methods that make direct changes in the image contents. They will be referred to in this paper as recomposition methods, as discussed next.

Cropping algorithms are limited in the sense that they crop the images from the borders. Cropping columns or rows in the middle of the image usually results in distortions. However, in some cases the important content of the image is close to the borders. There is, however, a class of algorithms named retargeting algorithms, which may crop the image to regions other than the borders only.

Retargeting algorithms are mainly designed for adapting an image to different rendering devices, such as mobile phones [1, 3, 24, 138]. The goal is to preserve the main content of the image while discarding unnecessary or redundant information in such a way the main content is more visible than if a simple resample were applied. Global energy optimization for the whole image may be used for image retargeting [127]. Face detection, text detection, and visual attention, all combined, may also be used for finding content in photos [24].

Another class of algorithms, similar to the retargeting algorithms is the class of recomposition algorithms. Recomposition algorithms present a very challenging area of research: the goal is to automatically change the image in order to obtain a more pleasant composition. Some examples of such changes include modifying the subject proportions, removing elements from the photo, cropping the image, etc. Most approaches are, as yet, semi-automatic in the sense they require human intervention to indicate which areas need improvement. In this survey, recomposition algorithms are considered as different from retargeting algorithms since they do not necessarily imply changing the original image dimensions or the original image proportions. The changes are usually artistic ones. Liu et al. [87] proposed a method for recomposition based on finding elements of interest, and applying composition rules (such as rule of thirds, diagonal guidance, and visual balance) to produce a better composed image. In a similar approach, Bhattacharya et al. [7] proposed a semi-automatic recomposition method which uses stress points (adapted from the rule of thirds) for optimal object placement and visual balance for improving composition. Experiments show that 73 % of recomposed images were considered better than original counterparts by human observers.

4. ANALYSIS

In this section, relevant work on photography analysis is presented. Methods in this area may be organized according to their purposes, as follows:

1) *Assessment.* The goal is to score photos on a given scale (e.g., from zero to ten, good or bad) according to some criterion: the image quality (related to some degradation in the image) or the aesthetics of the image could be assessed; and

2) *Information extraction.* The goal is to detect the presence and location of some pre-defined elements of interest, e.g., people and faces, in a photo. The relationship between photos could also be extracted.

In the following sections, each one of these groups of methods is described in more detail.

4.1 Assessment

Assessment algorithms typically assign a score to a photo based on some metric. This allows the creation of an ordering based on the returned metric values. Assessing (or ranking) a photo is a very difficult and controversial task, especially when dealing with consumer ones. Two main aspects can be evaluated: the quality and the aesthetics of the photo. While the image quality analysis, in this survey, is understood as the assessment of the degradation of the image (e.g., sensor noise, resolution, and compression artefacts), the aesthetics analysis is related to the visual appearance and appeal of the photo (e.g., the color harmony and photo composition). IQA is out of the scope of this survey.

Several photo composition techniques and rules of thumb have been defined by experienced photographers, based on heuristics and are considered as responsible for improving the aesthetic quality of a photo. Those rules, known as photographic composition rules, may be used to identify higher-quality photos, based on the assessment of features. Photo composition may be regarded as the most determinant factor to consumers when considering photo quality [134].

The application of a photo composition rule will not necessarily assure best aesthetic results. Notwithstanding, photos obeying such rules are likely to look more appealing to consumers than if they were shot without attention to the rules [17, 134]. However, it is not necessarily true that a photo must have composition rules obeyed to be considered appealing by consumers. This contradiction may be explained by the existence of other factors, apart from composition, e.g., people involved, photogeny and the place the photo was taken.

Some of the photo composition rules were lately explained by the theories of perception. The rule of thirds is a good example: it is known that when the subject of the photo is placed in one of the thirds of the image, the viewer is stimulated, due to the nature of human visual system, to perceive other regions of the photo. Other rules are not well defined in the specialized photography literature or are defined in terms of more subjective concepts, e.g., trying to obtain a more casual and spontaneous picture [12].

Photographic composition rules have been adopted for ranking photos in many researches [4, 14, 17,18, 39, 41, 73, 81, 87, 95, 139], in which relationships between some predefined rules and the human judgment have been identified. Rules may come from human visual system theories as well as from professional photographer's expertise.

The rule of thirds is the most explored photographic composition rule in the literature [4, 14, 17, 18,39, 74, 87]. One of the main reasons for that is because it is easily translated to algorithms. The rule of thirds states that one should preferentially place the subject in a third of the image width or height (depending on the image orientation). Existing works differ on how the subject of the photo is located, for example by using (1) face detection algorithms [14, 17, 18]; (2) low-level information, such as borders and regions found by the mean shift algorithm [4, 87]; or (3) by evaluating the differences of pixels positioned in those interest areas [39].

Other rules are also explored but with less consensus between authors. The zoom rule can be applied to classify photos according to the distance from the camera to the subject. Excessive or insufficient distances are penalized by the algorithm as inadequate compositions. Since a precise detection of the subject is required for this type of analysis, Cavalcanti et al. [18] and Byers et al. [14] used face detection as the main information to identify subject position. In a similar approach, Kahn et al. [74], used the ratio between the area of the face and the area of the image.

The integrity rule was proposed to identify undesired chopping of the main subject. The great drawback of this rule is the high cost of precisely detecting the subject in a photo. The use of anthropometric measures were shown to be effective to subjects in an upright frontal position. Using some reliable information, such as the coordinates, and the dimensions of a detected face [18, 139], it is possible to infer the position of the rest of the subject body, and detect possible chops.

Both zoom and integrity rules were designed considering that there is trusty high-level information such as the face coordinates. This is a great drawback, since an imprecise detection may lead to wrong conclusions. There are approaches that mainly rely on the intensities of pixels rather than on high-level information. One disadvantage is that color images may have their channels treated independently and may result in redundancy which must be treated by classification algorithms. For instance, in the work of Datta et al. [39], 56 initial rules were reduced to just 15 rules after the execution of support vector machines (SVM) and pruning [33], since there was redundancy in applying the same data extraction algorithm in all images.

Finally, the visual balance rule is also used for analyzing if the photo elements are well balanced, i.e., are placed in a photo in a way that observer attention is equally divided by the photo elements [7, 87,176].

Besides the use of photographic rules there are authors which evaluate low-level features (e.g., sharpness, brightness, and contrast) in order to identify the overall appearance of a photo [39, 73,80, 81, 108].

Higher level image analysis may also be employed for photo ranking. For instance, aesthetic analysis, may be achieved by learning how humans classify photos according to some subjective criteria. Although that might be difficult, there are studies focusing on the emotions evoked by artwork in humans [174]. The criteria may be diverse. For instance, the time a human spends evaluating an image can be a criterion for confidence on human assessment [45]. It is believed that the emotions evoked by a natural image can be understood by means of aesthetics gap concept. According to Datta et al. [40], "The aesthetics gap is the lack of coincidence between the information that one can extract from low-level visual data and the interpretation of emotions that the visual data may arouse in a particular user in a given scenario.". Color harmony can also be considered as an important feature to be considered [176]. Low-level information such as lighting, color [74, 80, 95], luminance [74], edges, and range of lightness

[48] are used for judging the harmony (a high-level subjective aspect) of a photo and videos [104].

Besides all the above presented factors, there are some other common sense factors that might influence human judgement. Below is a list of these additional factors:

- *People involved.* A photo may be considered more or less appealing depending on the identity of the shown people, e.g., even a badly composed and illuminated photo might be considered good if it contains people for which the consumer has affection, such as the photographer's child, a famous person, etc. The opposite might also happen: a well composed photo might be discarded if the person in the photo is unknown;

- *Place where the photo was taken.* Some photos are related to places rarely visited. Thus, even if a photo has problems, e.g., in composition or illumination, it is likely that it will not be discarded because of its uniqueness;

- *Photogeny.* Well-composed photos do not necessarily contain photogenic people. It is possible to find one or more group members talking or looking elsewhere in the moment the photo was shot, especially in group photos; and

- *Personal preferences.* Some people might prefer a photo without obeying composition rules.

Despite the above discussed factors, photo ranking might be useful for helping consumers to identify (at least in a group of pre-selected photos) the ones with more attributes related to a better looking or appealing impression.

4.2 Information extraction

This section includes a discussion on approaches for extracting elements of interest that might be important to a photographic analysis system. The reviewed work involves approaches for face and people detection, landscape analysis (e.g., horizon tilt evaluation), and identification of the image class (e.g., if it is a photo or a graphic image). The goal is neither to rank nor to classify the images but to extract information. This may be considered as an auxiliary source of information for image ranking methods (discussed in the previous section). Elements of interest might be anything the user is searching for: (1) a face; (2) a person; (3) regions with unwanted features such as dissection lines [139], (4) unfocused or blurred regions [151], (5) a sunset area [9], (6) text [153], and many others.

Generally, information extraction by different approaches involves the construction of a classification model for the targeted element (this can be performed, for example, through a learning process using a set of reference patterns). It is commonly accepted that the best technique to build a particular model for a given problem is dependant on specific features of the problem.

Decision trees [43, 130] are typically employed to identify classes that have a reduced number of constraints, both numerical and categorical, such as number of colors, number of people, etc. The ID3 classification algorithm [124] was used for classifying an image as either a digital photo or as artwork (e.g., a logo, a drawing, and other images artificially generated). The decision tree was trained with 1,200 images. An accuracy of 95.6 % was achieved when distinguishing the classes. This result was verified through a tenfold cross validation.

The SVM [33] is largely used for classification, which is useful for detecting features in photographs, such as indoor or outdoor scenes [137], the presence of a sunset [9], the level of expertise of the photographer [152], the presence of skin regions [64], among others. The SVM is normally used when the set of constraints is not small, and there is no clear linear separation of the data for each class. When defining an SVM model, a kernel must be specified. For instance, Serrano et al. [137] used a radial basis function. On the other hand, Boutell et al. [9] and Li et al. [80] used a gaussian function.

When there is a great amount of data, and a great number of components as well, the high correlation between those components may harm classification. Many authors use principal component analysis (PCA) [65] for reducing the dimensionality of the feature space [152].

Some information extraction methods are designed for detecting human-related information, such as face, eye, skin, pose, etc. Since most photos have people, such information is very important to any photographic analysis system.

Recent work in face detection focused on multi-view, rotation, and scale invariant face and eye detectors. Discriminant features [162], low-level features [42], Sobel edge detection, morphological operations, and thresholding [154] may be used for this goal.

Face recognition algorithms can be used for identifying photos which contain or do not contain a specific individual, as well as for finding relationships between images due to the presence of a given person or group [55]. The identification of a specific person might be used, according to a rule defined by Loui et al. [92], to infer the relevance of a given photo based on the relationship of the people to the photo owner. Recognition can be also used, along with human tagging and some logic formalism (e.g., Markov logic), to retrieve social connections in photo repositories [57, 75, 140, 187].

In a photo selection scenario, it is very important to identify the relationship between the people present in some image set. Such a relationship may be used for predicting the significance of such images to that set [91]. This can be done using local patterns of Gabor magnitude and phase [166]. Face recognition highly relies on face detection. Thus, imprecision on face detection may result in a poor face recognition. There are, however, approaches for misalignment-robust face recognition [171].

The use of face details, such as birthmarks [120] and clothes [54], are also used to improve face recognition. A Markov random field is used for recognizing people based on contextual clues such as clothing [2]. Gender can also be a clue for face recognition by means of spatial Gaussian mixture models (SGMM) [84].

Considering that low-level image features are considered by consumers to determine if a given photo is better than another [137], detecting the presence of such low-level features may be very useful for ranking photos. One of those features is the blur. Blur may be used for automatically ranking photos [73, 95]. Blurred images can be identified by the detection of some features, such as image color, gradient, and spectrum information [88]. The spectral analysis of an image gradient is also used for identifying blurring kernels in images [69]. Other features such as clarity, complexity, and color composition are also explored [39, 94].

Besides the face, skin regions are another important evidence for the presence of a human in a photo. Several approaches were proposed. Skin tone may be detected by a pixel-wise approach or by a region-based approach [76]. Both approaches use a color model [64]. Additionally, it might be possible to decompose skin tone in hemoglobin and melanin [169], which can be used for a better understanding of skin texture.

Skin classification may be performed by the use of SVM and region segmentation [64], as indicated earlier in this section. The approaches might be compared with receiver operating characteristic (ROC) analysis [136].

While evidence for people can be obtained by skin detection or face detection, there are also approaches by which humans can be directly detected in images. Recent approaches use local binary patterns (LBP) for human detection through two variants, semantic-LBP and Fourier-LBP [105]. People detection can also be achieved by the use of quantified fuzzy temporal rules for representing knowledge of human spatial data. This kind of data is learned with an evolutionary approach [106]. A head and shoulders detector can be also achieved by the use of a watershed and border detector, whose outputs are used to train a classifier using AdaBoost [168].

Some researches have been conducted for detecting people in a specific context, but might be extended to a more general scenario. For instance, it was shown that the use of region covariance features with radial basis function kernel SVM, and histograms of oriented gradients (HOG) with quadratic kernel SVM outperformed the use of local receptive fields with quadratic kernel SVM in the specific scenario of pedestrian detection [116]. In the same way, the detection of human activities, such as 'fighting' or 'assault', are recognized and encoded by using context-free grammars through a method which uses a description-based approach [131].

Besides people detection, other types of information may be useful for photography analysis. For example, the social context might be inferred by analyzing the distribution of people found within the image [56]. A graph-based approach has shown to be useful for finding rows of people [56].

The pose of the people is also important information about the photo. Each body part has a limited number of positions when compared relatively to other body parts. For instance, the head is directly connected to the shoulders and might not appear connected to the feet. Thus, if a face is found, the shoulders should come right below. There are several approaches for human pose estimation. Human pose may be estimated in video sequences using multi-dimensional boosting regression from Haar features [8]. In static images, pose can be classified through angular constraints and variations of body joints with the use of SVM [97], with observation a driven Gaussian process latent variable model (ODGPLVM) [61] and non-tree graph models [70], and with a conditional random field (CRF) if multiple views are available. A bottom-up parsing approach can be used to recognize the human body for performing pose estimation by segmenting multiple images.

Besides human subjects, other types of subjects may be considered in a photo. Different subjects (e.g., natural or man-made objects and animals) might appear alone or interacting with humans, resulting in a more complex photo. A shape-driven object detector [59, 129], SIFT [78], and sets of mattes [144] may also be employed for a more general object detector. It is also possible to identify the region-of-interest by using captured camera information stored in EXIF [83].

Instead of detecting a specific type of object, it is also effective to use the identification of regions within the image with some correspondence. In this sense, the image segmentation algorithm has fundamental importance for the photography analysis.

There are several approaches to image segmentation. Since in photography analysis, subjects and scenarios might vary widely, the more general the image segmentation algorithm is, the better the result.

Main methods for image segmentation are based on edge information [19, 159], fragment-based approaches [36, 79], point-wise repetition [182], tree partitioning under a normalized cut criterion [160], a nonparametric Bayesian model [115], a geometric active contour model [180], Markov random fields with region growing [123], Markov random fields and graph cut [25], and local Chan–Vese (LCV) model [163].

Most algorithms deal with both color and gray images. Some image segmentation algorithms are specific to color images [19, 181]. It is normally difficult to compare different image segmentation algorithms, but unsupervised objective assessment methods have been attempted for this task [185].

4.3 Grouping

Photo grouping is designed for setting associations between groups of photos. The associations may be set by either the semantic information found (such as number of faces detected, number of colors, etc.) or high-level information (e.g., Global Positioning System, GPS, position present in some image EXIF).

4.3.1 Classification and clustering

Classification algorithms are designed to identify the class which a given image belongs to. There are several goals for image classification, e.g., (1) identifying, in a set of image files, which ones are photos and which ones are graphics [114]; (2) identifying whether photos were obtained in an indoor or an outdoor environment [137]; and (3) identifying if images were obtained by an amateur photographer or a professional one [80, 94, 111, 151], among others.

It is not completely known how humans perform classification tasks. Vogel et al. [157] have shown, however, that humans use both local and global region-based configurations for scene categorization. This implies that human-inspired algorithms may consider both local and global region-based information for better results in image classification. It was also shown that the color plays an important role in image categorization for humans. Natural images were better classified when presented in color as opposed to gray levels [157]. Classification has a close relation to information extraction, as discussed in Sect. 4.2.

One of the main steps for an accurate image classification is the representation of the image which will later be used as input to a classifier. Representation can be performed by local descriptors [101], a topic histogram using probabilistic latent semantic analysis (pLSA) and expectation–maximization (EM) [93], multilevel representation [164], triangular representation, which is robust to viewpoint changes [67], resolution invariant image representation [161], and scale invariant feature transform (SIFT) [164], among other methods.

Some relevant classifiers proposed in the literature are: AdaBoost [93], SVM [101, 164], multiple kernel learning (MKL) [93], Bayesian belief networks [38], Bayesian active learning [122], and conditional random fields models [15, 184].

The main challenges in image classification are the computational cost and the classification accuracy. A local adaptive active learning (LA-AL) method was used for lowering the number of training samples needed [93]. The within-category confusion can be dealt with probabilistic patch descriptors, which encodes the appearance of an image fragment, and the variability within a category [101].

Clustering algorithms are intended to automatically group images when considering their extracted features. Given a set of photos, clustering can be used to identify the existing relationship between such photos.

Cooper et al. [30] presented an automatic temporal similarity-based method using EXIF data. Graph-based algorithms [52] and local discriminant models and global integration (LDMGI) [173] are common methods for image clustering.

Since clustering is not commonly a supervised process, system improvements are necessary for reducing errors in the system. Thus, user feedback is used as a way to bring out relevant feedback about system performance [11].

4.3.2 Summarization

Another recent area of interest is finding relationships between photos for producing summaries. Summaries are useful since finding information in large sets of images can be time consuming. Summaries are used for producing condensed displays of touristic destinations [117], simplifying photo browsing on personal collections [28, 141, 155], indexing [156], and storytelling [53, 110], among other applications. A specific problem related to the task of producing summaries or filtering out redundant information from a collection of photographs is the detection of near duplicates [28,126, 148].

Photos matching specific keywords [142] or GPS-tagged information [135] have been grouped to build 3D models of some sightseeing. On-line tools, such as Bing maps [102], used some of those technologies for building 3D models of such places.

4.3.3 Image retrieval

According to Marshall et al. [99], image retrieval techniques can be classed as content-based image retrieval (CBIR) and annotation-based image retrieval (ABIR). In CBIR, the images are processed for obtaining information while in ABIR, images are often annotated with textual information, such as place, time or photographer, and this information is used to retrieve images.

Most detection algorithms can be used as an intermediate step for retrieving images in CBIR [90, 99], such as recognized faces [121, 187] and events [37], among others.

Since manually tagging photos can be time consuming, recent work considers the use of information automatically obtained from EXIF [83, 85, 132, 148], SIFT [26, 148], face recognition and connections found in social networks [27, 113, 155], and georeferences, which might be obtained from GPS devices [16], people clues such as faces and clothes [146] or other high-level information [132].

4.4 Discussion

In this section, algorithms for photo analysis have been organized in three categories: assessment, information extraction, and grouping. From the performed review, assessment seems to be the less explored area. This may be explained by the highly subjective nature of the task, which makes it difficult to perform precise or universal analyses. The other two areas are more explored in the literature and present a richer set of approaches.

Besides the underlying limitations discussed in the next section, the approaches seem very promising to be included in a photography analysis system.

5. CRITICAL ANALYSIS

The main issues covered in the studies reviewed in this survey are considered in this section. To better discuss such issues, the following information about the articles were summarized: the source of the used image set, the size of the image set, the main goal, the metrics used for assessment, and the achieved results. The photo analysis algorithms are shown in Table 2 and the enhancement algorithms are in Table 3.

This section contains two subsections. In the first one, a review of the image sets used in the experiments is given. In the second one, commentaries about the validation processes are presented.

5.1 Image sets

For most of the image analysis algorithms reviewed in this survey, the purpose is to perform tasks in a human-like manner. Thus, it is fundamentally important to ensure the photo sample is representative for testing.

Some studies were performed to identify the user behaviour when photographing [96], sharing [103], analyzing [49], and managing [35]. However, based on the conducted literature review, strong evidence about the user preferences were not drawn, the assessment of most algorithms for photo enhancement and analysis are performed by means of subjective assessment.

According to the conducted literature review, there is no defined methodology for carrying out subjective experiments for photos analysis. Some methodology ought to be employed due to the number of factors that might influence subjective assessment. Some of these factors are:

1) *People involved.* While in professional photos, the people present in the photo are usually part of the subject, in consumer photos, people are mostly known and significant to the photo owner. Therefore, a photo assessment performed by consumers might be too strict in the absence of a known person and too flexible in the occurrence of, for instance, a family member;

2) *Place and event.* In some situations, the photo might not be technically good, but captured a place or a rare event. This could positively influence the judgement of the photos;

3) *Style used.* Different users adopt different photo habits. The individual style of a user might not be appreciated by other users;

Table 2. Summary of the reviewed work on analysis techniques

Authors	Image sources	Set size	Main goal	Assess. method: used metrics	Results
Liu et al. [90]	Photosig [10], NUS-WIDE [29], Kodak [172]	1,300,000	CBIR	Obj.: precision	14.5 %
Li et al. [83]	NI	70,000	ROI Detection	Obj.: precision and Recall	NI
Pang et al. [117]	Flickr [50]	50,000	Grouping	Sub.: scaled (1–5)	Average rank > 4
Sinha [141]	Flickr [50], Picasa [58]	40,000	Grouping	Obj.: JS Divergence	JS Div. < 0.3
Tong et al. [152]	Corel [32], MS	29,540	Assess.: home user x photographer	Obj.: MSE	11.1
Marshall [99]	MIR FLICKR 25000 [51]	25,000	CBIR	NI	NI
O'Hare [113]	Own	23,774	Grouping	Obj.: H-hit rule	NI
Dao et al. [37]	Picasa [58]	19,101	Grouping	Obj.: F-Measure	NI
Luo et al.[94]	Web	17,613	Assess.: high x low quality	Obj.: accuracy	95 %
Yao et al. [175]	Photo.net [60]	13,302	Assess.: ranking	Sub.: scale (0–100)	75.33 %
Ke et al. [73]	DpChallenge [20]	12,000	Assess.	Sub.: scale (1–10)	72 %
Yeh et al. [177]	DpChallenge [20], Flickr [50]	12,000	Assess.: ranking	Sub.: scale (1–10)	81 %
Yeh et al. [176]	DpChallenge [20], Flickr [50]	12,000	Assess.: ranking	Sub.: scale (1–10)	93 %
Sandnes [132]	Own	7,672	Grouping	Obj.: accuracy	88.1 %
Su et al. [145]	DpChallenge [20]	6,000	Assess.	Sub.: scale (1–10)	92.06 %
Boutell et al. [9]	Corel [32]/Own	5,770	Class.: sunset	accuracy	96.4 %
Singla et al. [140]	Own	4,500	Summ.	Obj.: precision and Recall	NI
Oliveira et al. [114]	Web	3,700	Class.: photo x graphic	Obj.: cross-validation	95.6 %
Datta et al. [39,41]	Photo.net [60]	3,581	Assess.: ranking	Sub.: scale (1–7)	70.12 %
Obrador et al. [111]	Photo.net [60]	3,141	Class.: high x low aesthetics	Sub.: scale (1–7)	66.5 %
Zhang et al. [187]	Own	2,597	Grouping	NI	NI
Tong et al. [151]	Corel [32]	2,355	Class.: blur	Obj.: Accuracy	98.6 %
Obrador [108]	NI	2,000	Assess.: ranking	Sub.: 6 grades	37.5 %
Shen et al. [139]	Web, Flickr [50]	2,000	Detect.: dissection lines	Sub.: TP + FP	80.87 and 33.61 %
Cooper et al. [30]	Own	1,449	Class.: event	Obj.: F-Measure	0.8568
Serrano et al. [137]	Web	1,200	Class.: indoor x Outdoor	Obj.: accuracy	90.2 %
Chu et al. [26]	Own	1,199	Grouping	Obj.: precision	0.68
Chu et al. [27,28]	Flickr [50]	1,024	Grouping	Sub.: scale (1–5)	Satisfaction > 4
Tang et al. [148]	Picasa [58]	975	Grouping	Obj.: precision and Recall	NI
Loui et al. [92]	NI	943	Grouping	Sub.: correlation	0.84
Lo Presti et al. [121]	Gallagher [54]	589	Retrieval	Obj.: error rate	27.68 %
Kim et al. [75]	Own	564	Grouping	Obj.: Precision at Top-N	MAP > 0.4
Li et al. [81]	Flickr [50]	500	Assess.: ranking	Sub.: choice	51 %
Li et al. [80]	Flickr [50]	500	Assess. & Class	Sub.: scale (0–10)	Residual sum-of-squares: 2.38
Khan et al. [74]	Li et al. [81]	500	Assess.: ranking	Sub.: choice	61.10 %
Jiang et al. [71]	Flickr [50], Kodak [172], Own	450	Assess.: ranking	Sub.: scale 0–100	MSE < 17
Obrador et al. [110]	Own	200	Grouping	Sub.: choice	75 %

4) *Number of Images.* There are an endless number of poses, camera settings, and subject positioning. Therefore, it is barely infeasible to represent this diversity of possibilities in a small set of images.

Table 3. Summary of the reviewed work on enhancement techniques.

Authors	Image sources	Set size	Main goal	Assess. method: used metrics	Results
Byers [13]	Own	3,008	In-camera photo composition	Sub.: user selection	35 %
Tian et al. [149]	Own	1,627	Photo Collage	Sub.: professional	Most results considered good
Liu et al. [87]	Web	900	Recomposition	Sub.: forced choice	93.7 %
Bhattacharya et al. [7]	Web	632	Recomposition	Sub.: forced choice	93.7 %
Yin et al. [179]	Own	600	Media Adaptation	NI	NI
Suh et al. [147]	Corbis [31]	150	Cropping	Sub.: recognition time	Faster using the approach
Zhang et al. [186]	Own	100	Cropping	Sub.: scaled	41 %
Chen et al. [24]	Web	56	Recomposition	Sub.: scaled	71.28 %
Santella et al. [133]	NI	50	Cropping	Sub.: forced choice	58.4 %
Setlur et al. [138]	NI	40	Retargeting	Sub.: forced choice	89.1 %
Achanta et al. [1]	Berkeley [100] and MSRA [89]	NI	Retargeting	NI	NI
Banerjee et al. [4]	NI	NI	Recomposition	NI	NI
Lim et al. [86]	NI	NI	Composite	NI	NI

In Tables 2 and 3, the second column (Image sources) indicates the databases from which the images were obtained. In this column, *Web* refers to web crawled images and *Own* refers to particular photos from the authors or contributors. The third column, (Set size), represents the number of images used in the experiments (if any). The fourth column indicates the main goal of the work. The fifth column briefly indicates how the approach has been evaluated, in which *Obj.*represents an objective assessment and *Sub.* a subjective assessment method. In the final column is shown the best reported performance of proposed algorithms. Tables 2 and 3 have been built based strictly on what was described in the papers. Whenever the information was not explicitly shown in the paper, results are shown in a non-numeric way or the information is not suitable for the discussed problem, *NI* (Not Informed) is used. Both tables are sorted based on the total number of images and then alphabetically by the name of authors.

By analyzing the Tables 2 and 3 it is possible to draw some conclusions about the number of images and their sources. First, there is no consensus on the database to be used. This makes it impossible to perform a direct comparison between the results in Tables 2 and 3, and to reproduce the experiments as well. Second, the number of images employed in the evaluations drastically vary. The average number of images employed in photo analysis work is 45,344 with a standard deviation of 212,556, and a median of 3,581 with an interquartile range of 12,278. If only photo enhancement work is considered, the average is 716 with a standard deviation of 952, and a median of 375 with an interquartile range of 766. Third, no work presented a categorization of the image set, e.g., not known is the distribution of the number of people among a given set. Finally, some papers only presented a simple visual verification of the results (e.g., Achanta et al. [1] and Banerjee et al. [4]).

It is important to highlight the non-utilization of a labeled and representative public image database for photographic analysis. Therefore, most authors crawled images from on-line repositories. Web crawlers can be employed for creating image sets which present a richer and diverse number of situations, and a higher number of pixels [24, 114, 137, 139]. Nevertheless, the great drawback is the lack of copyright licenses for public experiments. There are some public image databases that are free for academic research use (such as Flickr [50] and other databases under Creative Commons license [34]), yet they are not labeled. Regarding photo analysis, there are some web databases which have been used as a ground-truth for subjective quality analysis (e.g., DPChallenge [20] and Photo.net

[60]). However, since those databases were designed for photo contests, they typically do not represent the reality for consumer photography, which usually have less quality and less exigent evaluators.

Two authors have built datasets in order to make them available to the community. The first work, from Luo et al. [94], presented a dataset of 17,000 labeled photos. The set was built to be diverse, once photos are distributed over seven categories, they were labeled as high or low quality. The problem of this photo set lies in the labeling process. Some important information is not shown, such as the exact number of votes for each category, the origin and background of the photographer, and the personal information of the voters. Besides this, a more precise ranking (instead of only classifying images as high/low quality) could be used for a more general use in enhancement and analysis algorithms. The other work, from Bhattacharya et al. [7], presented a smaller photo set (only 632 images). Other factors, such as the ones analyzed on the Luo et al. [94] approach, could not be evaluated, since the image set built by Bhattacharya et al. [7] could not be downloaded due to a Web server error. Thus, it might be considered that the image set is no longer available.

One might suggest that if it is possible to learn an expert opinion about a photo, it would be possible to analyze a photo. However this is surprisingly not always true. Since average photography consumers do not have training in what a good photo is, they often do not agree with advice given by experts. There are several other factors that might influence a photography user's opinion, such as photo effects and the event from which the photo was obtained, rather than photographic rules.

In conclusion, it was not possible to identify comparative studies involving different approaches, which considered publicly available photo datasets. This causes difficulties to reliably compare techniques when dealing with consumer photography. The use of image sets from photography contests has also its disadvantages since both photographers and voters may have professional skills or are highly interested in photography. This may lead to results that are not related to ordinary photography consumer preferences.

5.2 Validation

This section contains a discussion on validation approaches. Photography might be considered an art form [66]. There is no simple way of deciding whether a photo is aesthetically pleasant or not. However, it might be possible to identify some metrics that would help photo assessment, and that would be a step further in this area.

Another important aspect to be considered is how approaches were validated. Since the reviewed work is about photo enhancement and analysis, the results are usually images (in the case of photo enhancement algorithms) or abstract information, e.g., color/gray-scale maps, statistics, and scores. Both have a very high subjective component, although some metrics might be defined for obtaining a more objective analysis in a specific scenario.

Validation methods can be classified as subjective or objective. Subjective methods involve subjective experiments in which humans are asked to give their opinion on photos of a pre-defined test set with respect to a given attribute or criterion. A participant may give his/her opinion based on the following methods [98]:

- *Single-stimulus rating.* The participant will give a score to a photo or a group of photos. The score might be continuous (such as 0–10) or categorical (e.g., excellent, good, fair, bad, and poor). During the rating process, each photo is typically showed to the participant for a fixed presentation time (e.g., 3 s);

- *Double-stimulus rating.* While analogous to the single-stimulus rating, in double-stimulus trials a reference photo and a test photo are presented in random order, one after another, for a fixed presentation time (e.g., 3 s);

- *Forced-Choice.* The participant is forced to choose only one within a group of photos, according to a given criterion;

- *Pairwise similarity judgement.* Similar to forced-choice but, besides choosing one from a group of photos, the participant has also to indicate on a continuous scale how large the difference in quality is between the two photos; and

- *Indirect.* The participant does not directly give his/her opinion. The quality may be inferred by some measurement such as the time needed for the participant to choose a photo.

Other details and comparing methods can be found in the work of Mantiuk et al. [98], in which a comparison between the first four above-mentioned methods is given. The better method is usually the one with higher correlation between human and automatic labeling. It was shown, however, that for comparing IQA algorithms, in which differences between images might be small, the forced-choice pairwise comparison is the most accurate and time-efficient [98].

Besides the comparing method, there are also other factors have an influence in the experimental assessment, since such experiments involve humans. Some of the factors are:

- *Number of participants.* Once the opinion about the quality of a photo may vary from one person to another, it is important to have a large number of participants in order to identify features that are more significant in human analysis;

- *Used equipment.* When the experiment is conducted in an uncontrolled environment, the equipment used might harm the results (e.g., the calibration of the screen in a color experiment might produce a different opinion);

- *Knowledge in photography.* Experts evaluate photos in a different way than consumers do. As an example, professional photos might be considered good by both expert and consumer while a consumer photo might be considered good by a consumer but bad by experts;

- *Cultural diversity.* The style and subject of the photo might influence the judgement depending on the participant's background and origin; and

- *Number of photos.* The number of photos in the experiment is a factor as crucial as the number of participants. If, on the one hand, a great number of photos might better represent the diversity of the photos, on the other hand, it might reduce the number of volunteer participants, since it becomes a more laborious experiment.

Since, according to the literature review, there is no database which considers all those factors, most of the conclusions drawn from subjective experiments might be considered partially biased. Besides the drastic influence of such factors, there is no consensus on what are the ideal values for them. Thus, most papers present some questionable decisions on the validation step, such as the number of participants (e.g., three participants [108]), knowledge in photography (e.g., most participants are experts [73]), and the number of images used (e.g., only 34 photos to represent the analysis sample [49]).

On the other hand, objective metrics present a set of well-defined criteria, and proposals are evaluated based on those criteria. For instance, the best algorithm might be the one which has lower false-positive rates in a face detection scenario.

Objective methods are usually less expensive since they do not rely on the availability and classification coherence of human participants. However, there are some important features that are not yet well-assessed by computational algorithms, such as the global visual aspect of a photo. Even humans may disagree with a classification result, what may imply a harder subjective assessment. Both approaches (objective and subjective) are important, each in its specific application scenario.

As it can be seen in Tables 2 and 3, the methodology of the assessment widely differs in the reviewed work, with regards to the following aspects: (1) the assessment method, (2) the metric used for assessment, and (3) the source of the photo set.

Although the results reported in those tables were obtained with different algorithms and different goals, it is possible to conclude that most approaches have opted for subjective assessment when dealing with image enhancement and analysis. The reason is probably the lack of consensus on the image set to be used as ground-truth and the essentially subjective task of comparing images.

There is also a lack of clarity regarding the number of people used in the subjective experiments, their confidence with the labeling, and the methodology of the experiment.

6. CONCLUSIONS

This survey reviewed state-of-the-art methods for photo enhancement and analysis. For better understanding of this research area, a taxonomy was defined based on the related work. The main conclusions of this survey are discussed next:

- According to the conducted literature review, this is the first survey on consumer photographic enhancement and analysis techniques;

- The interest in algorithms for photo enhancement and analysis has been growing recently, based on the number of recent papers published in this area;

- There is not a consensus on a methodology for conducting subjective photo analysis experiments;

- Although the results were obtained with different algorithms and different goals, it is possible to conclude that most approaches have opted for a subjective assessment due to the lack of a public and labeled image set that might work as a ground-truth for an objective assessment, and due to the inherently subjective task of comparing images. Therefore, in this scenario, direct comparisons between existing approaches might be unfair;

- Some work that indicates the photo sources are not reproducible, since the photos used for testing are not clearly identified due mostly to copyright reasons or the great number of images;

- There is no consensus on the number of images to be used in the experiments; and

- There is a lack of clarity regarding the number of people used in the subjective experiments, their confidence with the labeling provided, and the assessment methodology.

Thus, it is possible to conclude that, although there has been recent growth in photo enhancement and analysis techniques, this is an area with large potential. Experimental assessment needs to be improved, and assessment methodologies are required as well in order to obtain strong conclusions about methods and results.

ACKNOWLEDGMENTS

The authors wish to thank Conselho Nacional de Desenvolvimento Científico e Tecnológico (CNPq) for the financial support of part of this research.

REFERENCES

1. Achanta R, Süsstrunk, S (2009) Saliency detection for content-aware image resizing. In: Proceedings of the IEEE ICIP 2009. Piscataway, IEEE, pp 1005–1008

2. Anguelov, D, Lee KC, Gokturk SB, Sumengen B (2007) Contextual identity recognition in personal photo albums. In: Proceedings of the IEEE CVPR 2007. IEEE Computer Society, pp 1–7

3. Avidan S, Shamir A (2007) Seam carving for content-aware image resizing. ACM Trans Graphics 26(3):10.1-10.9

4. Banerjee S, Evans BL (2004) Unsupervised automation of photographic composition rules in digital still cameras. In: Proceedings of the SPIE Conference on sensors, color, cameras, and systems for digital photography, VI. pp 364–373

5. Benoit A, Caplier A, Durette B, Herault J (2010) Using human visual system modeling for bio-inspired low level image processing. Comput Vis Image Underst 114(7):758–773

6. Bertalmio M, Bugeau A, Caselles V, Sapiro G (2010) A comprehensive framework for image inpainting. IEEE Trans Image Process 19(10):2634–2645

7. Bhattacharya S, Sukthankar R, Shah M (2010) A framework for photo-quality assessment and enhancement based on visual aesthetics. In: Proceedings of the ACM MM 2010, pp 271–280

8. Bissacco A, Yang M, Soatto S (2007) Fast human pose estimation using appearance and motion via multi-dimensional boosting regression. In: Proceedings of the IEEE CVPR 2007, pp 1–8

9. Boutell M, Luo J, Gray RT (2003) Sunset scene classification using simulated image recomposition. In: Proceedings of the IEEE ICME 2003, pp 37–40

10. Boyce W, Wilkie S (2013) Photosig. http://www.photosig.com. Accessed 31 January 2013

11. Bruneau P, Picarougne F, Gelgon M (2010) Interactive unsupervised classification and visualization for browsing an image collection. Pattern Recogn 43(2):485–493

12. Busselle M (1999) Better picture guide to photographing people. RotoVision, Hove

13. Byers Z, Dixon M, Goodier K, Grimm CM, Smart WD (2003) An autonomous robot photographer. In: Proceedings IEEE/RSJ IROS 2003, pp 2636–2641

14. Byers Z, Dixon M, Smart W, Grimm C (2004) Say cheese!: experiences with a robot photographer. AAAI Mag 25(3):37–46 (this is an invited paper that wraps up all of the other Lewis papers)

15. Cao L, Luo J, Kautz H, Huang T (2008) Annotating collections of photos using hierarchical event and scene models. In: Proceedings of the IEEE CVPR 2008, pp 1–8

16. Cao L, Luo J, Kautz H, Huang T (2009) Image annotation within the context of personal photo collections using hierarchical event and scene models. IEEE Trans Multiméd 11(2):208–219

17. Cavalcanti C, Gomes H, Veloso L, Carvalho J, Lima Jr O (2010) Automatic single person composition analysis. In: Skala V (ed) Proceedings of the WSCG 2010. UNION Agency-Science Press, Plzen, pp 229–236

18. Cavalcanti CSVC, Gomes H, Meireles R, Guerra W (2006) Towards automating photographic composition of people. In: Proceedings of the IASTED VIIP 2006. ACTA Press, Anaheim, pp 25–30

19. Celik T, Tjahjadi T (2010) Unsupervised colour image segmentation using dual-tree complex wavelet transform. Comput Vis Image Underst 114(7):813–826

20. Challenging technologies: dpchallenge a digital photography contest (2013) http://www.dpchallenge.com. Accessed 31 January 2013

21. Charrier C, Knoblauch K, Moorthy AK, Bovik AC, Maloney LT (2010) Comparison of image quality assessment algorithms on compressed images. In: Proceedings of the SPIE, Image Quality and System Performance VII, 2010. pp 75, 290B–1-75, 290B–11

22. Chartier S, Renaud P (2008) An online noise filter for eye-tracker data recorded in a virtual environment. In: Proceedings of the ACM ETRA 2008, pp 153–156

23. Chen H (2008) Note: Focal length and registration correction for building panorama from photographs. Comput Vis Image Underst 112(2):225–230

24. Chen Lq, Xie X, Fan X, Ma WY, Zhang Hj, Zhou HQ (2003) A visual attention model for adapting images on small displays. Multiméd Syst 9:353–364

25. Chen S, Cao L, Wang Y, Liu J, Tang X (2010) Image segmentation by map-ml estimations. IEEE Trans Image Process 19(9): 2254–2264

26. Chu WT, Lee YL, Yu JY (2009) Using context information and local feature points in face clustering for consumer photos. In: Proceedings of the IEEE ICASSP 2009, pp 1141–1144

27. Chu WT, Li CJ, Tseng SC (2011) Travelmedia: an intelligent management system for media captured in travel representation. J Vis Commun Image 22(1):93–104

28. Chu WT, Lin CH (2010) J Vis Commun Image Rep. Consumer photo management and browsing facilitated by near-duplicate detection with feature filtering 21(3):256–268

29. Chua TS, Tang J, Hong R, Li H, Luo Z, Zheng YT (2009) Nus-wide: a real-world web image database from national university of singapore. In: Proceedings of ACM CIVR 2009, July 8–10

30. Cooper M, Foote J, Girgensohn A, Wilcox L (2005) Temporal event clustering for digital photo collections. ACM Trans Multiméd Comput Commun Appl 1(3):269–288

31. Corbis: Corbis image gallery (2001–2009). http://www.corbis.com. Accessed 31 January 2013

32. Corel Images: Corel images (2013) http://elib.cs.berkeley.edu/photos/corel/. Accessed 31 January 2013 (currently unavailable)

33. Cortes C, Vapnik V (1995) Support-vector networks. Mach Learn 20(3):273–297

34. Creative Commons: Creative commons (2012) http://creativecommons.org/. Accessed 31 January 2013

35. Cunningham SJ, Masoodian M (2007) Identifying personal photo digital library features. In: Proceedings of the ACM/IEEE-CS JCDL 2007, pp 400–401

36. Daliri MR, Torre V (2009) Classification of silhouettes using contour fragments. Comput Vis Image Underst 113(9):1017–1025

37. Dao MS, Dang-Nguyen DT, De Natale FG (2011) Signature-image-based event analysis for personal photo albums. In: Proceedings of the ACM MM 2011, pp 1481–1484

38. Das M, Loui AC (2009) Event classification in personal image collections. In: Proceedings of the IEEE ICME 2009. IEEE Press, New York, pp 1660–1663

39. Datta R, Joshi D, Li J, Wang JZ (2006) Studying aesthetics in photographic images using a computational approach. In: Proceedings of the ECCV 2006, pp 7–13

40. Datta R, Li J, Wang JZ (2008) Algorithmic inferencing of aesthetics and emotion in natural images: an exposition. In: Proceedings of the IEEE ICIP 2008, pp 105–108

41. Datta R, Wang JZ (2010) Acquine: aesthetic quality inference engine—real-time automatic rating of photo aesthetics. In: Proceedings of the ACM MIR 2010, pp 421–424

42. Destrero A, Mol C, Odone F, Verri A (2009) A regularized framework for feature selection in face detection and authentication. Int J Comput Vis 83(2):164–177

43. Duda RO, Stork DG, Hart PE (2000) Pattern classification and scene analysis. Part 1, Pattern classification, 2nd edn. Wiley, New York

44. Dunker P, Popp P, Cook R (2011) Content-aware auto-soundtracks for personal photo music slideshows. In: Proceedings of the IEEE ICME 2011, pp 1–5

45. Engelke U, Maeder AJ, Zepernick HJ (2009) On confidence and response times of human observers in subjective image quality assessment. In: Proceedings of the IEEE ICME 2009, pp 910–913

46. Ercegovac M, Lang T (1992) On-the-fly rounding (computing arithmetic). IEEE Trans Comput 41(12):1497–1503

47. Etchells D (2005) Canon expo 2005—a one-company trade show. http://www.imaging-resource.com/NEWS/1126887991.html. Accessed 31 January 2013

48. Fedorovskaya E, Neustaedter C, Hao W (2008) Image harmony for consumer images. In: Proceedings of the IEEE ICIP 2008, pp 121–124

49. Fedorovskaya E, Neustaedter C, Hao W (2008) Image harmony for consumer images. In: Proceedings of the IEEE ICIP 2008, pp 121–124.

50. Flickr (2013) Flickr photo sharing. http://www.flickr.com/. Accessed 31 January 2013

51. Flickr (2013) Mirflickr-25000. http://www.flickr.com/photos/tags/. Accessed 31 January 2013

52. Foggia P, Percannella G, Sansone C, Vento M (2008) Int J Pattern Recogn Artif Intell. A graph-based algorithm for cluster detection 22(5):843–860

53. Fujita H, Arikawa M (2007) Creating animation with personal photo collections and map for storytelling. In: Proceedings of the ACM EATIS 2007. ACM, New York, pp 1:1–1:8

54. Gallagher A, Chen T (2008) Clothing cosegmentation for recognizing people. In: Proceedings of the IEEE CVPR 2008, pp 1–8

55. Gallagher AC, Chen T (2007) Using group prior to identify people in consumer images. In: Proceedings of the IEEE CVPR 2007, vol 0. IEEE Computer Society, pp 1–8

56. Gallagher AC, Chen T (2009) Finding rows of people in group images. In: Proceedings of the IEEE ICME 2009. IEEE Press, New York, pp 602–6058

57. Golder S (2008) Measuring social networks with digital photograph collections. In: Proceedings of the ACM HT 2008, pp 43–48

58. Google: Picasa (2013) http://picasa.google.com/. Accessed 31 January 2013

59. Gorelick L, Basri R (2009) Shape based detection and top–down delineation using image segments. Int J Comput Vis 83(3): 211–232

60. Greenspun P (2013) Photo.net photography community. http://photo.net. Accessed 31 January 2013

61. Gupta A, Chen F, Kimber D, Davis LS (2008) Context and observation driven latent variable model for human pose estimation. In: Proceedings of the IEEE CVPR 2008, pp 1–8

62. Haddad Z, Beghdadi A, Serir A, Mokraoui A (2010) Image quality assessment based on wave atoms transform. In: Proceedings of the IEEE ICIP 2010, pp 305–308

63. Han HS, Kim DO, Park RH (2009) Structural information-based image quality assessment using lu factorization. IEEE Trans Consum Electron 55(1):165–171

64. Han J, Awad G, Sutherland A (2009) Automatic skin segmentation and tracking in sign language recognition. IET-CV 3(1):24–35

65. Haykin S (1999) Neural networks: a comprehensive foundation. Prentice Hall, Englewood Cliffs

66. Hedgecoe J (2009) New manual of ohotography. Dorling Kindersley, New York

67. Hoíng NV, Gouet-Brunet V, Rukoz M, Manouvrier M (2010) Embedding spatial information into image content description for scene retrieval. Pattern Recogn 43(9):3013–3024

68. Hsu SH, Jumpertz S, Cubaud P (2008) A tangible interface for browsing digital photo collections. In: Proceedings of the ACM TEI 2008, pp 31–32

69. Ji H, Liu C (2008) Motion blur identification from image gradients. In: Proceedings of the IEEE CVPR 2007, vol 0, IEEE Computer Society, pp 1–8

70. Jiang H, Martin D (2008) Global pose estimation using non-tree models. In: Proceedings of the IEEE CVPR 2008, pp 1–8

71. Jiang W, Loui A, Cerosaletti C (2010) Automatic aesthetic value assessment in photographic images. In: Proceedings of the IEEE ICME 2010, pp 920–925

72. Joshi N, Matusik W, Adelson EH, Kriegman DJ (2010) Personal photo enhancement using example images. ACM Trans Graphics 29(2):1–15

73. Ke Y, Tang X, Jing F (2006) The design of high-level features for photo quality assessment. In: Proceedings of the IEEE CVPR 2006, pp 419–426

74. Khan SS, Vogel D (2012) Evaluating visual aesthetics in photographic portraiture. In: Proceedings of the CAe 2012. Eurographics Association, pp 55–62

75. Kim HN, Saddik AE, Jung JG (2012) Leveraging personal photos to inferring friendships in social network services. Expert Syst Appl 39(8):6955–6966

76. Kruppa H, Bauer MA, Schiele B (2002) Skin patch detection in real-world images. In: Proceedings of the the 24th DAGM Symposium on Pattern Recognition. Springer LNCS, pp 109–117

77. Lee C, Schramm MT, Boutin M, Allebach JP (2009) An algorithm for automatic skin smoothing in digital portraits. In: Proceedings of the IEEE ICIP 2009. IEEE Press, New York, pp 3113–3116

78. Lee S, Kim K, Kim JY, Kim M, Yoo HJ (2010) Familiarity based unified visual attention model for fast and robust object recognition. Pattern Recogn 43(3):1116–1128

79. Levin A, Weiss Y (2009) Learning to combine bottom–up and top–down segmentation. Int J Comput Vis 81(1):105–118

80. Li C, Gallagher AC, Loui AC, Chen T (2010) Aesthetic quality assessment of consumer photos with faces. In: Proceedings of the IEEE ICIP 2010, pp 3221–3224

81. Li C, Loui AC, Chen T (2010) Towards aesthetics: a photo quality assessment and photo selection system. In: Proceedings of the ACM MM 2010, pp 827–830

82. Li X, Ling H (2009) Learning based thumbnail cropping. In: Proceedings of the IEEE ICME 2009. IEEE Press, New York, pp 558–561

83. Li Z, Luo H, Fan J (2009) Incorporating camera metadata for attended region detection and consumer photo classification. In: Proceedings of the ACM MM 2009, pp 517–520

84. Li Z, Zhou X, Huang TS (2009) Spatial gaussian mixture model for gender recognition. In: Proceedings of the IEEE ICIP 2009. IEEE Press, New York, pp 45–48

85. Liao WH (2009) A framework for attention-based personal photo manager. In: Proceedings of the the IEEE SMC 2009. IEEE Press, New York, pp 2128–2132

86. Lim SH, Lin Q, Petruszka A (2010) Automatic creation of face composite images for consumer applications. In: Proceedings of the IEEE ICASSP 2010, pp 1642–1645

87. Liu L, Chen R, Wolf L, Cohen-Or D (2010) Optimizing photo composition. In: Proceedings of the Eurographics, vol 29, pp 469–478

88. Liu R, Li Z, Jia J (2008) Image partial blur detection and classification. In: Proceedings of the IEEE CVPR 2007, vol 0. IEEE Computer Society, Los Alamitos, pp 1–8

89. Liu T, Yuan Z, Sun J, Wang J, Zheng N, Tang X, Shum HY (2011) Learning to detect a salient object. IEEE Trans Pattern Anal Mach Intell 33(2):353–367

90. Liu Y, Xu D, Tsang IW, Luo J (2011) Textual query of personal photos facilitated by large-scale web data. IEEE Trans Pattern Anal Mach Intell 33(5):1022–1036

91. Loui A, Wood M, Scalise A, Birkelund J (2008) Multidimensional image value assessment and rating for automated albuming and retrieval. In: Proceedings of the IEEE ICIP 2008, pp 97–100

92. Loui AC, Wood MD, Scalise A, Birkelund J (2008) Multidimensional image value assessment and rating for automated albuming and retrieval. In: Proceedings of the IEEE ICIP 2008, pp 97–100

93. Lu F, Yang X, Zhang R, Yu S (2009) Image classification based on pyramid histogram of topics. In: Proceedings of the IEEE ICME 2009. IEEE Press, New York, pp 398–401

94. Luo W, Wang X, Tang X (2011) Content-based photo quality assessment. In: Proceedings of the IEEE ICCV 2011, vol. 0. IEEE Computer Society, Los Alamitos, pp 2206–2213

95. Luo Y, Tang X (2008) Photo and video quality evaluation: focusing on the subject. In: Proceedings of the ECCV 2008. Springer, Heidelberg, pp 386–399

96. Lux M, Kogler M, del Fabro M (2010) Why did you take this photo: a study on user intentions in digital photo productions. In: Proceedings of the ACM SAPMIA 2010, pp 41–44

97. Maik V, Paik D, Lim J, Park K, Paik J (2010) Hierarchical pose classification based on human physiology for behaviour analysis. IET-CV 4(1):12–24

98. Mantiuk RK, Tomaszewska A, Mantiuk R (2012) Comparison of four subjective methods for image quality assessment. Comput Graphics Forum 31(8):2478–2491

99. Marshall B (2010) Taking the tags with you: Digital photograph provenance. In: Proceedings of the IEEE symposium on data, privacy, and E-Commerce 2010. IEEE Computer Society, Los Alamitos, pp 72–77

100. Martin D, Fowlkes C, Tal D, Malik J (2001) A database of human segmented natural images and its application to evaluating segmentation algorithms and measuring ecological statistics. In: Proceedings of the ICCV 2001, vol 2, pp 416–423

101. Mele K, Suc D, Maver J (2009) Local probabilistic descriptors for image categorisation. IET-CV 3(1):8–23

102. Microsoft Corporation: Bing maps (2012) http://www.bing.com/maps/. Accessed 31 January 2013

103. Miller AD, Edwards WK (2007) Give and take: a study of consumer photo-sharing culture and practice. In: Proceedings of the ACM SIGCHI 2007, pp 347–356

104. Moorthy AK, Obrador P, Oliver N (2010) Towards computational models of the visual aesthetic appeal of consumer videos. In: Proceedings of the ECCV 2010. Springer, Berlin/Heidelberg, pp 1–14

105. Mu Y, Yan S, Liu Y, Huang T, Zhou B (2008) Discriminative local binary patterns for human detection in personal album. In: Proceedings of the IEEE CVPR 2008, vol 0. New York, IEEE Computer Society, pp 1–8

106. Mucientes M, Bugarín A (2010) People detection through quantified fuzzy temporal rules. Pattern Recogn 43(4):1441–1453

107. Nikon Corporation: Nikon d90 advanced function (2008). http://chsvimg.nikon.com/products/imaging/lineup/d90/en/advanced-function/. Accessed 31 January 2013

108. Obrador P (2008) Region based image appeal metric for consumer photos. In: Proceedings of the IEEE Workshop on multimedia signal 2008, pp 696–701

109. Obrador P, Moroney N (2009) Automatic image selection by means of a hierarchical scalable collection representation. In: Proceedings of the SPIE visual communications and image processing, San Jose, vol 7257, pp 0W.1–0W.12

110. Obrador P, de Oliveira R, Oliver N (2010) Supporting personal photo storytelling for social albums. In: Proceedings of the ACM MM 2010, pp 561–570

111. Obrador P, Schmidt-Hackenberg L, Oliver N (2010) The role of image composition in image aesthetics. In: Proceedings of the IEEE ICIP 2010, pp 3185–3188

112. O'Hare N, Lee H, Cooray S, Gurrin C, Jones G, Malobabic J, O'Connor N, Smeaton AF, Uscilowski, B (2006) Mediassist: Using content-based analysis and context to manage personal photo collections. In: Proceedings of the CIVR 2006, vol 4071. Springer, Heidelberg, pp 529–532

113. O'Hare N, Smeaton AF (2009) Context-aware person identification in personal photo collections. IEEE Trans Multiméd 11(2):220–228

114. Oliveira CJS, Araújo AdeA, Severiano CA Jr, Gomes DR (2002) Classifying images collected on the World Wide Web. In: Proceedings of

the SIBGRAPI 2002, IEEE Computer Society Press, Fortaleza, pp 327–334

115. Orbanz P, Buhmann JM (2008) Nonparametric bayesian image segmentation. Int J Comput Visi 77(1–3):25–45

116. Paisitkriangkrai S, Shen C, Zhang J (2008) Performance evaluation of local features in human classification and detection. IET-CV 2(4):236–246

117. Pang Y, Hao Q, Yuan Y, Hu T, Cai R, Zhang L (2011) Summarizing tourist destinations by mining user-generated travelogues and photos. Comput Vis Image Underst 115(3):352–363

118. Park HJ, Har DH (2011) Subjective image quality assessment based on objective image quality measurement factors. IEEE Trans Consumer Electron 57(3):1176–1184

119. Peres M (2007) Focal encyclopedia of photography: digital imaging, theory and applications, history, and science. Elsevier Science Inc./Focal Press, Boston

120. Pierrard JS, Vetter T (2007) Skin detail analysis for face recognition. In: Proceedings of the IEEE CVPR 2007, pp 1–8

121. Presti LL, Cascia ML (2012) An on-line learning method for face association in personal photo collection. Image Vis Comput 30 (4–5):306–316

122. Qi GJ, Hua XS, Rui Y, Tang J, Zhang HJ (2008) Two-dimensional active learning for image classification. In: Proceedings of the IEEE CVPR 2008, pp 1–8

123. Qin AK, Clausi DA (2010) Multivariate image segmentation using semantic region growing with adaptive edge penalty. IEEE Trans Image Process 19(8):2157–2170

124. Quinlan JR (1986) Induction of decision trees. Mach Learn 1(1):81–106

125. Rahman M, Gamadia M, Kehtarnavaz N (2008) Real-time face-based auto-focus for digital still and cell-phone cameras. In:

Proceedings of the IEEE SSIAI 2008. IEEE Computer Society, Los Alamitos, pp 177–180

126. Redi JA, Heynderickx I (2012) Image integrity and aesthetics: towards a more encompassing definition of visual quality. In: Proceedings of the SPIE human vision and electronic imaging XVII 2012, vol 8291. SPIE, San Jose, pp 15.1–15.10

127. Ren T, Liu Y, Wu G (2009) Image retargeting based on global energy optimization. In: Proceedings of the IEEE ICME 2009. IEEE Press, New York, pp 406–409

128. Ren X, Fowlkes CC, Malik J (2008) Learning probabilistic models for contour completion in natural images. Int J Comput Vis 77 (1–3):47–63

129. Rousson M, Paragios N (2008) Prior knowledge, level set representations & visual grouping. Int J Comput Vis 76(3):231–243

130. Russell SJ, Norvig P (2009) Artificial intelligence: a modern approach, 3rd edn. Prentice Hall, New Delhi

131. Ryoo MS, Aggarwal JK (2009) Semantic representation and recognition of continued and recursive human activities. Int J Comput Vis 82(1):1–24

132. Sandnes F (2010) Unsupervised and fast continent classification of digital image collections using time. In: Proceedings of the ICSSE 2010, pp 516–520

133. Santella A, Agrawala M, Decarlo D, Salesin D, Cohen M (2006) Proceedings of the gaze-based interaction for semi-automatic photo cropping. In: Proceedings of the ACM SIGCHI 2006. ACM Press, New York, pp 771–780

134. Savakis AE, Etz SP, Loui ACP (2000) Evaluation of image appeal in consumer photography. In: Proceedings of the SPIE human vision and electronic imaging V, vol 3959. SPIE, San Jose, pp 111–120

135. Schindler G, Krishnamurthy P, Lublinerman R, Liu Y, Dellaert F (2008) Detecting and matching repeated patterns for automatic geo-tagging in urban environments. In: Proceedings of the IEEE CVPR 2008, pp 208–219

136. Schmugge SJ, Jayaram S, Shin MC, Tsap LV (2007) Objective evaluation of approaches of skin detection using roc analysis. Comput Vis Image Underst 108(1–2):41–51

137. Serrano N, Savakis A, Luo J (2002) A computationally efficient approach to indoor/outdoor scene classification. In: Proceedings of the IEEE ICPR 2002. IEEE Computer Society, Los Alamitos, pp 146–149

138. Setlur V, Takagi S, Raskar R, Gleicher M, Gooch B (2005) Automatic image retargeting. In: Proceedings of the ACM MUM 2005. ACM Press, New York, pp 59–68

139. Shen CT, Liu JC, Shih SW, Hong JS (2009) Towards intelligent photo composition-automatic detection of unintentional dissection lines in environmental portrait photos. Expert Syst Appl 36(5):9024–9030

140. Singla P, Kautz H, Gallagher A (2008) Discovery of social relationships in consumer photo collections using markov logic. In: Proceedings of the IEEE CVPR 2008 Workshops, pp 1–7

141. Sinha P (2011) Summarization of archived and shared personal photo collections. In: Proceedings of the ACM WWW 2011, pp 421–426

142. Snavely N, Seitz SM, Szeliski R (2008) Modeling the world from internet photo collections. Int J Comput Vis 80(2):189–210

143. Sony Corporation: Sony party-shot automatic photographer (2009). http://store.sony.com/webapp/wcs/stores/servlet/ProductDisplay?catalogId=10551%26storeId=10151%26langId=-1%26partNumber=IPTDS1. Accessed 31 January 2013

144. Stein A, Stepleton T, Hebert M (2008) Towards unsupervised whole-object segmentation: Combining automated matting with boundary detection. In: Proceedings of the IEEE CVPR 2008, pp 1–8

145. Su HH, Chen TW, Kao CC, Hsu WH, Chien SY (2011) Scenic photo quality assessment with bag of aesthetics-preserving features. In: Proceedings of the ACM MM 2011, pp 1213–1216

146. Suh B, Bederson BB (2007) Semi-automatic photo annotation strategies using event based clustering and clothing based person recognition. Interact Comput 19(4):524–544

147. Suh B, Ling H, Bederson BB, Jacobs DW (2003) Automatic thumbnail cropping and its effectiveness. In: Proceedings of the ACM UIST 2003. ACM Press, New york, pp 95–104

148. Tang F, Gao Y (2009) Fast near duplicate detection for personal image collections. In: Proceedings of the ACM MM 2009, pp 701–704

149. Tian A, Zhang X, Tretter DR (2011) Content-aware photo-on-photo composition for consumer photos. In: Proceedings of the ACM MM 2011, pp 1549–1552

150. Tómasson G, Sigurp'orsson H, Jónsson B, Amsaleg L (2011) Photocube: effective and efficient multi-dimensional browsing of personal photo collections. In: Proceedings of the ACM ICMR 2011, pp 70:1–70:2

151. Tong H, Li M, Zhang H, Zhang C (2004) Blur detection for digital images using wavelet transform. In: Proceedings of the IEEE ICME 2004, pp 17–20

152. Tong H, Li M, Zhang HJ, He J, Zhang C (2004) Classification of digital photos taken by photographers or home users. In: Proceedings of the Pacific Rim Conference on Multimedia. Springer, Heidelberg, pp 198–205

153. Tran C, Wijnhoven R, de With P (2011) Text detection in personal image collections. In: Proceedings of the IEEE ICCE 2011, pp 85–86

154. Tsao WK, Lee AJT, Liu YH, Chang TW, Lin HH (2010) A data mining approach to face detection. Pattern Recogn 43(3): 1039–1049

155. Tsay KE, Wu YL, Hor MK, Tang CY (2009) Personal photo organizer based on automated annotation framework. International Conference on Intelligent Information Hiding and Multimedia Signal Processing, pp 507–510

156. Valle E, Cord M, Philipp-Foliguet S, Gorisse D (2010) Indexing personal image collections: a flexible, scalable solution. IEEE Trans Consumer Electron 56(3):1167–1175

157. Vogel J, Schwaninger A, Wallraven C, Bülthoff HH (2007) Categorization of natural scenes: Local versus global information and the role of color. ACM Trans Appl Percept 4(3):19.1–19.21

158. Wan D, Zhou J (2008) Stereo vision using two ptz cameras. Comput Vis Image Underst 112(2):184–194

159. Wang H, Oliensis J (2010) Generalizing edge detection to contour detection for image segmentation. Comput Vis Image Underst 114(7):731–744

160. Wang J, Jia Y, Hua XS, Zhang C, Quan L (2008) Normalized tree partitioning for image segmentation. In: Proceeings of the IEEE CVPR 2008, vol 0. IEEE Computer Society, Los Alamitos, pp 1–8

161. Wang J, Zhu S, Gong Y (2009) Resolution-invariant image representation for content-based zooming. In: Proceedings of the IEEE ICME 2009. IEEE Press, New York, pp 918–921

162. Wang P, Ji Q (2007) Multi-view face and eye detection using discriminant features. Comput Vis Image Underst 105(2):99–111

163. Wang XF, Huang DS, Xu H (2010) An efficient local chan-vese model for image segmentation. Pattern Recogn 43(3):603–618

164. Wang Y, Huang Q, Gao W (2009) Pornographic image detection based on multilevel representation. IJPRAI 23(8):1633–1655

165. Wichmann FA, Drewes J, Rosas P, Gegenfurtner KR (2010) Animal detection in natural scenes: critical features revisited. J Vis 10(4):6.1–27

166. Xie S, Shan S, Chen X, Chen J (2010) Fusing local patterns of gabor magnitude and phase for face recognition. IEEE Trans Image Process 19(5):1349–1361

167. Xie ZX, Wang ZF (2010) Color image quality assessment based on image quality parameters perceived by human vision system. In: Proceedings of the ICMT 2010, pp 1–4

168. Xin H, Ai H, Chao H (2011) Tretter D Human head-shoulder segmentation. In: Proceedings of the IEEE FG 2011, pp 227–232

169. Xu S, Ye X, Wu Y, Giron F, Leveque JL, Querleux B (2008) Automatic skin decomposition based on single image. Comput Vis Image Underst 110(1):1–6

170. Xu Z, Sun J (2010) Image inpainting by patch propagation using patch sparsity. IEEE Trans on Image Process 19(5):1153–1165

171. Yan S, Wang H, Liu J, Tang X, Huang TS (2010) Misalignment-robust face recognition. IEEE Trans Image Process 19(4): 1087–1096

172. Yanagawa A, Loui AC, Luo J, Chang SF, Ellis D, Jiang W, Kennedy L, Lee K (2008) Kodak consumer video benchmark data set: concept definition and annotation. Columbia University, Technical report

173. Yang Y, Xu D, Nie F, Yan S, Zhuang Y (2010) Image clustering using local discriminant models and global integration. IEEE Trans Image Process 19(10):2761–2773

174. Yanulevskaya V, van Gemert J, Roth K, Herbold A, Sebe N, Geusebroek J (2008) Emotional valence categorization using holistic image features. In: Proceedings of the IEEE ICIP 2008, pp 101–104

175. Yao L, Suryanarayan P, Qiao M, Wang JZ, Li J (2012) Oscar: on-site composition and aesthetics feedback through exemplars for photographers. Int J Comput Vis 96(3):353–383

176. Yeh CH, Ho YC, Barsky BA, Ouhyoung M (2010) Personalized photograph ranking and selection system. In: Proceedings of the ACM MM 2010, pp 211–220

177. Yeh CH, Ng WS, Barsky BA, Ouhyoung M (2009) An esthetics rule-based ranking system for amateur photos. In: Proceedings of the ACM SIGGRAPH 2009, pp 24:1–24:1

178. Yi Y, Yu X, Wang L, Yang Z (2008) Image quality assessment based on structural distortion and image definition. In: Proceedings of the international conference on computer science and software engineering 2008(6):253–256

179. Yin W, Luo J, Chen CW (2010) Semantic adaptation of consumer photo for mobile device access. In: Proceedimgs of the ISCAS 2010, pp 1173–1176

180. Ying Z, Guangyao L, Xiehua S, Xinmin Z (2009) Geometric active contours without re-initialization for image segmentation. Pattern Recogn 42(9):1970–1976

181. Yu Z, Au OC, Zou R, Yu W, Tian J (2010) An adaptive unsupervised approach toward pixel clustering and color image segmentation. Pattern Recogn 43(5):1889–1906

182. Zeng G, Gool LV (2008) Multi-label image segmentation via point-wise repetition. In: Proceedings of the IEEE CVPR 2008, vol 0. IEEE Computer Society, Los Alamitos, pp 1–8

183. Zeng YC (2009) Automatic local contrast enhancement using adaptive histogram adjustment. In: Proceedings of the IEEE ICME 2009. IEEE Press, New York, pp 1318–1321

184. Zha ZJ, Hua XS, Mei T, Wang J, Qi GJ, Wang Z (2008) Joint multi-label multi-instance learning for image classification. In: Proceedings of the IEEE CVPR 2008, vol 0. IEEE Computer Society, Los Alamitos, pp 1–8

185. Zhang H, Fritts JE, Goldman SA (2008) Image segmentation evaluation: a survey of unsupervised methods. Comput Vis Image Underst 110(2):260–280

186. Zhang M, Zhang L, Sun Y, Feng L, Ma W (2005) Auto Cropping for Digital Photographs. In: Proceedings of the IEEE ICME 2005, pp 438–441

187. Zhang T, Chao H, Willis C, Tretter D (2010) Consumer image retrieval by estimating relation tree from family photo collections. In: Proceedings of the ACM CIVR 2010, pp 143–150

188. Zhou C, Lin S (2007) Removal of image artifacts due to sensor dust. In: Proceedings of the IEEE CVPR 2007, vol 0. IEEE Computer Society, Los Alamitos, pp 1–8

Index

V